Endorsements

"Mike Bent has taught many people who have become very successful comedians, writers, and actors. They all (I'm in touch with many of them) still speak highly of him. That is reason enough to buy this book. Also, he's unique and very funny."

—**Eugene Mirman**, actor, *Flight of the Conchords* and author,
The Will to Whatevs: A Guide to Modern Life

"Mike Bent has been an institution in Boston comedy for more than a quarter of a century. He has the two things every comic wishes he had: a unique, creative voice and a really cool name. He's able to pass on to his students what he's learned from performing in just about every theater, comedy club, college pub, Elk's hall, and church basement in New England. Learn from him."

—**Brian Kiley**, Emmy-award winning staff writer, *Late Night with Conan O'Brien* and *The Tonight Show with Conan O'Brien*

"Mike Bent is a true comic genius and a fantastic teacher. From monologue jokes to sitcom scripts, Mike will make your material sharper, stronger, and way funnier."

—**Paul Starke**, Emmy-award winning senior producer,
The Tyra Banks Show

"You never forget your great teachers. For me, Mike Bent is one of those teachers. There's nothing deadlier to comedy than analyzing it, but Mike knows how to take it apart and show you the guts while keeping it alive with a sense of discovery and fun. Great fun."

—**Eric Drysdale**, Emmy-award winning writer,
The Daily Show and *The Colbert Report*

"Mike Bent knows more about comedy than Aristophenes, Henny Youngman, and Noam Chomsky combined—and Chomsky killed it at Comic Relief in '94. He's a great guy, and this is a great book."

—**Joe Randazzo**, editor, *The Onion*

THE
EVERYTHING
GUIDE TO
COMEDY WRITING

Dear Reader,

By the time you read this, I will be dead. Well, probably not, but I start every letter that way. Someday I'll be right, and that'll show 'em.

But seriously, whenever someone finds out that I teach comedy writing at Emerson College, they invariably ask, "Can you teach someone how to be funny?" My answer is always, "Yes—but not you." The truth is, although you can't really "teach" someone to be funny, you can help them to teach themselves how to be funnier, and uncover their unique comedy voice.

Comedy is the best way to express yourself. You get to say things no one else would dare say. Even better, you can get away with it. There's no better sound than laughter. There are easier ways to make a living but none are as creatively rewarding. There's no better way to tell the world that you are one of a kind.

The best thing about teaching hundreds of students is that it has kept the creative process fresh and fun for me. You can't help but feed off the excitement when great ideas are bouncing around the room. I leave the classroom with a million ideas racing through my head.

That's what I like most about comedy, that kinetic energy. Comedy is always moving forward; it's never done. A joke or idea always has the potential to be better, funnier. If you look for them, you'll find great ideas everywhere. I hope that this book helps you discover your comedy voice and teaches you to trust it. Take risks. Be passionate about your ideas. And, above all, have fun!

Yours from the grave (eventually),

Mike Bent

P.S. Boo!

Welcome to the EVERYTHING® Series!

These handy, accessible books give you all you need to tackle a difficult project, gain a new hobby, comprehend a fascinating topic, prepare for an exam, or even brush up on something you learned back in school but have since forgotten.

You can choose to read an *Everything®* book from cover to cover or just pick out the information you want from our four useful boxes: e-questions, e-facts, e-alerts, and e-ssentials.

We give you everything you need to know on the subject, but throw in a lot of fun stuff along the way, too.

We now have more than 400 *Everything®* books in print, spanning such wide-ranging categories as weddings, pregnancy, cooking, music instruction, foreign language, crafts, pets, New Age, and so much more. When you're done reading them all, you can finally say you know *Everything®*!

E-QUESTION
Answers to common questions

FACTS
Important snippets of information

ALERTS!
Urgent warnings

Quick handy tips

PUBLISHER Karen Cooper

DIRECTOR OF ACQUISITIONS AND INNOVATION Paula Munier

MANAGING EDITOR, EVERYTHING SERIES Lisa Laing

COPY CHIEF Casey Ebert

ACQUISITIONS EDITOR Lisa Laing

ASSISTANT DEVELOPMENT EDITOR Elizabeth Kassab

EDITORIAL ASSISTANT Hillary Thompson

Visit the entire Everything® series at *www.everything.com*

THE
EVERYTHING®
GUIDE TO
COMEDY WRITING

From stand-up to sketch—all you need
to succeed in the world of comedy

Mike Bent

Avon, Massachusetts

This book (or "my manifesto" as it came to be called)
is for my wife Linda and my daughter Nora. It's for their love,
support, and most of all, for giving me everything that I have ever
wanted from life, and so much more than I ever expected.
Oh yeah, and they're hilarious.

An Everything® Series Book.
Everything® and everything.com® are registered trademarks of F+W Media, Inc.

Published by Adams Media, a division of F+W Media, Inc.
57 Littlefield Street, Avon, MA 02322 U.S.A.
www.adamsmedia.com

ISBN 10: 1-60550-168-9
ISBN 13: 978-1-60550-168-0

Printed in the United States of America.

J   I   H   G   F   E   D   C   B   A

Library of Congress Cataloging-in-Publication Data
is available from the publisher.

This publication is designed to provide accurate and authoritative information with regard to the subject matter covered. It is sold with the understanding that the publisher is not engaged in rendering legal, accounting, or other professional advice. If legal advice or other expert assistance is required, the services of a competent professional person should be sought.

—From a *Declaration of Principles* jointly adopted by a Committee of the American Bar Association and a Committee of Publishers and Associations

Many of the designations used by manufacturers and sellers to distinguish their products are claimed as trademarks. Where those designations appear in this book and Adams Media was aware of a trademark claim, the designations have been printed with initial capital letters.

This book is available at quantity discounts for bulk purchases.
For information, please call 1-800-289-0963.

Contents

Acknowledgments

I want to thank all the comedians who have made me laugh, and through the joy of that laughter, have taught me everything I know about comedy writing. I also want to thank all the comedy writers who were interviewed for this book. It was great to reconnect with old friends and make new ones as well. And, thanks to all my magic buddies—you know who you are.

Top 10 Things You Should Know about Comedy Writing

1. Writing comedy is hard work, but the work can feel like play if you approach it the right way.

2. Comedy is important; for thousands of years, it has reflected and even transformed society (just look at how three Stooges and a couple of pies could take down the aristocracy).

3. There are no bad ideas—they're just steps on the way to great ideas.

4. The "rules" of comedy writing were made to be broken.

5. Keeping a good notebook is the comedy writer's lifeline.

6. There are many different ways to use your comedy skills. Stand-up and sitcoms are just the tip of the iceberg.

7. Insightful, inside information from some of the industry's most talented writers will help you write funnier material.

8. Originality is the key to your success.

9. We live in the age of do-it-yourself success—your future, and the future of comedy, is literally in your hands.

10. Trust your instincts and have confidence in what you write.

Introduction

▶ COMEDY WRITING IS REALLY comedy thinking. The writing part is much easier than the comedy part. It all starts with ideas—unique observations about the world that make people laugh out loud.

Maybe you've heard this old saying: "There's no such thing as an original joke. Comedians just retell the same old jokes in slightly different ways." Well, that's just not true. That's the creed of hacks—comics who are lazy and unoriginal. There are countless new jokes just waiting to be discovered by writers with the creativity to find them, the drive to develop them, and the guts to try them out. Dating? Airline travel? They might sound like tired topics, but you haven't had *your* say on them yet, and your unique take might be the funniest one yet.

The key to comedy writing is having a system, a thought process for generating and developing comedy ideas. No book can teach you that system, because it's different for every writer. You can't just fill in the blanks and get comedy. The goal of this book is to guide you to develop your own system by exploring your personal way of looking at things.

So what do you do now? Read through the book and try the exercises at the end of each chapter. If a strategy works for you, keep it, use it, modify it. If it doesn't, just move on to the next one. You'll be doing all the work, and the jokes you come up with will be all yours. You won't merely think outside the box; you'll forget that big, stupid box even exists.

Remember, there's no right or wrong with comedy. One comedian may be quiet, thoughtful, and deadpan (think Steven Wright), while another is loud, crazy, and all over the place (Robin Williams, anyone?).

They are polar opposites, and guess what? They're both right, because they're doing exactly what's right for them and making millions of people laugh in the process. The lesson for you, the student of comedy writing, is that you should learn from both styles—and everything in between—as you figure out what's right for you.

These are exciting times for comedy. Writers have more freedom than ever before. In the old days (like ten years ago), you had to get permission from someone to get your comedy out into the world, and you often had to win that permission by making compromises—watering down your comic vision to make it work for a mass audience. But the explosion of new media outlets means you don't have to make artistic compromises to find an audience—in fact, your audience might even find you. You still have to be funny to be successful, but there's no filter wearing a suit between you and the audience.

So what are you waiting for? Get started! In the time you've spent reading this introduction, two guys walked into a bar and said: "Line?"

That's your cue.

CHAPTER 1

What Are You— a Comedian?

Have you ever watched a comic on stage and thought, "I could do that!" Have you ever watched a television comedy sketch and thought, "You know, a better ending would have been . . . " Do you tell funny stories that are so great people pass them on to others? If you have, you just might have what it takes to make it in the field of comedy writing.

The Best Job in the World

Being able to write comedy—and get paid for it—is a dream job. You can make a living by doing the very thing you are driven to do. When you work with other comedians, you have a great time and write some great comedy in the process. If you respect your job and your talent, everything else is just icing on the cake. Just be warned—most people won't get what you do. You'll be at a dinner party, and someone will ask what you do for a living. If you say, "I'm a comedian," their next question will likely be, "Wow, that's great, but what do you do for a *living*?"

Society craves comedy yet dismisses it as a career. But that's not important. You will be doing something that makes a big difference in people's lives. Being a comedian is also one of the most important jobs in the world. And it's a blast! If you have a high opinion of yourself and love what you do, it won't matter what others think.

"No Respect, I Tell Ya!"

The late great Rodney Dangerfield spoke for all comedians when he said, "I don't get no respect!" Beginning in grade school, comedians get a bad rep. "Stop kidding around!" "Stop acting like a clown!" "What are you, some kind of comedian?" Comedians and comedy writers tend to be treated by society as second-class artists. What comedians do is fine, but it's not that important. A comedy movie isn't as important as a drama. A stand-up comedian isn't as important as a poet. A comedy writer is never as important as a "serious" novelist.

FACT

In the eighty-year history of the Academy Awards, only three comedies have won the Best Picture Award—*It Happened One Night* (1934), *You Can't Take it With You* (1938), and *Annie Hall* (1977). Tons of classic comedies weren't considered worthy of the honor, even such great films as *Animal Crackers* (1930), *Some Like it Hot* (1960), *Dr. Strangelove or How I Learned to Stop Worrying and Love the Bomb* (1964), and *Tootsie* (1982).

What people don't realize is it that comedy is just as important as the "serious" arts. Where would we be without humor? Comedy is what gets us by, and the world needs more of it. If there were no one around to make fun of all the stupid things that happen everyday, we'd just be stuck with, well, the stupid things that happen every day. If people in authority couldn't be taken down a peg, we'd have to (gasp!) take them seriously.

Respect Yourself

Remember, in the Middle Ages, only the jester could call the king's actions into question. Today, comedy can do more to make a change in public opinion than most people realize. Think about it: Do politicians care about what *Saturday Night Live*, *The Tonight Show*, *The Daily Show*, and *The Colbert Report* say about them? You bet they do.

A barrage of jokes can bring someone down faster than an editorial in the *New York Times*. Comedians tend to be prosecutors for the people in the court of public opinion. It's serious stuff, this comedy thing. And, while it struggles to get artistic respect, it's always in high demand in film, TV, comedy clubs, novels, and just about any form of entertainment the public consumes.

FACT

In the 2008 presidential election, Tina Fey's impression of Sarah Palin on *Saturday Night Live* became a major news story. Record audiences tuned in to *SNL* and Fey's NBC series *30 Rock*. It could be argued that a lot of people formed their opinion of the mostly unknown vice presidential candidate after seeing Fey's hilarious portrayal—her impression was as newsworthy as the candidate herself.

Then why doesn't comedy writing get its due? It's because good comedians make it look easy, effortless, like they're not even trying. People don't see the work—the writing—involved in what comedians do, if they do it right. And comedy writing is work—hard work—but guess what? It's a blast! When you write a joke that works, there's no better feeling in the world. It makes all the work, and the second-class status, worthwhile. Maybe Rodney got no respect, but he respected himself, and he could make an audience laugh until they cried. That was all that mattered. If you respect yourself, that's all that should matter to you.

Everybody's Funny—Except Maybe Dick Cheney

Everyone has a sense of humor. Others might not seem all that funny to you, or they might not laugh at the things that make you laugh. But everyone has their own sense of what's funny to them.

Were you the class clown? The kid who was always on, always trying to crack everyone up? Or were you the quiet kid who mostly kept to herself and barely spoke, but when you did chime in, you would say something that was *really* funny?

Go online and look at anything comedy-related that has "user comments"—such as a YouTube video or a comedy DVD for sale at *www .amazon.com*. Look at those comments and compare them to a similar noncomedy item. Notice how nasty and personal the comments are whenever someone feels that their funny bone has been violated.

Everyone can be funny—you just need to find your style. You need to figure out how to communicate what you think is funny to your audience, in your own way, and make them think it's funny too.

People also guard their sense of humor passionately. That's the blessing and the curse of comedy—immediate feedback. If someone goes to a play featuring an actress who isn't that great, she might make a snide comment to her friends after the show, but she won't stand up and shout, "You suck!" in the middle of Act One. But when comedy isn't funny, the audience will tell you. On the spot. You can count on it.

If you make a funny comment, professionally or not, people will let you know that they don't find you witty at all. They won't even hesitate; it's almost a defensive reaction: "How dare you assault my sense of humor!"

Kidding Around: Getting in Touch With Your Inner Child

Boy, does "getting in touch with your inner child" sound hokey or what? But this is not meant in a New Age way at all. It is simply that you need to get back to your sense of play if you want to be a successful comedy writer.

Every child at play is a consummate improvisation expert. When playing with other children, rules don't apply. One minute a kid is Mommy and her doll is the baby and the next minute she's Batman and the doll is a bomb she needs to defuse. Children are totally committed to each character they play and the premise they're following—and they can flow to the next "set" effortlessly. Why? Because they don't care what people think. Their friends aren't going to judge them, because they're all acting the same way.

Notice how easily children laugh, truly laugh—that full body, side-splitting, rolling-on-the-floor type of laughter. Why is it so different with adults? Because kids willingly accept the fantasy of the comedy premise presented. They *want* to laugh; they are actively looking for things that make them laugh. Kids aren't easier to crack up than adults, but they are more willing to let you make them laugh.

"Act your age." Those three words are the enemy of creativity. We've always been told "Stop kidding around!" or "You're too old to behave that way!" Well, if you want to write comedy, you had better *start* kidding around. You need to let your mind free-associate the same way a child does. You need to stop worrying about what people are going to think. If you don't, you'll never take any chances with your comedy, and taking chances is what good comedy is all about. Playing it safe is what mediocre comedy is all about.

What This Book Will And Won't Do

It is impossible to teach someone to be funny. It just can't be done. So if you don't really believe you're funny, this book can't fix that. But obviously, since you're reading it, you must think you've got some funny in you. Deep down inside, you think you're a funny person. The goal of this book is to make you *know* you are funny. Using the exercises in this book and learning to let go of your inhibitions will get you started on the road to being a comedy writer. It will act like a coach, teaching you to trust your comedic instincts and encouraging you to get your comedy out there to the world.

You'll mostly be working with sketches and stand-up in this book. They are the most immediate use for your ideas, but of course, your ideas can be used for anything. This book will ask a *ton* of questions. Asking yourself questions is the key to good comedy. Questioning everything is the only way to get ideas. This book won't make you funny—but if you're willing to put the work into it, you'll make *yourself* funnier.

No Shortcuts

How do you get to Carnegie Hall? Practice! Some people are just naturally funny. If you're one of them, congratulations. But the rest of us have to work at it. Comedy writing is a lot of work, coming up with ideas, working through them, writing them effectively, and performing, refining, and polishing. If you do it properly, no one will even notice all the work.

It's different for everybody, but on average only 5 percent of a comedy writer's ideas work as a joke, and probably only one out of 100 jokes works really well. You have to sift through a lot of rocks to find a nugget of comedy gold.

But if it works, it's all worth the effort. A well-crafted joke is something you will be really proud of.

Rules? We Don't Need No Stinking Rules!

You won't be learning comedy by "filling in the blanks" with a bunch of comedy formulas. None of that: "He's so stupid, he thinks _____ is _____!" Why? Because your end product will sound like formula writing. You want material that's fresh and unique—stuff that's "you." Why start by imitating stuff that's already been done?

E-QUESTION

What is the difference between a comedian, a comic, and a comedy writer?
There's an old saying, usually attributed to radio comedian Ed Wynn: "A comic says funny things; a comedian says things funny." But for all practical purposes, there is no difference between a comedian, a comic, and a comedy writer. And, unless you're French, *never* use the word comedienne for a female comedian.

You won't be learning a lot of comedy rules in this book because there are no hard-and-fast rules in comedy. Remember, comedy is all about *breaking* the rules of society, so don't get bound by them in your writing. You'll approach comedy writing from a more organic path, from an idea-to-idea basis. You'll learn how to come up with good ideas and make them better using some very simple techniques. You'll figure out which ideas work for you and which ones don't. The goal here is to help you develop comedy that reflects your own unique and original point of view.

Profile in Comedy: Mary Jo Pehl

Mary Jo Pehl is a former writer for *Mystery Science Theater 3000*, where she also played evil nemesis Pearl Forrester. She is currently a writer, producer, and actor for *Cinematic Titanic*, a direct-to-DVD series. Mary Jo is a regular contributor to *Minnesota Monthly*, and her work has appeared in many other publications. She has contributed to several anthologies, including *Life's A Stitch: The Best of Contemporary Women's Humor* and *Travelers' Tales: The Thong Also Rises*. In addition, her commentaries have aired on NPR's *All Things Considered* and *Weekend America* and *The Savvy Traveler* on Public Radio International. She has appeared in various stage productions from New York to Los Angeles, including live shows of *Cinematic Titanic*.

When did you first realize that you were uniquely funny?

Actually, I'm still wondering about that! I think I had an inkling that perhaps I was out of step humor-wise when I saw *The Sound of Music* for the first time. I was pretty young, maybe 6, and there's a part where Maria is on her way to the Von Trapps after singing a lusty, bravada song about how confident she is. She arrives at their giant gate, and says, "Oh, help." I cracked up at the irony and I was the only one (as I recollect) laughing in the theater.

Who do you think were your influences?

Carol Burnett, *Laugh In* (when I could sneak in a viewing without my parents' knowledge), my Mom, my whole family, my best friend Kitti in high school, *Monty Python* (and each member's individual projects), *The Onion*, John Kennedy Toole with *Confederacy of Dunces*, *Saturday Night Live*, and as I made my way up the standup comedy ranks, my tremendously funny friends and colleagues. Stop me!

When did you realize that comedy was something you had to do for a living?

The "universe" backed me into a corner. I kept getting fired or laid off from all the cube corporate jobs I tried to fit in at. I didn't get corporate politics. Apparently I was "ineffective" as an employee. I had an "attitude." And several companies I worked for went out of business. At one point, I'd gotten fired right when I got a long-term gig doing a comedy show. I knew I would survive for a couple of months on that, and I decided to give it a go. I felt like I didn't have any choice, really!

What was your first job comedy writing / performance?

I used to do sketchs and/or impersonations in high school talent shows but I'd say the REAL first was when I started a sketch comedy group with a couple of friends of mine. We called ourselves the Boneless Hams. We wrote and performed sketch comedy and stand-up bits, and performed at a bar in an office building off an interstate exchange during happy hour.

How did you first get involved with *Mystery Science Theater 3000*?
I knew most of the gang working on the show from the Minneapolis comedy scene. When the show got picked up by Comedy Central, I heard they were looking for a new writer. So I called Mike Nelson, the head writer, and expressed my interest. They asked me in for an audition; I was there for two weeks, then they forgot I was there and I just stayed.

What are you currently working on?
I'm a writer/producer for *Cinematic Titanic* and I'm working on a book, as well as some other creative projects that are in the tadpole stage.

What is the biggest difficulty you've encountered being a comedy writer?
Not being funny! Sometimes the funny fails. Sometimes you have no idea what's funny anymore. The subjectivity of humor and justifying my humor to people who don't share the same sensibilities as me. Trying to come up with something specific for a spot in the film, as in the case of *MST3K* or *Cinematic Titanic*. People who dismiss women in whole as "not funny" just because they are women. Having to hear really bad, disgusting, vile jokes because "Hey, you have a sense of humor—you'll love this—"

Are there jokes that you do just for you?
Sure—mostly in my stand-up comedy act, and sometimes a sort of joke that might show up in an episode of *Mystery Science Theater 3000* and now *Cinematic Titanic*.

What are the differences between writing for yourself and writing for others?
Obviously, the voices and point of view are different. So you have to figure out a way to make someone else funny, which might not be as organic. Fortunately, on *Mystery Science Theater 3000*—and now *Cinematic Titanic*—we all worked together a long time and get each other's sensibilities, so it's easier to do.

Where do you think the future of comedy is headed?

I really couldn't say. I think it's getting harder to be funny because so many real life events are so preposterous you couldn't make them. Real life beats comedians to the punch.

What is the best thing about being a comedy writer?

There is nothing like making people laugh. There is nothing that compares to meeting people or getting an e-mail that thanks you for making them laugh and getting them through hard times. There is nothing like saying something funny on stage and hearing laughter.

Do you have any advice for up and coming comedy writers?

First of all, be a good writer. Secondly, figure out a way to do it. In this day and age, there are so many outlets and venues to get your work out there. Comedy and writing is no longer dependent on a publisher or a TV network—it's all DIY.

Brainstorm

In this book, any time you see the word "joke," it basically means a funny idea or concept. The ideas you'll be brainstorming can have many uses—a one-liner, a sketch, a movie idea, a short story, etc. In the beginning, just concentrate on the jokes—worry about their uses later.

Take some time to think about why you want to be a comedian or comedy writer. Why did you buy this book? Are you willing to put the work into creating some funny stuff? There are many reasons people become comedians, but you can basically boil them down to two. Some will say, "I do it because I just love making people laugh." Others say, "I love making people laugh (at how funny *I* am)!" Either way, they are both great motivators to make you want to be a comedy writer.

Is comedy something you *have* to do? Something you know deep down you'll be really good at? Start thinking about what you want to do with comedy. Is it stand-up or sketches? Screenplays, sitcoms, or novels? Maybe your goal is simpler than that. Maybe you just want to write funnier speeches and presentations. Maybe you're a "serious" writer who just wants to lighten up a little. Or perhaps you're just a comedy aficionado who appreciates seeing how it all works. Whatever your reasons, there will be something for you here.

FACT

The ultimate goal in comedy is to make your comedy voice unique. You want your writing to reflect you. You want to write jokes that no one else in the world would even think of. If your name is Joe Smith and you write a joke, you want people to say, "Wow, that's a real Joe Smith joke!"

Also, begin thinking about the potential markets for your work. Is there a comedy club near you with an open-mic night? Do you want to start a blog? Do you want to get millions of hits on your YouTube video? Should you start getting re-aquatinted with that friend who has a cousin who knows someone who used to date someone who works in television? Do you have friends with a similar or compatible sense of humor with whom you might like to write or perform?

Open your mind to the possibilities that are out there for you. Start noticing where you might fit into the world of comedy.

Notebook

Buy a notebook and start jotting your ideas in it. Don't worry about structure and formatting; just keep it with you at all times. When you think of something funny, write it down. Throughout this book there will be exercises to help you start filling up the first of what will be many notebooks to come.

This first exercise is going to sound really weird, but try it out or at least embrace the principles behind it. Write down your observations in your notebook. There are two options you can try; if you're really adventurous, try both.

Can Billy Come Out and Play?

Find a kid. If you have one lying around the house, great. If you don't, ask a friend or relative if you can borrow his for a few minutes. Get down on the floor and play with whatever the kid's playing with—Barbies, action figures, stuffed animals, whatever.

Watch how the child plays and follow his lead. If the baby wants to drive the minivan, let the baby drive the minivan. You know that's not logical, but don't contradict the fun with reality. Have some fun and notice how effortlessly the child improvises and how quickly he makes decisions when he isn't being judged.

Staples: The Mini-Series

Try this when you are alone or you might have a lot of explaining to do. Look at the things on your desk. What have you got? A stapler? A coffee mug? A Mr. T bobblehead? Start treating the objects as characters—living, breathing entities—and have them interact with each other. Is the stapler having an affair with the pencil behind the keyboard's back? Is your "World's Greatest Dad" mug worried because he falling behind on his child support payments? Are the pens and paper being downsized by the computer? For a week or so, create your own little desktop soap opera. Commit to it. Keep the action going and have fun with it.

Why are you doing this? You want to start looking for relationships and connections between random things. Start seeing things from a new perspective, and soon you'll see the world in a different light.

CHAPTER 2

You Know More Than You Think You Do

Even though you may not have realized it, you've been preparing to be a comedy writer your entire life. Every time you've laughed or made someone else laugh—that's comedy. In fact, you're an expert on comedy. You just need to work on refining the basic techniques you already know and start figuring out interesting topics you want to write about.

Become a Comedy Sponge (Squarepants Optional)

Let's get started. You know a lot more about comedy and comedy writing than you think you do. As a consumer of comedy, just think about how much comedy you have experienced in your lifetime. You've seen it all, from Bugs Bunny cartoons to late-night talk shows. How many times have you seen Lucy pitching Vitavitavegimin on reruns of *I Love Lucy*? How many of Gary Larson's *Far Side* cartoons have you laughed at? How many times have you seen Homer Simpson try to jump over Springfield Gorge? Sitcoms, movies, newspaper articles, books, stand-up, talk shows, cartoons, the list goes on and on. You've seen what works and what doesn't, and you know what you like and don't like. You've seen countless examples that others have presented to the world as their comedic point of view. Now it's time to show the world yours.

Are You the Life of the Party?

On a personal level, you've been funny with your family, friends, and coworkers. You've probably made people you don't even know laugh. You've done it all—just not professionally. Your comic voice and timing will come from everything that has made you laugh, all the funny things that have happened to you, and all the funny thoughts you've had. Your comedy point of view will be shaped by all the comedy you have consumed. So if good stuff has been coming into your mind during your life, good stuff will come out. But even though you've been influenced by others (who were, in turn, influenced by those who came before them), your comedy voice will be uniquely yours. You have a wealth of material just waiting to get out. And believe it or not, you also know all the techniques needed to make it happen.

Are You a Good Listener?

When people see a great performer they always say, "What a great sense of timing she has." Timing comes from having a good ear, from watching so much comedy that you know the patterns and the beats that make people laugh. It comes from listening. Listening is also important in order to get a

sense of how people talk, in order to create believable dialogue and interesting characters. Everyone's timing is unique. Two comedians telling that
same joke would tell it in two completely different ways. A good comedian
doesn't have to think about the timing of a joke; she instinctively *knows* the
timing.

To "Kill" in Comedy: Start Packing Comedy "Heat"

It's weird that comedy, which in most cases is meant to make people laugh
and be happy, has such a violent lexicon. Think about it—if you really connect with an audience, you "kill." The audience laughed so hard "they almost
died." On the other hand, if the audience isn't responsive, they're "dead" or
"a bunch of stiffs." With that kind of crowd you "bomb." Your lines failed to
pack a "punch." Rough stuff!

E-QUESTION

Has anyone ever actually died from laughing?
According to Snopes.com, in 1975 a man named Alex Mitchell of Nor-
folk, England, died from laughing too hard at a sketch he saw on the
television show, *The Goodies.* He could not stop laughing for twenty-five
minutes and suffered a fatal heart attack. Now that's a sketch that literally killed.

Well, you might as well extend the metaphor with your comedy
"weaponry." In the upcoming chapters, you'll learn lots of techniques to
fully stock your armory, but for now let's look at what's already in your
arsenal.

So, Tell Me About Yourself

What's your story? Did you grow up in the city, the suburbs, or the country? Were you an only child or from a large family? Were you the oldest or

the youngest? Public or private school? Football hero or band geek? Everything about your upbringing will affect your comedy voice.

What are the things that make you unique? Maybe your dad was a mortician, a professional wrestler, or an ex-Navy Seal. And your mother—maybe she was an astrologer, a stripper, or a soccer mom. Were you a spelling-bee champion, a child prodigy, or an altar boy?

Audiences love hearing about things they have only experienced from "the other side." If you say that your parents were ex-hippies who didn't believe in discipline, two things will happen: You'll instantly connect with those who had a similar background, and you'll draw in those who always wondered what that would be like. Look for the things that may seem normal to you but might be interesting to everyone else. Think about it—if a comic says he worked at Disney World while he was in college, wouldn't you be dying to find out what that's like? It's a chance to take a peek behind the scenes and find out what it's really like to work at the Magic Kingdom. Don't you want to find out what makes Goofy so . . . goofy?

Tell Me a Story

If you had to tell someone a funny story about something that happened to you, what story would you tell? Do you have a story that you've told before that works? Let's call it your "Date Story"—you know, that great little icebreaker you have, a story you've told lots of times and usually gets a laugh. Maybe you've even refined your story over the years. You've cut out some parts of the story and maybe exaggerated others to make it even funnier. If you've done that, you've written comedy.

Maybe it's a favorite joke. A street joke, as comics call it, is a joke of unknown origin that just gets passed around by word of mouth. They typically fall into the "two guys walk into a bar . . . " or "a priest, a rabbi, and a gorilla are stuck if a lifeboat . . . " category. Is there a joke you've heard, liked, and repeated? Maybe you've even changed it around or added funny voices to make it even funnier. If you have, you've performed comedy. (If you haven't, don't worry—lots of comedians, including some of the funniest, can't tell a street joke to save their lives.)

The Funniest Joke

In 2001, Professor Richard Wiseman and the British Association for the Advancement of Science set out to find the world's funniest joke, After 40,000 jokes and 1.5 million responses, here is the winner: *A couple of New Jersey hunters are out in the woods when one of them falls to the ground. He doesn't seem to be breathing and his eyes are rolled back in his head. The other guy whips out his cell phone and calls the emergency services. He gasps to the operator, "My friend is dead! What can I do?" The operator, in a calm soothing voice, says, "Just take it easy. I can help. First, let's make sure he's dead." There is a silence, then a shot is heard. The guy's voice comes back on the line. He says, "Okay, now what?"* Is it the funniest joke? Is it even close? You decide.

Trust Your Instincts

Here's the bottom line: If *you* think something is funny, it *is* funny. There's no doubt about it, it's funny—to you. The question is: Is it funny to anyone else? Sometimes it will be, sometimes it won't. It might be funny to some and not to others, but it will never be funny to everyone.

There is a classic Monty Python sketch about a joke that was so funny that whoever heard it would literally die laughing. The joke was so powerful that it was used in warfare as a secret weapon. It's a great concept, but there is no surefire joke. There will always be somebody who just doesn't get it.

The Marx Brothers were hilarious in their heyday, and still are today. But their leading lady never got their jokes. Margaret Dumont, who usually played the wealthy dowager the brothers simultaneously tried to woo and scam, never understood what was funny. Perhaps this is why she played the perfect straight "man" to the brothers Marx.

If you've ever seen a comedy amateur night, you've probably seen fledgling comedians who really thought they were funny but didn't connect with the crowd at all. You need to figure out how to communicate your comedy to your audience so that most of them see it in the same way you do. You know the expression "you had to be there"? You need to make the audience feel as if they *are* there.

Play The Odds

Comedy is about percentages. As a comedy writer, sometimes you'll gamble that about 80 percent of the audience will get a certain joke, 90 percent will get another, and maybe only 10 percent or less will get some jokes. If that 10 percent thinks those jokes are *really* funny, the other 90 percent of the audience feels left out and will now pay even closer attention to what you're saying.

A Target Audience

Gaining a following is easier today because audiences are segmented, and there are so many opportunities to reach them. In the old days of just three networks—ABC, CBS, and NBC—you had to play it safe. You had to have a large audience, a wide range of people of different ages and backgrounds, think your show was funny. But with hundreds of channels to choose from, audiences will seek out the kind of comedy that appeals to them. You don't have to play it safe to be successful. People who like your style of comedy will find you, and those who wouldn't get it probably won't even know it exists.

ALERT!

Hitting that 100 percent mark, where everyone thinks a joke is funny, is pretty much impossible. So don't waste your time trying to find it. Do what *you* think is funny and you'll attract a following that thinks it's funny too.

In the big scheme of things, even if a relatively small number of people check out a blog because it speaks to them, it doesn't need huge numbers to be a success. Advertisers will buy ads on your blog space and will thank you for helping them sell to a specific market segment. Some film comedies have bombed at the box office but have developed a cult following, which led to a second or third life on video or DVD.

Trying to please everybody is a fool's errand. Be yourself, trust your instincts, present your comic view of the world, and you'll attract your audience.

Profile in Comedy: Jonathan Katz

Jonathan Katz co-created and starred in Comedy Central's hilarious, Emmy award-winning animated series *Dr. Katz: Professional Therapist*, which ran for six seasons. He has also appeared in three of David Mamet's films, *State and Main*, *Things Change*, and *The Spanish Prisoner*, and cowrote the story for Mamet's *House of Games*. He recently released a comedy CD, *Caffeinated*, and has his own podcast called *Hey, We're Back*. He is also one of the funniest people on the face of the earth.

When did you first realize that you were uniquely funny?
When my wife got an obscene phone call and even though it wasn't me, she thought it was and she laughed hysterically and then started wheezing and then the guy said, "Are you alright?"

Who do you think were your influences?
Johnny Carson, Ronnie Shakes, Dom Irrera, David Mamet, Tom Snyder, A. Whitney Brown, Norm McDonald, and Rita Rudner.

Do you remember your first original joke?
"I have been called a white Paul Simon."

When did you realize that comedy was something that you had to do for a living?
The first laugh in a club, the first time I got paid, and then the acceptance of other comedians at the bar. I am a compulsive comedian. The fact that I get paid sometimes just makes it more legit.

What was your first job comedy writing / performance?
My first comedy writing gig was for *New York Magazine*. I wrote an article called "The Peeing Man's Guide to Midtown Manhattan." It never got published. My

first performance was in a revue at Goddard College called *Camel* and it was written by my friend of forty-three years, David Mamet.

What is the biggest difficulty you've encountered being a comedy writer?
Giving jokes away for free and not knowing my audience. I have a very dark side and sometimes it comes out in broad daylight.

Are there jokes that you do just for you?
Sometimes I will tell a joke I like as a litmus test of the audience.

You created one of the most stolen jokes in comedy history ("I had dinner with my father last night and I made a classic Freudian slip. I meant to say, 'Please pass the salt,' but it came out, 'You putz, you ruined my childhood.'"). How do you feel about that?
Flattered and bitter.

Do you need to be in Los Angeles or New York to have a comedy writing career?
Absolutely not.

What are the differences between writing for yourself and writing for others?
You have to trust that they can make your comedy work. Writing for Bill Maher was fun, because he can soft sell a joke.

What do you find exciting about comedy right now?
Bad taste is tasting better than ever.

Where do you think the future of comedy is headed?
Back to vaudeville.

What is the best thing about being a comedy writer?
I get to think of things that make me laugh.

Do you have any advice for up-and-coming comedy writers?
Get a notebook and don't discard anything. Don't be afraid to use jokes in a new context.

FACT

Police Squad, the Abrahams, Zucker, and Zucker parody of cheesy '70s police shows, was a critical success but a ratings bomb. The show went on to become the very successful *Naked Gun* series of films. *Police Squad* is also important because it was one of the first TV comedies not filmed in front of a live audience that didn't have a laugh track.

Brainstorm

Stop being a passive consumer and start being an active comedy analyst. Watch all the comedy that you see and hear with a critical eye. Look at a show and ask: Who is this written for? What is the intended audience? Who wouldn't get this at all? Would my friends like this? Would my grandmother? Start looking for the comedy that fits your sensibilities—the shows and movies you like, the stand-up you think is funny, and the authors that make you laugh. Then try to figure out the audience for each of the things you like. This will help you find yourself and your audience—an audience that is like-minded.

Notebook

Ready to start writing some jokes or at least kick-start your brain's joke-generating engine? Be careful: Once you start asking your brain to come up with jokes it might not be able to stop.

"Something From Nothing"

You can use this exercise anytime. Try it when you have down time—when you're riding the subway, waiting at the doctor's office, anytime you're bored. Boredom can be a comic's best friend. When your mind starts to wander, that's when it's ready for comedy.

This exercise is called "Something From Nothing" because it's a quick and fun way to come up with lots of ideas from absolutely nothing. It's like plucking jokes from thin air. Some might be great, and others, well, not-so-great. But that's okay. The object is to get ideas and start making those random brain connections that make up comedy. One idea—good or bad—will always lead to another. That's how the process works.

Here's how it works: Take out a sheet of paper and draw a line lengthwise down the middle. Make a list of thirty to forty nouns, people, places, and things on one side. On the other side, write thirty to forty more. Don't overthink your word choices; just let it flow. Don't try to be funny yet—simply write down words that are interesting but not too specific. Here's a sample list to get you started:

SOMETHING FROM NOTHING

dog	microwave oven	teacher	fossil
taxi	wallet	dinosaur	remote control
potato	Barbie	ventriloquist	calculator
elephant	newspaper	dictionary	gift basket
monster	monkey	lunchbox	piggy bank
toaster	robot	office chair	answering machine
computer	evil genius	vampire	secret recipe
backpack	fast food	toothpaste	ATM
astronaut	kitten	laser	genie lamp
bowling ball	blanket	microphone	cell phone
iPod	hybrid car	mullet	stuffed animal
crayons	blender	telephone	eyeglasses
doll	diary	ambulance	camel
milk carton	policeman	dog groomer	parrot

Now that you have a list, set aside an hour or so and get ready to play. The goal is to take a word from Column A and pair it with any of the words from Column B and see if any funny ideas come to mind. It could be anything—a quick joke, a sketch idea, even a premise for a short story. Feel free to jump around the list; there are no real rules here. If an idea makes you think of something totally different and takes you in another direction, don't be afraid to go there; that's the whole point of this exercise. As you make matches, jot your ideas down, draw pictures, and doodle. Grab your notebook and let's get started.

ALERT!

Be warned, once you start asking your brain to look for comedy all the time, it will do just that—look for comedy *all* the time, even at the most inappropriate times. Funerals, colonoscopies, and waiting in line at the DMV will never be the same. You'll need to find a balance of allowing your brain to wander and asking it for extreme focus as an idea comes up.

The following is an attempt to capture the thought process on paper. Your results will vary—and hopefully they'll be funnier!

Dog paired with Microwave

Hmmm, there's an urban legend about an old lady who tried to dry her wet dog in the microwave with disastrous results. It probably never happened, but what if it did? Hot Paw-kets? . . . How do urban legends start anyway? How about a sketch about an office full of guys whose job it is to write urban legends and get them out to the public . . . Or, what about this—a support group for people who were in urban legends telling their stories. You could have the microwaved-dog lady, the woman who was parked in lover's lane with her boyfriend and later found a bloody hook on the car door handle, and the kid who made a funny face and it froze that way. They could all be talking about their problems when a newcomer is introduced to the group. There might be something there.

Dog paired with Secret Recipe

Cans of pet food have flavor names like "Hearty Stew" and "Seafood Fiesta Select." Do people test them? Is there someone whose job it is to taste test dog food? Is there a temperamental master chef behind these creations? Dogs and cats eat weird stuff on their own. They even eat out of the garbage and drink out of the toilet bowl. Why not give the foods names that reflect that. Names like "Rancid Month-Old Chinese-Food Leftovers Medley," "Coffee Grounds and Q-Tips Blend," "I Can't Believe it's Not Poop" and "Diaper Surprise!"

Dog paired with Fossil

What would a prehistoric dog look like? Would it look like Dino from The Flintstones? *What if archeologists actually found the Flintstones-like home in a dig? The pig/garbage disposal, the bird/record player, etc. That could be interesting. What if a dog skeleton was actually made out of Milk Bones? That could be a cool prop. It proves you are what you eat.*

Elephant paired with Newspaper

Why would an elephant be reading a newspaper? What section, the personals? Maybe it could take out an ad. What would animal personals be like? What if two animals that were mortal enemies, like a lion and a wildebeest, fell in love in a chat room, then finally met each other on a blind date? How awkward would that be? . . . How about the job listings? Maybe the elephant is sick of its job at the zoo or circus and wants a different career? What job would it apply for, and how would the interview go? That could be a fun sketch. . . . What's another "weird" job that someone could be sick of? The Tooth Fairy, the Boogyman, the Jolly Green Giant, and Santa might be fun choices to try. . . . How about this: Have a job interview where someone is applying for the job of Boogyman—"My strengths? Well, I'm really bad with kids . . . " Or, instead of a job interview—a blind date. The Boogyman on a blind date—that could be a funny sketch or it could be a single-panel comic strip. Or what if the Tooth Fairy's job was outsourced to India?

Get the idea? Not everything was funny, but weak ideas led to stronger premises. The key is not to judge ideas as they come up, just let them flow. If you've tried to make a connection but a word pairing isn't giving you ideas, just move on. Don't make speed bumps on your path to an idea by deciding if a thought is funny or not. Just jot it down and keep going. Do this exercise whenever you can and remember even if you only get one good idea from it—it's worth it.

If you don't get *any* good ideas from this exercise, don't worry about it. Put the list aside and try again tomorrow. This can't be a chore; it has to be fun. If you're not in the right mood, you're not going to get much, or all your ideas will reflect that mood. Maybe you're too close to the list. Maybe it's just a bad list. Ask a friend to make you a list. Better yet, make it really random by asking a few friends to give you four or five items.

CHAPTER 3

The Funny Five

Every comedian's arsenal includes some go-to joke formats that get the job done. They aren't really rules or formulas; they're just familiar joke patterns that work. Become familiar with them and they just might help you craft your ideas into comedy gold. There are a lot of tricks of the trade, but there are five that are pretty much sure-fire techniques. These funny five—creating set-ups and punch lines, surprise, building tension and releasing it, the rule of threes, and using funny-sounding words—will help you start using your ideas right away.

Set-Ups and Punch Lines

The set-up is the most common type of joke. You've heard it thousands of times; it's pretty much the staple of stand-up, late-night talk shows, and some sitcoms. It's a simple yet effective format: You state a fact or opinion, then give it a comedic twist. The audience expects one thing, but it gets much more than it expected—a joke. It's especially good for topical monologues because it's a good, quick way to use disposable information—something that happened in the news that day. You use the joke once and then move on. Here's an example of a set-up:

NASA announced that the Mars Rover found possible signs of life on Mars today . . .

It's just a statement of fact. That's it, nothing more—but notice the ellipse. That pause tells the audience the joke is coming. Here's the punch line:

A homeless Martian tried to squeegee its windshield.

This technique can also be used on a personal level:

I had French toast this morning. . . . Well, actually it was just regular toast—but it had a really snotty attitude.

There can be multiple punch lines for the same set-up. Think of how many jokes Jeff Foxworthy has come up with for the set-up: "You know you're a redneck if . . . ." He's probably used it hundreds, if not thousands, of different ways. There are probably thousands more to come, and they all work. In most cases, a comic will come up with a couple of possible contenders for the punch line before she chooses the one that works best. That might happen after she tries different punch lines on stage. Through trial and error, she finds the best fit.

The set-up and punch doesn't have to be a quick one-two punch. You can add an extra joke or two after the punch line to keep the laughter going. This is called a tag. The tag basically turns the original punch line into a set-up and usually catches the audience completely off-guard. Think of it as a knockout punch line. Even better, a tag can be used to show how your character relates to the punch line. Here's an example:

I'm convinced that my car is possessed by the devil. The other day, I parked it, went into the store for a couple of minutes, and when I came back out—mysteriously, the words "WASH ME" had appeared on it.

And here's the reaction tag:

So I abandoned it. I'm not driving home in some haunted voodoo car.

It does two things; it adds an extra joke *and* tells the audience something about your character.

A good way to practice this format and flex your comedy muscles at the same time is to watch the late-night television monologues and write down the set-up—just the first part of the joke—and then try to think of alternate punch lines. You might even come up with one that is funnier than the one the host delivered.

The Element of Surprise

Monty Python said it best: "Nobody expects the Spanish Inquisition!" The element of surprise takes the set-up and punch line format to a whole new level. It's all about distraction, leading the audience down the garden path—then siccing the dogs on them. You make them expect something, and then you *really* twist it. It's like watching a good magic trick; it's all about deception.

Imagine what it was like for the first person in history to be handed a can of salted peanuts only to have cloth-covered spring snakes fly out of the can. That's what the element of surprise is all about.

Here's a great example of the element of surprise: In 1985, comedy magician Harry Anderson hosted *Saturday Night Live*. At that time, he was the star of the successful sitcom *Night Court*. In his opening monologue, he spoke about how the audience wouldn't be seeing the "old Harry" any more—No more shoving a needle in his arm, or dropping his pants on stage. Now that he was a star he had to provide only "good, clean fun . . . family entertainment."

ALERT!

> Be careful not to overuse the element of surprise. It's all based on trust. If you continue to violate the audience's trust in you, eventually they'll get wise to you and won't take the bait. Any of these techniques can be overused; it's up to you to know when to stop.

Then he introduced his new best friend, a cute little guinea pig named Skippy. After trying to get Skippy to do some simple tricks and failing, Harry finally said, "Well, Skip . . . you know the rules—you don't work, you don't live." Then he proceeded to shove the guinea pig into his mouth and eat him, mumbling, "We'll be right back!"

Now that's a surprise! The audience probably knew *something* was going to happen, but nobody expected that. As it turned out, *they* were the guinea pigs in a bizarre comedy experiment. (By the way, Skippy was in on the gag and lived out his life in Boca Raton.) The element of surprise manipulates the audience's expectations, then takes them somewhere completely different.

Tension and Release

Tension and release is great for sketch and film work. You control the audience by making them as uncomfortable as possible by creating tension, then releasing that tension with a joke just at the right time. The members of Monty Python were masters of this format.

On their 1972 album *Monty Python's Previous Record* there is a sketch called "Travel Agent," where a man (Eric Idle) walks into the office of a travel agent (Terry Jones) to arrange a vacation. The man drones on about all the problems with his past trips, not letting the exasperated agent get a word in edgewise. It's funny at first, then it's funny because it's gone on too long, then it gets annoying, then it ends up being really annoying. It actually makes the listener squirm in his seat, wondering when it's going to end. Finally, the travel agent literally begs the listener to lift the needle off the album to end his torment. Now that's connecting with the audience!

For more great examples of tension and release sketches, check out the following Monty Python sketches: "Anne Elk," " The Cheese Shop," and, of course, the famous "Dead Parrot Sketch." Also, check out the comedy album *Bob & Ray: A Night of Two Stars*, which features probably the best example of the tension and release format, "The Slow Talkers of America."

Three is a Magic Number

There were four Marx Brothers, but only three of them were funny. Good things come in threes: Musketeers, Wise Men, and Stooges. The same goes for comedy. Think of the Rule of Three as a laundry list where the third item is the punch line. Why three? It's the minimum number needed to set up and break a pattern. You build to a climax.

I've always had a great memory. Probably my earliest memory is from when I was a baby. I can even remember my christening like it was yesterday: lots of people, the noise—Queen Elizabeth hitting me over the head with a champagne bottle.

This technique lengthens the set-up by adding a list. The first two items on the list reinforce or "prove" the statement of fact at the beginning, and the third item on the list is the twist.

FACT

One great facet of the Rule of Three is that the audience is preconditioned to expect something funny at the punch line. They've heard the format so many times, it's almost as if they're in on the joke. They expect the joke to be funny at the point you want it to be funny—they know it's coming.

Sometimes the audience is so used to the Rule of Three that the best way to get them to laugh is to violate it. Make them expect the joke on the third beat, but drag it out in a funny way.

In this classic example from *Monty Python and the Holy Grail* (1975), the instructions for the Holy Hand Grenade of Antioch are solemnly read:

> *And the Lord spake, saying, "First shalt thou take out the Holy Pin. Then shalt thou count to three, no more, no less. Three shall be the number thou shalt count, and the number of the counting shall be three. Four shalt thou not count, neither count thou two, excepting that thou then proceed to three. Five is right out. Once the number three, being the third number, be reached, then lobbest thou thy Holy Hand Grenade of Antioch toward thy foe, who, being naughty in my sight, shall snuff it.*

The audience thinks the joke is coming at three, but three is just the beginning. So whether you choose to use—or misuse—the rule of three, it will probably be funny. It works because you're playing with the audiences' expectations either way. It's all about timing; performers have timing when they tell a joke, but audiences have their own timing based on what they expect from a joke.

Funny Sounds: No, Not Those Funny Sounds

There's no doubt about it, *k* is the funniest letter of the alphabet. Whenever you have a choice to use a word with a hard *k* sound over one that doesn't, go with the *k*. The letter *p* is also funny, but not as funny as *k*. What's funnier: vomit, throw-up, or puke? (Up-chuck would be a close second.) What's funnier: "Boy, am I in trouble!" or "Boy, am I in a pickle!"? What's funnier: "A robin walks into a bar." or "A duck walks into a bar."? (Ducks are always funny.) Killjoy, kumquat, kiwi, hockey puck, Krusty the Klown, hiccup—they all work. You can't go wrong with *k*.

Another sound that works is a double consonant sound: Pepperoni, wobble, tummy, bossy, bratty. What's funnier: Oreo or Nutter Butter? "Does this tuna fish smell bad?" or "Does this tuna fish smell funny?"? Apple pie or apple cobbler? Again, if you have a choice, choose the word with the double consonant.

A single word can make the difference in whether a joke works or fails. Good comedians are always searching for that perfect word that sells the joke. Sometimes it takes a while to find it, but you'll know the perfect word when you see it.

Words that have a *k* sound and a double consonant—Catskills, cuddle, commune, clapper—are comedy gold. And don't forget "cowbell." This staple in our pop culture lexicon came from Christopher Walken's now classic *Saturday Night Live* sketch about the Blue Oyster Cult in which he demanded "more cowbell." Phrases with alliteration can also work: pepperoni pizza, wobbly wheel, dead duck.

Some General Writing Tips

Now that you know the Funny Five, here are a few more personal rules or tips you can use to make your writing—and the writing process—more effective:

- **Find time to write.** Make sure to set aside some time every day to write something or at least look over the notes you may have jotted down during the day.
- **Don't force it.** If ideas aren't coming, take a break. Walk away from what you're writing and come back to it later. Sometimes seeing your work with a fresh set of eyes can work wonders.
- **Expand your vocabulary.** Always have a dictionary and a thesaurus handy. A slang dictionary can be especially useful.
- **If you're having trouble writing something, say it out loud.** Walk around and verbally brainstorm it. Also, try drawing your thoughts on paper.
- **Doodle.** Keep a sketch pad handy when you're relaxing and watching TV. This free form of expression is good for helping you subconsciously release ideas.

- **Comedy writing is like sculpting; you really get your hands dirty crafting jokes.** Add a little here, and take away some there. You are basically organizing chaos, so expect it to be messy.

- **Be suspicious of an idea that comes too quickly.** Beware of jokes that just "happen." There is always the chance that you're just remembering something you heard somewhere before. It happens to everyone. If you run across a suspect joke, check it out. Do a web search. Ask other comics. Once you get the all clear, it's all yours.

- **Write your pacing into the jokes by using ellipses.** It may not be grammatically correct, but remember, you're out to break the rules. To the reader what's more effective: "Ready, set, go!" or "Ready . . . set . . . go!"? Timing is really important in comedy, and your writing should show it.

When you're writing, or even just trying to get the creative juices flowing, keep these tips in mind. And remember, this is comedy. Don't put too much pressure on yourself; make it fun!

E-QUESTION

If I think of a joke, perform it on stage, but never actually put pen to paper and write it down, is that still writing?
Absolutely! You can write things without writing them down. In fact, sometimes it's best to just say your ideas out loud. Comedy writing is just the process of thinking of funny thoughts. Someone says something and you think of something funny, on the spot, as a response. That's writing, plain and simple.

Profile in Comedy: Jimmy Tingle

Jimmy Tingle's down-to-earth and approachable style has helped him perform his political and satirical comedy and get big laughs even from those who disagree with him. He has appeared as a commentator on PBS, NBC, MSNBC, CNN, and the BBC. He was the weekly humorist on *60 Minutes II*.

He even owned his own comedy theater, and he has appeared in the films *Next Stop Wonderland* and *Head of State*.

When did you first realize that you were uniquely funny?
When you asked me to contribute to this book.

Who do you think were your influences?
Daniel Boone, Lenny Bruce, my mother.

Do you remember your first original joke?
Yes, but I cannot repeat it here. My first real material was song parodies that I would perform in a trench coat, sunglasses, and felt hat, a la *The Blues Brothers*. I was trying to be the comedian with the blues and I had several songs; "Thank God I'm a City Boy" and "Thank God I'm a 'Burbite" were takeoffs on the John Denver "Thank God I'm a Country Boy." "The Test Tube Baby Blues" was in response to the birth of the first test tube baby, and "The Pooper Scooper Blues" was a protest song against the newly enacted pooper scooper legislation, which I opposed. Looking back on it I realize I was actually advocating for poop on the sidewalk.

When did you realize that comedy was something you had to do for a living?
When I first performed on Lenny Clark's open-mic night in 1980. Forty friends showed up and after I was done with all my songs, they cheered wildly. The rest of the audience was probably cheering just because the songs were over, but regardless—I was hooked.

What was your first job in comedy writing or performance?
I have only had two official jobs with a consistent paycheck. One was as a contributor to MSNBC when they first went on the air in 1996. The other was with *60 Minutes II* where I was a commentator for two seasons in 1999 and 2000. Other than that, it has always been a series of one-nighters or a week at a comedy club or a month or two at a theater. My first job that paid was probably street performing. My first official paycheck I think was at a gong show or talent contest. Most of the open mike nights gave the performers a free beer.

What is the biggest difficulty you have encountered being a comedy writer?

The biggest difficulty is trying to please everyone—the audience, producer or client, and myself—at the same time.

Are there jokes that you do just for you?

Jokes just for me? Not really. They are all for me; if they don't get laughs I don't do them anymore. There are pieces I do that are not funny but they are important to the story I am telling so I do them. This is only true in theater shows, not clubs or private parties where they are hiring me to be funny.

As a political comedian, what is your biggest challenge?

Biggest challenge as political comedian is to make a point and be funny to people who do not agree with you. It is also a challenge to say something about the issue or individual without resorting to their obvious attributes or flaws—height, weight, hair, dress—but rather something about the policy or political positions they are taking. The greatest thrill is to make people laugh at a point of view on a hot button issue they do not agree with, like immigration or gun control.

How did your schedule work, writing your spot for a weekly TV show?

I did not really have a set schedule. Some bits I wrote that week or day. Others I did were bits I had been doing for years and were tried-and-true pieces that worked great for TV. It was always a challenge to write well and consistently on deadline. That was a muscle I was not really required to use as a stand-up comic, but for weekly TV show it is indispensable.

What do you find exciting about comedy right now?

What's exciting now is all the outlets and a really well-informed public concerning social and political issues.

Where do you think the future of comedy is headed?

I think comedy will continue to improve just like everything else. Ball players are better and faster and smarter than twenty years ago, technology is better. I would say the same will hold true for comedy; it will always reflect where society is at that moment. With all the outlets there will be less filters so more voices will be heard.

As audiences are becoming more specific and more segmented, is that making your job easier or more difficult?

I think with the interest in politics and the proliferation of media outlets it makes my job easier and more mainstream than when I started in 1980.

What is the best thing about being a comedy writer?

The best thing for me is to be able to articulate what I'm feeling most of the time. To be paid for something I love doing. To be able to use the craft to actually effect social change and to help deserving people and causes.

Do you have any advice for up-and-coming comedy writers?

Advice? Do what you love, follow your heart, follow your passion. In 1980 before I had even done an open-mic night in Cambridge I was traveling around Europe with a friend with the Eurail pass. Soon I was out of money and took to street performing for beer money and food. A very kind man amused by the test-tube baby blues bought my friend and me fish and chips and a pint or two. He said something I will ever forget as we said our good-byes: "Sing your song, lad, sing your song."

Brainstorm

Start studying the work of others and look at their word choices, phrasing, and use of pauses. Keep track of words and phrases that you find interesting. As you begin writing your jokes, look at your word choices and identify the words that tell the story efficiently. The faster you can get to the joke, the better.

Notebook

Here are some set-ups that you can use to help you practice writing punch lines. Don't worry about set-ups being boring. Sometimes the simpler they are, the more effective the punch line can be. But they can also be weird statements that catch the audience's attention.

- "I feel weird being naked in front of my dog."
- "I'm not a good cook."
- "I hate getting my hair cut."
- "They say that one out of every 300 cars is stolen."
- "Did you know that dolphins sleep with one eye open?"
- "Women are smarter than men"
- "I'm bad with money."
- "I read a study that said women thought bald men were sexier than men with hair."
- "Paris Hilton has a new show coming soon."
- "I like pencils better than pens."
- "Television commercials confuse me."
- "I hate taking the subway."
- "I hate getting my picture taken."

Those are just a few to get you started. When you're writing your punch lines, try using the different techniques you've learned to see where they might fit best. Always keep in mind what the audience is thinking when they hear the set-up. What are their expectations, and how can you play with those expectations to make it funny?

Feel free to alter the set-up to get you thinking. Instead of: "I hate taking the subway" try "I love taking the subway!" or "I always get nervous taking the subway." You might actually hate taking the subway, but your hatred might come through better if you start out saying you love it. The audience will assume your statement is true and your hatred will become the twist.

CHAPTER 4

Comedy Secret No. 1: We're All in the Same Boat

Like it or not, you're human. And, while each human experience is unique, there are parts of it that aren't. There are things you've experienced or thoughts you've had that might seem deeply personal to you, but in fact, they're quite common.

Quiz: The Dirty Dozen

Many of the things we have in common aren't obvious. They're things that you don't think of or talk about very often—or at all.

Here are twelve questions to get you started. Just jot down your responses, but make sure to give each one a lot of thought. They might seem kind of weird, but there is a point here—promise.

If a question makes you feel uncomfortable, just skip it. We want to find embarrassing moments here, not deep-rooted personal traumas! Lighten up, this is supposed to be fun.

1. **What was the worst present you ever got?** How old were you when you received it? Were you disappointed because you were expecting something else? Was it something practical when you wanted something fun? Was it obviously "regifted?" Was it insulting or embarrassing? Did it show that the person who gave it to you had no clue about your likes and dislikes?

2. **What was the worst job you ever had?** Were you bad at it? Was it embarrassing? Below your skill level? Above your skill level? Did you work with weird people? Was it doing something disgusting? How did you get the job? Were you fired? Did you quit? How did you leave?

3. **What is a guilty pleasure of yours?** What is something that you really like, but never really admit that you like? Are you really macho and love a certain heart-wrenching chick flick? Are you quiet and demure but love violent and gory action movies? Is it something you have to do on your own, in secret, because you're too embarrassed to admit it?

4. **What is something that you are supposed to like that you just don't get?** Is it a classic film that you just can't stand? A popular food that people think you're weird for not liking? A singer or band that is universally loved—just not by you? Do you usually play along and pretend you like it, or do you have an argument about it every time it comes up?

5. **What is something that you used to be really into, but now you can't see why you ever liked it?** Was it a TV show you were obsessed about as a kid, but now have absolutely no interest in whatsoever? Was it a hobby or sport you were passionate about that now seems really lame to you? At what point did your feelings about it change?

6. **Have you ever said something and immediately wished you could take it back?** What was it? Was it socially embarrassing? Did it just sound stupid? Were you using e-mail to gossip about someone, then accidentally forwarded the e-mail to that person? How did you get out of the situation?

7. **What was the worst date you ever had?** Was it a blind date? An online romance that fizzled when you met face-to-face? A crush who you finally won over, and turned out to be completely different from what you imagined? Was it not the person but the date itself that caused the problems?

8. **Describe the worst photo of you that was ever taken?** Was it just a hair day from hell? Is it a photo that went out for everyone to see, like a newspaper photo, photo ID, or yearbook photo? Was it a photo that you thought at the time made you look really cool, but is now hopelessly dated?

9. **Do you have a pet peeve?** Is there some small thing that really gets on your nerves and drives you crazy but seems so insignificant, petty, or silly that you're almost too embarrassed to even mention it? Do you know anyone that shares your pet peeve or are you pretty much alone on this one?

10. **Did you ever unintentionally lie about something small that you are now stuck with and have to live with?** Was it an attempt to gain approval from others? Do you continue to perpetuate that lie just out of habit?

11. **Is there someone you know fairly well, someone you see all the time, whose name you don't know?** Is it a friend or a coworker? Even worse, is it a relative? Have you ever been with that person and prayed that you wouldn't have to introduce him to anyone? Are you embarrassed to ask for help with this? Are you afraid it might get back to that person?

12. **Is there anything embarrassing or stupid you've done, an event or a moment that still occasionally haunts you?** Have you ever been walking along, having a great day, and suddenly this embarrassing thing enters your head and ruins your whole day?

Okay, pencils down, pass your papers to the front. Was it hard to answer these questions, or was it painfully easy? Everyone has these kinds of personal thoughts. Everyone has socially awkward moments, things they'd like to forget but can't, things they just don't talk about—unless they're comedians. By bringing these personal, unspoken topics up and making fun of them, you can make the audience feel that they are not alone.

It's Like You're Reading My Mind!

Everyone has thoughts or experiences that they never share with others. These are things that people tend to think are unique to them. However, while the exact situations may be exceptional, the overall experiences are commonplace.

These kinds of thoughts can be very useful for comedy writing. It's almost like mind reading. Magicians call it cold-reading. They are the staples of phony psychics, astrologers, and mediums. They are very general statements that can be said about anyone but seem deeply personal to *everyone*.

It's pure magic when the audience arrives at the joke at the exact moment you deliver the punch line, where they practically complete your sentence. Connections like that are hard to make, but they are worth the work for the effect they have on an audience.

Here is a classic dating scenario: At some point in the date you mention that you like the *Simpsons*. Your date exclaims: "Oh my God! I love the *Simpsons!*" Then you proceed to talk about your favorite episodes and memorable moments from the show. Now, this isn't exactly an amazing coincidence. Lots of people love the *Simpsons*. It's a great show, and it's the longest-running American sitcom. And people who do like it tend to be rabid about it; they know their favorite episodes and moments, and many can practically recite whole episodes from memory.

What makes this scenario seem amazing is the *moment*. You and your date have made a connection. You've shared something personal about yourselves.

Comedy is a lot like dating. Sometimes you and your audience hit it off well, and sometimes you don't. If you don't, it was nothing personal, just a mismatch. Those connections are what help make comedy work consistently. Making strong connections is like courting the audience and eventually making them fall in love with you.

ALERT!

Be careful not to share too much with the audience. Remember, an air of mystery keeps a romance alive. Don't make the stage your private confessional. Performing and writing can be therapeutic, but don't ask the audience to be your therapist. Making the audience uncomfortable without a strong comedic payoff will create lots of tension between you and the audience—and not the good kind.

If you can make connections and elicit laughs with things that audience members have thought but never told anyone, you own that audience. They are drawn in and will listen to every word you say. They will become your biggest fans, read everything you write, see every show you do, buy every album you record, and be devoted followers for life.

Get Inside the Audience's Head

Mystery Science Theater 3000, Joel Hodgson's amazing cult series that mixed really bad movies with hundreds of hilarious pop-culture references, is a great example of comedy that truly made viewers feel special and made them devoted fans for life. There were so many jokes that there was literally something for everyone. There were some references you got and others you didn't. But it didn't matter. If you got one of those jokes, you felt that Joel and his 'bots were directly talking to you. You probably felt as if you were the only person who got that joke. They got inside your head and spoke directly to the things that make you tick, the things that make you—you.

When the audience gets a connection like that, they are drawn closer to you. If you make a connection with them that touches something deep inside, it creates a bond between you and them. That bond makes it easier to entertain them. They have hitched themselves to your wagon and are along for the ride.

Paula Poundstone does a brilliant bit that perfectly illustrates the concept of getting inside the audience members' heads. She does a routine where she justifies eating a whole box of Pop-Tarts in one sitting. She mirrors exactly the way people make silly justifications in their minds for the things they do.

Likewise, if you make too many references or jokes that exclude the audience and make them feel left out, you create a barrier between yourself and the audience—a chasm that can be difficult to overcome. If they like you, a few missed connections will be overlooked. In fact, the audience might be drawn in even closer if they don't get a joke, because they feel like they're missing out on the fun. But if there are too many, you'll shut them out and they won't even try to get back in. People love feeling included and hate feeling excluded.

Profile in Comedy: Gary Gulman

Gary Gulman has appeared on *The Tonight Show with Jay Leno*, *Late Show with David Letterman*, *The Late Late Show* on CBS, *Last Call with Carson Daly*, and *Jimmy Kimmel Live*. He was second runner up on Season 2 of *Last Comic Standing* and a finalist on Season 3. He has made specials for Showtime and Comedy Central and written and starred in pilots for CBS, Fox, and Showtime. He was also a star on HBO's *Tourgasm*. His CD *Conversations with Inanimate Objects* is really good—seriously.

When did you first realize that you were uniquely funny?
Uniquely?! Gadzooks! I'll let you know when I'm unique. I'm getting there, though.

Who do you think were your influences?
Chris Elliott, David Brenner, Paul Reiser, Garry Shandling.

Do you remember your first original joke?

I remember saying a funny quip in first grade. The teacher asked what a chick was. Another kid said a baby chicken and I said, out of turn, "or a girl!" Killed! Even the teacher was broken up by it. I still get the same feeling in my stomach when something comes to me. It never gets old.

When did you realize that comedy was something you had to do for a living?

I have to make a distinction between "for a living" and "full time." With any artistic endeavor there are immensely talented people who never "make a living" in their chosen field. There's a lot of luck involved so I hate to make the idea of making a living a necessary hurdle to being a comedian. I think after getting my first job after college with an international CPA I thought, this is it? This is adulthood and I'll be in this for forty more years, best case. Fuck that! I want to do something meaningful or at least fun. You couldn't pay me enough to go back.

What was your first job in comedy writing or performance?

My first comedian job was hosting a show (for Rob Steen) above an Italian restaurant in Beverly, Massachusetts, called the Casa De Luca. I sold tickets, set up the chairs, sat the audience, ran the sound system, paid the comics, and emceed the show. For that I received $25 in CASH! It was as enjoyable as any of the more higher profile/lucrative jobs I've had.

My first writing job was a $200 project writing for some guy making a wedding video for his sister-in-law. I don't think he used any of my ideas, but the check cleared.

ALERT!

Be a smart and clever comedy writer, but don't be elitist. This type of comedy usually serves only one thing—your ego. You can write intelligent, personal, and funny comedy and be approachable at the same time. Check your ego from time to time and make sure you have a good balance between originality and approachability.

My first WGA [Writers Guild of America]-certified writing job was for a 20th Century Fox pilot for Fox television based on my standup comedy (this was 1999; I think you got a development deal just for showing up at the Montreal Comedy Festival back then) called My Gary. It hasn't been picked up . . . YET!

What is the biggest difficulty you've encountered being a comedy writer?
The waiting! I think everyone is so afraid to offend anyone in Hollywood that they never give you a clear no. I honestly have never heard a no to any of the four pilots I wrote on.

How much of a reality show is "reality" and how much is "show"?
In the case of Last Comic Standing, all of the standup was legitimate. They may have edited some of the head-to-head match-ups to make it look closer, but I think for the most part it was "reality." The off-stage stuff was definitely put together to make dramatic arcs, but again there was nothing that was just plain false.

How long does it take you to prepare for a comedy special?
I did my first one about six years in, so in a way that one took six years. Right? You're always preparing to get your work out there. I found out I was doing it in June and then did as many spots as I could until August when I shot it. So I worked on assembling and "testing" the content of the special for a little over a month. My second special I shot a week after it was offered to me. I had to put my topics on a teleprompter so I wouldn't leave anything out. The second one came out better but I also had another three years under my belt.

Are there jokes that you do just for you?
For me at this point I do all the jokes for me, not in a self-indulgent way, but there's nothing I say just to get a laugh. I do a joke because it's funny or clever or meaningful to me. That hasn't always been the case. For years it was a mixed bag. I did some jokes just because they worked and gave me that oxygen we need. I was looking to get hired, which is a terrible motivator for an artist, but I've evolved, hopefully. The greatest thing I ever heard related to this was in the Curb Your Enthusiasm pilot. Someone, it may have been Jerry Seinfeld, said that Larry had unwavering convictions as

to what he thought was funny. That's essential to becoming unique/original and it's hard to stay true to in an environment where the audience's laughter is (wrongly I feel) considered so important in measuring a performer's talents.

What are the differences between writing for yourself and writing for others?

I only wrote anything for someone other than me once. My friend was roasting Pam Anderson and I sat with him and some other comedians pitching jokes. Surprisingly, it was fun and I didn't have any paternal feelings about the jokes. The main objective was making the other comedians laugh.

What do you find exciting about comedy right now?

So much! I don't think there's ever been a better time to be a comedian. When I first started in the '90s we used to lament the fact that "the Boom" was over. Nobody was making a killing in the clubs and there were very few people who were well known just for being comedians. Now between YouTube and Comedy Central there are (I think and I'd love to hear your thoughts on this) more comedians known only, or predominantly, as comedians than any time in my lifetime. There are no overnight-type successes like when Carson ruled, but I think those stories, and again I may be wrong, for the most part were either incredibly rare or overblown. I remember Tom Dreesen telling me on the night I did my first Leno that when he did *The Tonight Show* you were famous the next day. Meanwhile, I had honestly never heard of him.

Also while very mainstream comedy is still drawing much of the audience (I'm talking Leno and the Blue Collar guys and Two and a Half Men) it's nice to see what I like to call comedy of bad comedy or the uncomfortably unfunny (mastered by the Christopher Guest troupe and Ricky Gervais) become really popular. I've always found the unfunny trying to be funny so f-ing funny!

Where do you think the future of comedy is headed?

Hopefully the postmodern Andy Kindler thing will become more accepted. I just can't imagine audiences will continue to respond to the same hackneyed premises in the next decade, but I didn't think it would last this long. I would think that Steve Martin would have snuffed out that crap, but it's still here, am I right, fellas?!

As audiences become more specific and more segmented, is your job becoming easier or more difficult?

I think easier for everyone because while it's still a completely different ball game, once you're able to develop an audience that is there specifically for you, there are more venues where a quirky comedian can find a receptive audience. Mainstream comics will always have the majority of the clubs, but I have noticed there are some major clubs that cater to a more progressive (SMARTER!) audience.

What is the best thing about being a comedy writer?

It's a rejection of the 9 to 5 empty bullshit. It's rebellious but without risking your life on a motorcycle.

Do you have any advice for up-and-coming comedy writers?

Be original. Be persistent. Be lucky. Be-lieve.

Brainstorm

Look over your responses to the questions at the beginning of this chapter, and take an educated guess about what might click with an audience—things that they might identify with. Remember, it's not the specifics of the bad job or the pet peeve, it's the *idea* of it. They will respond to *any* bad job or *any* pet peeve, because they can empathize with you. And if your job was even worse than theirs, they might even feel better about themselves because you've helped them put things in perspective. They have had similar situations as well. Start looking for more things that you can share with your audience, and they'll start sharing their laughs with you.

Notebook

Here's an exercise that helps you start looking at everyday, mundane things with a new set of eyes. It may help you realize that the things you notice about everyday life are the things that others notice as well.

In his 1983 book *Crackpot: The Obsessions of John Waters*, John Waters, director of *Hairspray*, *Cry Baby*, and *Serial Mom* wrote an essay called "Hatchet Piece (101 Things I Hate)." It is basically an exaggerated day in the life of John Waters written in narrative form, from an extremely negative perspective. He actually numbers each of the things that annoy him as he journeys through his day.

Try to write your own original version of his piece. Start by writing down everything that happens to you in a day, from the moment you wake up to the moment you fall asleep. Don't overlook the small things like brushing your teeth, checking your mail, and walking the dog. Then run through your day again, but this time focus on all the things that really bother you, all the unnecessary annoyances, problems, and time-wasters that we all face every day. From waking up far too early, driving in traffic, dealing with spam e-mail or annoying coworkers, to trying to relax at home only to realize there is nothing to watch on any of the hundreds of television channels.

For example, let's try something with brushing your teeth. What could go wrong here? You could drop your toothbrush on the floor, or worse yet, into the toilet. If you're in a rush, do you use it anyway, or do you brush your teeth with your finger? Maybe you pick up a different tube of something besides toothpaste? Do you accidentally brush your teeth with athlete's foot cream or Preparation H? Have you ever brushed your teeth and then tried to drink orange juice right after? Not a great taste combination.

Exaggerate it further: Maybe you're brushing your teeth while showering to save time, multitasking your morning routine because you're late for work. Take the worst-case scenario and make it even worse.

Remember, no moment is too small; in fact, the smaller the moment, the more you want to explore it. Again, you want to work with the things that everybody notices and deals with every day but don't talk about. Have fun with it!

CHAPTER 5

Worship the Notebook

You've been using your notebook to write down the exercises from the previous chapters. Now is the time to take a closer look at the notebook itself and the note-taking process. For comedy writing, the notebook is essential to keep track of and organize your thoughts. What is the point of having all these great ideas if you can't remember them when you need them? That's why you need a notebook and the discipline to use it consistently. If you develop a successful system of tracking your ideas, you'll always have more ideas that you'll be able to use.

An External Hard Drive for Your Brain

Your notebook is like an extra brain. It's not a place to store ideas that won't fit in your head; it's a place to store all the ideas that you can't use right now but want to save for later. You might be thinking: "Well, if it's a good idea, I'll remember it. I don't have to write it down." And that's exactly the reason that you do need to write it down—it's a good idea! You will forget your ideas, no matter how good they are. That's just the way it is. You can't rely on the unlikely chance that you will instantly recall an idea when you need it.

FACT

As a comedian, there is nothing like looking through your notebook and laughing out loud at something you wrote down months before and then completely forgot about. Why is it funnier to you now than it was before? Maybe you were just too close to it before, and now you see it with a fresh set of eyes.

Also, the idea might not seem all that viable at first; it might take some time and distance to make it better. Do you think you'll have instant access to these alternative ideas as well? How about all the thoughts that aren't even a full idea yet? Probably not. If you want to be a successful comedy writer, you really need to develop a system for keeping track of your thoughts.

Write Down Everything—You Might Need It Someday

So far you've been using your notebook almost like a workbook for the previous exercises. What else goes in the notebook? Everything you think might have some comedy potential, no matter how small or obvious it may be. It could be an unusual or uncommon event from your day—getting a haircut, waiting for the cable guy, or running into an unusual person.

For example, let's say that you take your car in for a repair. The mechanic looks at it while you nervously wait in the waiting room. When he comes out and tells you what's wrong with the car, he's using technical terms that might as well be in a different language. You nod your head, pretending you understand, and give him the go-ahead to fix the car, although you're worried about cost and whether or not you're being taken advantage of.

Have you been in that situation? It's not all that fun at the time, but it could be funny later. While you're waiting for your car, what could you put in your notebook? Are you really in the mood or do you have the time to write a sketch right then and there based on your predicament? Probably not. In fact, if it's going to be expensive or a major inconvenience, you may feel like there won't be anything funny to write about ever again.

Well, comedy is a great way to get revenge on a situation that annoys you. And a situation like this is something that everyone can relate to. Are you going to let this great opportunity for comedy get away from you just because you're having a bad day? Not if you have your notebook with you.

Here's an example of what you could jot down about this situation:

Auto Repair
- Waiting room has weird magazines.
- The coffee is horrible and the machine is hard to use.
- The TV is tuned to a boring channel and it's too high to change it.
- I feel like a moron when they ask or tell me anything about the car.
- I pretend I know what I'm talking about.
- When they ask me if I change the oil on a regular basis, it's like the dental hygienist asking me if I floss.
- I know that the mechanics are talking about how big a sucker I am.
- Should the repair really cost that much?
- Are they making me wait longer to get it fixed just to justify the cost, thus doubly annoying me?
- Why do mechanics have names that sound like they're mechanics, like Chuck or Bubba?
- How come there are no mechanics named Chad, Blaine, or Stephan?
- What would a trendy garage be like? Would it be like a fancy hair salon?

Okay, so you jot these ideas down but nothing really hits you at the time as being particularly funny. No big deal. If the ideas are in your notebook, they're not going anywhere. You can come back to them any time.

ALERT!

When you are brainstorming your ideas with others or have a great ad-lib on stage, make sure you write your ideas into the notebook. If you don't, you might as well throw all the work that you've done out the window. An ad lib isn't just a thing that happens; it's part of the writing process, so write it down!

After some time has passed and you've calmed down about the high repair bill, these ideas are still sitting in your notebook, waiting for your magic touch. With a fresh set of eyes, you look back at your notes and start to brainstorm. Some of the ideas from your notes might be developed as follows:

- A company that designs waiting rooms to be as uncomfortable as possible. They show a model of the perfect waiting room design and point out all the things they have done to make it unlivable. The TV controls are exactly two inches away from the average person's reach, the chairs are made to produce maximum back pain, etc.
- The waiting room is really a research project and you are secretly being monitored as part of a university psychology project or a hidden camera television show.
- Maybe a sketch that features the conversation between a mechanic and a customer, but you hear the thoughts of each person that don't exactly mirror their words.
- A super-fancy reality show like *Project Runway* that is for auto mechanics. There could be a weekly challenge, such as who can sell a customer the most unnecessary repairs and services.

"Someday we'll look back at this and laugh." Every time you hear that, you probably want to pummel the person who's saying it. But that's the beauty of a notebook—time. It puts a little distance between you and your thoughts.

The notebook helps you as a writer organize your thoughts on paper so you can focus on looking for connections. When you want to write something, your notebook should be your starting point. It's where you store all your ideas before you turn them into a joke, story, or sketch. Having good notes ensures that you'll never run out of ideas to write about.

Types of Notebooks

The word notebook might bring back unpleasant memories from high school or college. You had to keep notes to get a good grade on the final. As soon as the class was over, the notebook was put away, never to be looked at again.

In comedy, the notebook should be fun, something you always want to have with you and enjoy rereading over and over again. You need to find a notebook or notebook system to fit your needs and your lifestyle. There are many different choices available to you:

- **A standard 8.5" x 11" spiral bound notebook.** Easy to write in but hard to carry around with you.
- **A smaller bound notebook like a Moleskine product.** These are easy to fit in a pocket but can be awkward to write in.
- **An audio recorder.** These small electronic versions of your notebook are easy to carry and may already be built into your cell phone. However, these notes are impossible to browse through unless they are later transcribed, which most comedy writers are too lazy to do. There are lots of comedians who have shoeboxes full of mini-cassettes with notes still waiting to be deciphered.
- **A computer file notebook.** Keeping your notes on a computer is great as long as you back them up religiously and print out a hard copy that you can browse through. This way, you can simply jot down ideas on any writing surface available—cocktail napkins, receipts, scrap paper, etc. When you get home, you can empty your pockets (and your mind) into a box that you can then type into your notebook. But make sure that you do. There are a lot of

comedians who have shoeboxes . . . well, you get the idea. Consider getting a small leather jotter that holds a single index card that might accommodate a full day's worth of notes. You can also go paperless and use your cell phone, Blackberry, or iPhone to text yourself your ideas.

- **A computer database.** You can easily make a database for your ideas using a program like FileMaker Pro, but the downside is that it's a little clinical and every idea is separate from the others.

Start experimenting with a notebook system that fits your needs and helps you organize your thoughts. Once you find a system, stick with it. Whatever system you choose, make sure you use it consistently. The more you make a habit of writing your down your thoughts, the more your mind will seek out new ideas. Creativity will become a habit—one you won't want to kick. As you fill a notebook, save it and move onto the next, but keep the previous one handy for instant access when you need it.

E-QUESTION

What is the difference between a notebook and a journal?
If you keep a journal or diary, you already have the discipline to record your thoughts. A notebook is a place to keep all the half-ideas and random thoughts you're not ready to develop. If you already keep a journal, continue to do so.

How You'll Use Your Notebook

You should always have your notebook with you. When an idea hits you, write it down. If you hear a funny word or phrase, write it down. Anything you find funny or interesting should go into your notes.

The key is to write down your ideas without judging them. That's a task for a later date. If you try to brainstorm an idea on the spot, you probably won't get very far. You might just get frustrated and reject the idea entirely, and it won't make it into the notebook. And if that's the case, you've wasted a potentially great idea.

Everything in your notebook doesn't have to be in writing. Feel free to sketch, doodle, tape in news clippings, or whatever suits your style. Do anything you need to do to make it work for you.

When you have some free time, sit down with your notebook and flip through it in no particular order. Look for ideas that strike you as being funny. You can even do this while watching TV; it doesn't always need to be an active process. You just want to refresh your memory with the things you have written down to see if anything clicks.

If one idea spawns another (and it will), jot it down. You don't have to stick to your original premise. Expand on those ideas and soon you'll have one that works. You might even notice that a really great idea is actually a combination of two ideas separated by a few pages in your notebook.

Keep track of your notebook and don't lose it! If you do, you'll lose a lot of work and ideas that might never come to you again. Make sure that your contact information is visible so that if you do lose it, at least there's a chance you'll get it back. If you don't think a notebook is all that important, just wait until you lose one.

In high school or college you might have had to read aloud in class from your notebook or journal, or maybe you even had to turn it into the teacher for a grade. What a way to stifle creativity! Your notebook is for you, no one else. Don't let others look at it or you'll always be judging ideas before you write them down. You don't want people to think that you're weird, do you? (Well, maybe you do and that's why you got into comedy.)

Your ideas should be private and you shouldn't have to explain them to anyone. The notebook is just a place to empty your brain on paper. What you think is nobody's business but your own.

Profile in Comedy: Brian Kiley

Brian Kiley is one of the smartest comedy writers in the country. He has appeared on *The Tonight Show with Jay Leno* and *Late Night with Conan O'Brien*, where he has been a staff writer from day one and has been nominated for seven Emmy Awards. He has also appeared on *Late Night with David Letterman* and *Evening at the Improv*.

When did you first realize that you were uniquely funny?

In elementary school when a kid would make a joke and someone else would say, "That sounds like a Kiley joke."

Who do you think were your influences?

Woody Allen, Rodney Dangerfield, Bob Newhart, Steve Wright, my older brother Paul, my Aunt Essie.

Do you remember your first original joke?

When I was four years old, my Mom was driving down California Street and I said to my older brother, "I almost got a sunburn on California Street" and my family laughed. I remember thinking, "That's a keeper."

When did you realize that comedy was something that you had to do for a living?

When I was thirteen I realized I wasn't going to make it to the Red Sox or the NFL. I decided I wanted to be a comedian or a comedy writer like Rob Petrie on *The Dick Van Dyke Show*.

What was your first job in comedy writing or performance?

I took a class at Emerson College during the summer taught by Denis Leary. For the final class, we had to do stand-up in front of invited guests. A working comic named Andrea Eisenberg told me that I should pursue this as a career. (She may have been kidding.)

What is the biggest difficulty you've encountered being a comedy writer?

If as a stand-up you come up with a great joke about Michael Jackson, you can do it for twenty years. As a comedy writer, the show does it once and it's gone. The next day the host wants another great Michael Jackson joke. The hard part is writing your 200th Michael Jackson joke. Going to the same well every day is the hardest part.

Are there jokes that you do just for you?

The jokes I do for me, I do in the car to myself on the way to the gig. I can stay home and entertain myself—the job is to entertain other people. I only do jokes I think other people will like.

How did you prepare for your job writing Conan O'Brien's monologue jokes?

I used to do a lot of topical jokes in my act, so reading the papers every day and trying to find what's funny in the news and then trying those jokes on stage gave me a good sense of what crowds will laugh at and not laugh at. Jokes about tragedies may be funny to you or to other comics but they're not funny to normal crowds.

What's it like working on a daily deadline? What's your daily routine like?

It's fun and it's exciting but it's also a lot of pressure. You have to produce every day. If you don't, your jokes fall flat on national television. I read about five papers (ignoring the tragic stuff) and I go to several different news sites on the Internet. I work on my own, brainstorm with another guy, type up my stuff, compile it with the other writers, then we give our stuff to Conan. He tells us what he likes and what he wants more of. We write more, he picks 'em, we tweak 'em, and he does the show.

What are the differences between writing for yourself and writing for others?

Writing for yourself you get to make all the decisions. If you like a joke you write, you do it. I'm lucky in that my "voice" isn't too different from Conan's. Generally, if I write a joke I really like, he usually likes it too and does it. But when you're a stand-up you get the laughs. It's more gratifying than someone else getting the laughs on something you wrote. The highs are higher writing for yourself, but the lows are lower.

What do you find exciting about comedy right now?

It seems that more basic cable networks are making an effort to produce shows. I'm hoping that means more opportunities for comedy. The reality thing seems to be waning, thank God.

Where do you think the future of comedy is headed?

I wish I knew.

As audiences become more specific and more segmented, is your job becoming easier or more difficult?

I don't really notice a difference in the audiences.

What is the best thing about being a comedy writer?

Working with a bunch of people who make me laugh.

Do you have any advice for up-and-coming comedy writers?

Find your own voice, write every day, lose the rap song bit.

Brainstorm

Become a master spy. Part of what you put in your notebook are your observations of others. Picture this scenario: You're having lunch, listening to your iPod in a busy restaurant, and writing in your notebook. What if the iPod wasn't turned on? You could listen to all the conversations around you, but it wouldn't look like you were listening. You're in a public place within earshot of all these conversations, so why not? Is it ethical? That's up to you to decide. But it is a great way to get a sense of dialogue and really hear the way people speak. Is there a customer giving the waiter a hard time? That could be a sketch. Is someone talking loudly on his cell phone? The other side of the conversation, the side you can't hear, might be a sketch. Here's a conversation overheard while waiting in line at a bank:

Bob: *So what are you doing tonight?*

Steve (frustrated): *I have to go see Karen.*

Bob: *Oh, I don't envy you. Good luck with that.*

Steve (letting it all out): *Tell me about it. She is the most selfish person I have ever known. It's all about her. I just have to sit there and listen to her cry* *about her problems. She is so needy! She never asks about my problems, it's just all about her!*

Wow! Why are they friends with her? If she's that needy, why do they stay with her?

What if Karen were an infant? That would explain it all—the crying, only caring about her own needs. There's a sketch. You have the conversation, then reveal that Karen is three months old.

ALERT!

Make sure to date your notebook when you start one, and date it again when it's full. This will help you if there is ever a dispute over the ownership of a joke; it will give you a range of time that tells you when you came up with the idea. It might even show you the context of the origin of the idea.

Get out there and listen. See if you can get ideas from conversations. If you feel weird about it, try this: Look at people who are way out of earshot and try to imagine what they are saying. Or turn on the TV, turn down the sound, and try putting your words in the characters' mouths. Or watch a TV show or a movie in a language you don't understand and try to make up your own story.

Notebook

Look through what you've written in your notebook so far. Read through it from the beginning to the end and see if there are any ideas that seem fresh to you or connections between two ideas that might form a joke. Pull at least one idea from your notes and work on it as a joke, sketch, or story. Expand on that original idea and work until you have a finished piece that you are happy with. For example, take some of the set-ups and punch lines that you wrote for Chapter 3 and work them into a short stand-up piece. Now backtrack and ask yourself if you would have remembered the idea you chose if you hadn't written it down.

CHAPTER 6

Comedy Secret No. 2: The Power of Lists

We all deal with lists every day: to-do lists, shopping lists, home improvement lists, organizing lists. Most of these are lists of chores, things you don't want to do but *have* to do. Lists are usually things you want to avoid, but in comedy, lists can be great tools that you'll look forward to working with every day.

Use Lists as a Springboard for Great Ideas

When you're writing about a specific topic, be it a monologue on dating or an essay about spending the holidays with your family, making a list of everything you can think of associated with that topic can really help you come up with jokes or ideas that you might have otherwise overlooked. You already worked with lists in Chapter 2 and Chapter 4, but now you'll take it a bit further.

Brainstorm a List

Try this experiment: Pick a general topic that you would like to talk about. It could be anything—going on vacation, a holiday, or even something a lot less exciting like going to the dentist, buying shoes, or grocery shopping. Let's try a topic that everyone has had some experience with: a birthday. Now write down every basic fact that you can think of on the topic of birthdays. They don't have to be funny; you just want to get all your thoughts down on paper. Don't be afraid of including the most obvious things; just write it down. Write down everything you can to cover as much of the topic as possible. Set a goal—make your list at least thirty items long. It might really be difficult coming up with those last few items on the list, but that's the point. You want to bring all the thoughts in the back of your mind to the front. Okay, what comes to mind when you think of birthdays? Your list might include the following:

BIRTHDAYS	
1.	Every year you have a birthday party.
2.	People give you cards and presents on your birthday.
3.	They sing "Happy Birthday to You."
4.	If you go to a restaurant and say it's your birthday, they might give you a free dessert and the staff might sing to you as well.
5.	The song "Happy Birthday to You" is copyrighted. Chain restaurants usually have their own birthday song to avoid paying royalties.
6.	People try to embarrass you on your birthday.
7.	When you are a kid, birthdays are lots of fun.
8.	As an adult, they are more reminders of getting older.

BIRTHDAYS

9.	People who are born on February 29 during a leap year only have birthdays every four years.
10.	In some cultures, your birthday is based upon your conception date.
11.	There are fun presents, practical presents, and "gag" presents.
12.	Sometimes people throw you a surprise party.
13.	You usually have a birthday cake.
14.	They put a candle on the cake for every year you've lived.
15.	You blow out the candles and make a wish. If you don't blow out all the candles, or if you tell anybody what you wished for, your wish won't come true.
16.	At kids' parties they have piñatas, sometimes based on different characters.
17.	Birthday parties sometimes have themes.
18.	Balloons are used to celebrate birthdays.
19.	Sometimes you have a "friend" party and a "family" party.
20.	Certain birthday milestones are celebrated more than others.
21.	If you live to be 100, you might get your picture in the newspaper or be mentioned on TV.
22.	At some parties you play "Pin the Tail on the Donkey."
23.	On your first birthday, people make a big fuss, but you are oblivious to everything that happens.
24.	Sometimes, especially when you are a kid, you might have entertainment at your party: a magician, a clown, or a face painter.
25.	Some people really go overboard with expensive kids' parties.
26.	A bar or bat mitzvah, quinceañera, or "sweet 16" party is a big deal.
27.	On your twenty-first birthday, you finally can legally drink; on your eighteenth birthday you legally become an adult.
28.	As you age, you enter phases: teens, twenties, thirties, forties, etc.
29.	At age sixty-five, you become a senior citizen and get special discounts.
30.	When you are younger, you want to be older. When you are older, you want to be younger.

Is that everything? Not by a long shot. But it's a good beginning at least. Now it's time to analyze the list and see if you can come up with some jokes, sketch ideas, or funny stories.

I'm Beginning to See a Pattern Here . . .

Now look over your list and see if there are any unusual connections between items. Also look for patterns. For example, this list shows that some things about birthdays have a pattern: Your first couple of birthdays are great, then they start to go downhill, then as you get really old they become a big deal again. What can you do with this?

Working with a Pattern

Think about your first and last birthday if you were to live to be 100. On your first birthday, you really don't know what's going on. There are a lot of people around that you don't know. You're in diapers; you don't have any teeth; you have to gum your cake. Are you beginning to see the connection? When you turn 100, chances are you really don't know what's going on. You're surrounded by people you don't know. You're in diapers; you don't have any teeth; and you have to gum your cake.

Try using Google or other online reference tools to research your topics. You might find the actual origins of things we all take for granted. Or you could uncover weird facts that might add interest to your topics. Brainstorm on your own first, but use the Internet to help you expand your ideas.

You could even argue that on your twenty-first birthday, when your friends get you drunk, you don't know what's going on or who all those people are. You might have lost all your teeth in a bar fight. And when you wake up in the morning, you realize that a diaper might have been a good idea.

Back to Basics

Now take the list and look at each point carefully. Look at each item with a critical eye, almost as if someone is telling you about birthday parties for the very first time. Question each item; ask yourself "Why?" Why do we do this at birthday parties? Who came up with the idea of a birthday cake? Why do we give each other presents? Why are certain birthdays more important than others? Who wrote "Happy Birthday to You"?

E-QUESTION

Why do I have to make a list? Why can't I just write funny thoughts on the topic as I think of them?
You can, but it's nice to separate the grunt work from the creative process. If you do them at the same time, you're asking your brain to do two different things at once. Splitting the tasks makes it easier; you've collected all the information you need and now can just play with what you have.

Now start jotting down the things that catch your interest in your notebook and start developing your ideas a bit further. Here are a few examples:

- **Piñatas.** If a kid's favorite TV character is Dora the Explorer, why do parents think it's a good idea to get a Dora piñata, fill it with candy, and encourage the kids to beat her head in with a stick? Do kids think everyone's head is filled with candy? Would you have a Matlock piñata filled with laxatives for a senior citizen party? What would make a really lame piñata for a kid's party?
- **"Happy Birthday to You."** What were the origins of the song? Is it owned by an individual or a massive corporation? How is the copyright enforced? How about a sketch that shows a family singing "Happy Birthday" to their child when a SWAT team from the American Society of Composers, Authors, and Publishers (ASCAP) bursts into the party and arrests the family for violating the copyright? How about a sketch that shows a family celebrating at a restaurant being shut down by the manager when they start to sing "Happy Birthday,"

because the corporate office insists that only the official restaurant birthday song can be sung on the premises.

- **Clowns.** A mom hires a clown to entertain at their child's seventh birthday party, but instead of a happy-go-lucky funny clown, the entertainment agency sends a weird, surreal, and confusing Cirque du Soleil-type clown, who (in a French accent) talks to the children about how they are now one step closer to death.

Now try expanding your ideas even further into jokes or sketches, knowing that you have covered all your bases, done your homework, and become an expert on the topic you want to write about.

Lists Are All Around You

If you look at the world around you, you'll see that you can sort almost anything into lists. Your friends are a list (and there's even an order to the list, starting with your *best* friend). You can organize the world's religions into a list. Everything around you is a list—of stuff.

Here's a challenge. Imagine this scenario: Right now, at this very moment, neutron bombs go off all over the world and kill every living thing on earth, but they leave the infrastructure intact. So you're dead and so is everyone else, but all the stuff around you is exactly as you left it. Fast forward a thousand years, and aliens from another universe land on Earth knowing absolutely nothing about us. The very first site their scientists excavate is the room you're in right now.

Okay, so you've already started to look at things objectively. Now try looking at the things around you *really* objectively. How would aliens interpret things, commonplace to you, that they have never encountered?

List all the things in your room—lamps, a TV set, an air conditioner, a CD player, an iPod, a trash can, curtains, chairs, remote controls, a computer, a printer, tables, rugs, photos, paintings, magazines, books, pillows, clothes, DVDs, pens, pencils, etc. What would aliens think each thing was used for? Let your mind play with looking at commonplace things from an entirely different perspective. Also, ask yourself what the aliens look like. Do they look like us or are they six inches tall? How would they look at a chair that they couldn't even climb, let alone sit in? What if they assumed that we were the same size as them?

In a class at Emerson College, a student once came up with a great premise from this exercise: What if the aliens noticed a copy of *TV Guide* in everyone's home and misunderstood it to be the bible of our civilization? What if they used it to form their own religion based upon ours as they conceived it. An alien sermon went something like this:

> PREACHER
> Now let us turn to the Book of Tuesday, chapter 5:30 P.M. to 6:00 P.M., channel 38. "'Gilligan's Island: Gilligan discovers that they are not alone on the island; headhunters are in their midst.'"
>
> HE CLOSES THE *TV GUIDE*.
>
> PREACHER
> What can we learn from Saint Gilligan to help us deal with the personal headhunters that we all have in our midst?

Profile in Comedy: Brendon Small

Brendon Small is a talented stand-up comedian, musician, actor, composer, and writer. He is best known as the co-creator of the animated series *Home Movies* and the cult hit *Metalocalypse*.

When did you first realize that you were uniquely funny?

I don't know that I am. . . . At least, I don't say that I'm uniquely funny. But sure, same story as everybody—your friends say you're funny and/or you just have that urge to do stupid things in front of audiences. And even though I spent a good portion of my life with near paralyzing stage fright, I still felt like I needed to try to be funny in front of people. So somewhere during the end of music school I took your class and it was such a breath of fresh air for a few reasons. I needed to stop learning about music—it was driving me crazy. But comedy writing made me use different parts of my brain and think differently and use different avenues to come to funny conclusions.

Who do you think were your influences?

Easy, I grew up with Woody Allen, Albert Brooks, and the Marx Brothers. (Of course Monty Python too.) I think of all those guys when I write. They wrote amazing characters and set pieces. Another reason I love them is because they (mostly Woody Allen and Albert Brooks) weren't afraid to write stories with mildly unsympathetic characters—they experimented, with a darker style of comedy.

Do you remember your first original joke?

Oh dear God. I'm told by my parents that I wrote a great joke when I was four and it went something like this, "Why did the hair go to the bathroom? There was no toilet paper." No, it doesn't make sense. And yes it was a little racy but at least I wrote what I knew. . . . And to this day I stand by that joke.

When did you realize that comedy was something you had to do for a living?

Somewhere around the time I realized there was no way I could make any money as a musician. But it was funny; I'm a pretty good guitarist and I could play better than a lot of other students, but I had no idea what I was going to do with music. I thought maybe I'd get into film scoring or jingle writing (but before my last year of school I interned at jingle houses in New York and realized I'd rather shoot myself in the face than work in post production). But the thing I noticed well into my first year of stand-up was that there were talent scouts from major networks peering around the edges of every crappy comedy club in Boston. I mean, there were people who wanted to find the next funny person. Nobody was looking for a guitarist, but everybody in Hollywood is constantly looking for a unique funny personality—it's their job. And the more uniquely yourself you are, the less competition there is—I mean there's only one *you* out there. Nobody can compete with that. Again, there are a million billion guitarists. . . . So g'bye guitar; hello checkered jacket and squirting flower.

What was your first job in comedy writing or performance?

My first comedy performance was when I did stand-up before a friend's drum recital at Berklee College of Music. There were about sixteen people and my jokes were stupid. I spoke with that lilt at the end of my sentences which gave the illusion that I was telling a joke. Some people politely fake-laughed so as to kill the awkwardness in the room. But a couple good things did happen: one, I technically DID stand up; and two, I didn't cry. But, I still had a lot to learn.

About a year later I had a "good night" at the Hong Kong in Harvard Square and met Loren Bouchard, who was producing *Dr Katz: Professional Therapist* at the time. He had an opportunity to put a show together and I was local. Next thing I knew we'd created *Home Movies* together. So that was technically my first job. Let me reiterate that I am incredibly lucky. . . . I was ready for the challenge, but still, without luck I'd be nowhere.

What is the biggest difficulty you've encountered being a comedy writer?

I think when you start out as a comic is the most difficult time of being a comic/writer. First off because (I speak for myself only) I sucked donkey dick. It took me a really long time to find out what was funny about myself. Every other night I would eat shit. But during that time I was also spending a lot of time writing—writing stories, sketches, little jokes, and character scenes— and I'd spend a couple hours filling up pages with crap every day. I'd force myself to write two hours a day. Maybe it was from music, but I was used to discipline to come along with a craft—doing endless scales on my guitar with a metronome. So writing or doing something that seemed mundane for a given time always made sense to me.

What makes writing for animation different from other outlets?

The real reason animation works for me is not necessarily the writing because your characters and story should function like they would in live action—so there's no difference there. The main difference in animation is in post production. The ability to throw away scenes or save them using audio, rudimentary animation tricks, and music can really save a project from sucking. It's much easier to save stuff in post with animation.

How do music and comedy work together?

I think music helps tell a story more than it's funny. Because I don't really like "funny" music. I like good music. When you're really trying to hit a story point home, music can help you sell those ideas. I mean it can really draw attention to the comedy—like a hacky rimshot or muted trumpets. But I'll think of music more as score or I'll think of little songs for the shows I do. Music always divides up the energy of the episodes and gives you something hopefully to remember.

Are there jokes that you do just for you?

I don't do anything for anybody else—entertainment-wise. Yes, it's selfish. But, that's what art is. It's an experiment to see if you're in the same mood as me. If you're not—no big deal. But seriously, I think if you do any art for anybody other than yourself you should quit. It's like I'd rather hang out with somebody who's comfortable in their own skin and means what they're saying rather than a person who's faking it to impress you.

What are the differences between writing for yourself and writing for others?

I've had a lucky career where I cast myself in as the characters (in the animated projects I do). But still I write for character first. Even when I bring in another actor to voice something, it's usually about how much they understand the character and joke and then how their voice fits in to those things.

What do you find exciting about comedy right now?

I'm sure there are tons of things that are awesome in comedy right now but I've just been keeping my head down and working. Ricky Gervais is brilliant and so is Sacha Baron Cohen. Those two are saving it for me right now. It's funny, but the more I do comedy the more of a comedy snob I become. Or maybe comedy is getting less funny. Who knows? I'm not sure.

Where do you think the future of comedy is headed?

I hope people start making unique movies with unique casting choices. Sorry for the bland answer, but I've had the same philosophy since I started: "Please do something new or get out of the business so that somebody else can."

What is the best thing about being a comedy writer?

Seeing matinees and being creative. Seriously. If I couldn't be creative and make a project that I wanted to be a part of then I'd just work at Starbucks. I mean, they have pretty good benefits and I like their coffee—not joking.

Do you have any advice for up-and-coming comedy writers?

I wish somebody would have grabbed and told me the following: one, just because you wrote it doesn't mean it's any good. Try to be objective. Try it out onstage. Two, don't be a dick. Nobody wants to work with a cocky dick. Nobody cares how funny you think you are. Three, oh and again, "Please do something new or get out of the business so that somebody else can."

Brainstorm

Try using a list to brainstorm ideas for topics you think you might want to write about, things that interest you. You can choose big events, like a job interview or a vacation trip. But don't overlook the small everyday things as well, like getting a haircut or riding the subway. You can write them as a monologue, a story, or a sketch. Try combining this with other techniques you've learned for maximum effect.

Notebook

Here's a fun exercise that will help you practice your list-making skill and also get you started thinking about characters as well. Write a letter from a child at camp to his parents at home. Don't make it any random child; make it a famous person as a child. It can be a real person, such as Albert Einstein, Atilla the Hun, Moses, Abraham Lincoln, Donald Trump, or Bill Clinton, or it can be a fictional character like Sherlock Holmes, Santa Claus, or Dr. Frankenstein.

Start by making a list of everything you know about that person. For example, Abraham Lincoln:

1. He wore a stovepipe hat.
2. He had a beard.
3. He was assassinated by an actor.
4. He was president during the Civil War.
5. He wrote speeches on the backs of envelopes.

Now start thinking about how all these facts about the man would apply to Lincoln as a child. What if the Civil War is a camp colors war instead of a violent conflict? How does he get in the habit of writing things on envelopes? Is young John Wilkes Booth a camper at the nearby theater camp? Is his bunkmate a young General Grant? Did he make a hat out of an actual stovepipe for Funny Hat Day and the look just stuck?

You get the idea. You want to use the letter to hint at the person Lincoln would someday become.

CHAPTER 7

The Power of Questions

With comedy, sometimes it's not about knowing all the answers, it's about asking the right questions—constantly. By questioning everything around you and within you, you'll create strong, memorable comedy. In this chapter you'll learn how to use questions as a creative force to move your comedy writing skills forward. By asking questions, you'll never run out of ideas.

Everything You Know is Wrong

The members of Firesign Theater said it all when they named their 1974 album "Everything You Know is Wrong." That's the attitude you have to take. You need to question everything around you. You can't just accept things as they are; you need to consistently challenge the status quo. That doesn't mean you have to be an outcast from society; it just means you need to look at things differently.

Question Everything

You need to become that three-year-old in the backseat of her mother's car who won't stop asking questions: Why is the sky blue? Can I have a cookie? When can I have a cookie? Why can't I have a cookie now? Are we there yet? When will we be there? Can I have a cookie now? Why can't I have a cookie now?

That's basically what comedians do. They ask, "Who said it should be this way?" Look at any TV commercial that show a group of "regular" people talking to each other with, of course, the product that's for sale. Millions of people see that commercial multiple times and do nothing. In most cases, the ad barely even registers; it just becomes background noise.

Turning Questions into Comedy

Comedians don't accept anything at face value. Look at that commercial and start questioning it. Have I ever had a conversation with anyone who spoke like the people in this ad? How stupid do they think we are? If you actually stop and think about what they are saying, you'll be amazed at how stupid the creators of the ad think people are. But most people are used to it so they accept it. They accept things as they are.

A comedian will look at that same ad and say, "That is the dumbest thing I have ever seen. I must tell the world. How can I make fun of that?" and they might mention it in a stand-up routine or write a commercial parody sketch about it. But what else could you do with that premise?

How about a sketch that shows a group therapy session for commercial actors who can't stop speaking that way? Or you could show a woman in her living room who says to herself, "How am I going to get that juice stain off the carpet?" Then suddenly, a booming announcer voice starts talking to her about a new cleaning product. Instead of her acting like someone in a commercial who finds that normal, what if she freaks out and thinks she's going crazy? As she's trying to make the voices stop, you could compound her troubles by having the product appear in her hand or have a talking cartoon character walk into the living room.

> The brilliant Steven Wright is the stand-up king of perception. His weird, funny, and quirky observations are truly original. Check out his CDs *I Have a Pony* and *I Still Have a Pony*, and just try to guess how his mind works—he's incredible.

What if there were a drug to help people who talk like people in drug commercials? You know, people who only talk about warnings or side effects. You could also write a satire of these ads that illustrates the very real problem of people asking for drugs that they don't need because a commercial convinced them they did. Ask yourself how a doctor would respond if she were confronted with a perfectly healthy patient convinced he needed the medications he saw advertised on TV.

Twist things around and ask yourself what an advertising agency meeting would be like with executives trying to make a boring item, like a garbage bag or paper towels, sexy and exciting. By asking questions, you can take the ordinary and make people notice that there's more to it than they thought.

The Two Most Important Words in Comedy: "What If?"

Why are the words "what if" so important? They advance your thinking process. If you start with a premise and keep asking "what if?" it will let you fully explore that premise. Keep the process going for as long as possible. If you start going off on a weird tangent, that's fine. You can always go back to your original thought, but if you explore it a little further, you might come up with something that might even be funnier than your original premise.

If you ask "what if?" and it leads to a dead end, just move on. Don't dwell on something that doesn't work. This goes for group brainstorming sessions as well. Once a train of thought has been derailed, it can be hard to get back on track.

One of the key rules of improvisation is to go with the premise no matter what. For example, two performers are on stage and one says, "I can't believe I've been in this lifeboat for ten days without food, water, or . . . cable." The other person says, "We're not in a rowboat; we're on the space shuttle." Two things happen.

The audience is confused and disappointed, and the second person has made the first look foolish. Don't deny the premise. Here's an example of how the "what if?" process might go:

- Every hurricane has its own name. Who picks the names? What if they had a meeting of nerdy meteorologists sitting around and picking the names for the next batch of hurricanes? What if they named them after all the girls who turned them down for a date in high school or after all the guys who gave them wedgies? What if hurricanes had a first and last name? "Today, Hurricane Hugo Kowolski formed off the coast of Cuba. . . ."

- If hurricanes are scary, why not give them scary names like Hurricane Frankenstein or Hurricane Jack The Ripper?

- What if they started running out of names and had to use less threatening names like Hurricane Bambi or Hurricane Tiffany? Would anyone be afraid of a hurricane named Tiffany? Would newscasters giggle whenever they said the name? Would big, tough guys evacuate for Hurricane Ashley?

- What if the meteorologists who oversee the process sold the naming rights to corporations? We would have Hurricane Pepsi, Hurricane Staples, Hurricane Toshiba, and Hurricane Lean Cuisine. What if corporations named them after their competition? Burger King would name a hurricane McDonalds. So when the newscasters said, "Today Hurricane McDonalds destroyed a children's orphanage today . . . " it would hurt the competition's image.

The questions you ask keep the thought process going. Imagine if someone threw a wrench in the works during the process and said, "Well actually, there is a six-year cycle of names that are reused over and over and a name is 'retired' only if a hurricane that has that name is particularly devastating. Then and only then would they add a new name, blah, blah, blah . . . " The truth would get in the way and stop the whole process. Sure you might be making stuff up, but that's your job. Some say only the truth is funny. But the real truth is, in some cases, sometimes truth gets in funny's way. Truth needs to learn to not take itself so seriously.

Never Take Anything at Face Value

Things are not always as they seem. Remember how Norman Bates seemed like such a nice guy? Well, you know the rest of the story. You can't just accept things the way they seem. You need to look at things differently, question everyone else's reality, and replace it with your own comedic view.

Reimagining Everyday Situations

You may see a man walking his dog, but maybe the dog is walking the man. Or, maybe it's a blind dog being led by a seeing-eye person.

Reinterpreting Famous Works of Art

Take a second look at famous photographs, ones you've seen a thousand times before: the sailor kissing the nurse in Times Square on VJ Day, the Beatles crossing Abby Road, Albert Einstein sticking his tongue out at the camera, and Bigfoot taking a stroll in the woods. How can you change those familiar photos and make them funny? Well, the Abby Road cover has been parodied by everyone from the Muppets to the Simpsons. In 1996, *The New Yorker* had a cover with a satirical parody of the VJ Day photo showing the sailor kissing another sailor, to address a political hot spot—

gays in the military. Why not show Albert Einstein with a punk Mohawk showing off his tongue piercing?

Let's look at classic paintings—Grant Wood's *American Gothic* or da Vinci's *Mona Lisa*. How many times have you seen those? What if you changed Wood's painting to show the farmer standing alone with a slightly crazed look in his eye and just a trace of blood on the points of the pitchfork? Comedy writer Ernie Kovacs once showed the audience why the Mona Lisa was smiling: a cat was licking her foot.

Film Favorites

Look what *Mystery Science Theater 3000* did with bad movies. They didn't accept them the way they were; they over-dubbed lines and made comments throughout every film, with hilarious results. Today, comedians are doing the same thing with the video mash-up, where two pop culture items are mashed together to make them funny. This may have started with short movie trailers shown on 1992's *The Ben Stiller Show*. One presented Eddie Munster getting revenge on the person who cancelled his show in the parody *Cape Munster*, and another was the Boy Scout version of *A Few Good Men*, called *A Few Good Scouts*.

Another great example of this was created by the Boston-based Emerson College sketch troupe Chocolate Cake City. In 2006 they combined *Brokeback Mountain* with *Back to the Future* and came up with *Brokeback to the Future*. In someone else's hands this could have been a disaster—just a one-word, one-note joke—but in the right hands it became an Internet masterpiece.

If you're looking for footage to make up your own mash-ups, check out *www.archive.org*, a collection of hundreds of weird ephemera films, most of which are in the public domain and ready for download in most popular movie formats. Browse through the collection and you're sure to come up with some great ideas.

Profile in Comedy: Eric Drysdale

After working his way through the New York alternative comedy scene in the late '90s, Eric Drysdale spent nearly eight years in the fake news business. He worked as a writer on *The Daily Show* with Jon Stewart from 2000 to 2005, earning five Emmy awards along the way. He then moved to *The Colbert Report*, where he stayed until late 2007, adding a Writers Guild award to his shelf. He also contributed to bestselling books based on both of those shows. As a stand-up comedian, he's appeared on NBC's *Late Friday* and Comedy Central's *Premium Blend*. He's also written and produced several live shows at New York's Upright Citizens Brigade Theatre. Oh, and he's also a graduate of the author's comedy class at Emerson College. He is now pursuing his own projects.

When did you first realize that you were uniquely funny?

When I was very young I realized that I liked making my parents and their friends laugh. I definitely liked the attention. Whether I was actually funny or not, I don't know. Later, in high school, one of my teachers confiscated a notebook in which I was writing these little weird essays sort of based on the "Deep Thoughts" column in National Lampoon. I would pass it around in class to make people laugh (especially girls). He grabbed it and made me come see him in his office later in the day. When I got there, he half-heartedly admonished me for disturbing his class, and then said he thought the stuff was really funny and encouraged me to write more.

Who do you think were your influences?

Well, the things that made me want to do comedy were *Saturday Night Live*, the NBC David Letterman years, Woody Allen, Monty Python, George Carlin, Steve Martin, Pee-Wee Herman, Stephen Wright, Jake Johannsen, and SCTV. But I think my earliest exposure to comedy—stuff I liked when I was preteen—was just as influential if not more so. *The Muppet Show* and *Sesame Street*, for sure. *The Electric Company*, which I must have watched when I was four, was just a great ensemble sketch-comedy show. *Mad Magazine* was a favorite—I especially love Al Jaffee and had all his books. I loved *Rocky and Bullwinkle*, and that show is super-smart. Also, I just obsessed over the early *Peanuts* comic strips, which I had in those

Fawcett-Crest paperbacks. I loved the K-Tel novelty record compilations—especially the *Coasters*. I could go on forever.

Do you remember your first original joke?

As some guests were leaving our house after a dinner when I was a kid, maybe four years old. My parents report this exchange: Guest: "Well, Eric, I hope we get to see more of you." Eric: "But this is all of me there is." I can't imagine that I made that joke on purpose, but my parents swear I knew exactly what I was doing.

When did you realize that comedy was something you had to do for a living?

I quit for a while in the mid '90s because of the instability of it all. I soon realized that I sucked at everything else, and, more importantly, didn't enjoy anything else.

What was your first job in comedy writing or performance?

When I was nineteen, I lucked into a job writing a "teen" late-night comedy show for the Canadian Broadcasting Company. They had an open casting call and I showed up with a writing packet instead of a headshot. You've got balls when you're nineteen! The show was pretty bad, and was cancelled as a favor to the Canadian people after a couple of months, but I had lots of great experiences. I worked with Valri Bromfield, who was Dan Aykroyd's partner at Second City, appeared on the very first episode of SNL, and then later wrote for SCTV. She made a big impression on me. The Kids in the Hall made a very early appearance on the show. It was great, but it took me twelve years to land my next job in the business.

What is the biggest difficulty you've encountered being a comedy writer?

Writing comedy.

As a stand-up you have all the time in the world to get a joke right. What's it like to have to get it right with daily deadline?

At first it's terrifying. When you're on a staff, it becomes about your "batting average," to some degree. You keep track of how many jokes you get on. Eventually, the fear dies away and you get used to throwing away a lot of material. (That is, getting lots of material rejected.) The fact is, you can only get it mostly right. Sometimes not even that. And when you do get it right, someone else might get it even more right. That's why these shows have many writers. Learning to throw away so much material is the hardest but most important lesson of a job like that. You build that confidence that there's another joke up in your head. And there is. Eventually.

When working on fake news, what is the daily routine like?
It sort of functions like a real newsroom plus jokes. We have a meeting all together first thing in the morning to discuss what "top stories" we're going to cover and how. In the morning we're writing stuff based on that day's news, usually individually. In the afternoon we work, usually in teams, on longer-term segments. On *The Daily Show,* that could be things like field pieces or other segments with correspondents. On *The Colbert Report*, that would be features like "Better Know a District" or "Formidable Opponent." It's a great blend of working by yourself, collaborating with one or two others, and working with everyone. The nice thing about a show based on daily news is that you can't plan that far ahead. The script is due at 4 or 5 P.M., and the rehearsal is soon after that. There are some rewrites between then and the taping, which can be really high-pressure, but then that's about it. So a lot of the time you get to go home at the end of the day—it's like a regular 9 to 5 job in some ways. More like 9 to 7, but still, not many comedy jobs are like that.

What are the differences between writing for yourself and writing for others?
In a way, I find writing for others somewhat easier, as they more or less tell you what to do. I certainly got used to that at *The Daily Show* and *The Colbert Report*. Every day we were sent off to write with a pretty clear assignment. Writing for myself, I can do anything, and I'm somewhat paralyzed by the possibilities sometimes.

What do you find exciting about comedy right now?
I guess the idea that anyone can just make something that can make an impact on the Internet. Sure, there are a lot of people who can be funny once for five minutes on YouTube. But once in a while you get something like those Yacht Rock guys, who took a simple concept and made something really great out of it.

Where do you think comedy is headed?

If I knew, I'd do something along those lines and make a fortune.

As audiences are becoming more specific and more segmented, is that making your job easier or more difficult?

It's making it easier in that even weird-ass stuff like "Adult Swim" can find an audience, but harder in that it's more challenging to eke out a decent living catering to those smaller groups.

What is the best thing about being a comedy writer?

Well, being on staff at a show like *The Daily Show* or *Colbert* is just heaven, because you are making some of the funniest people in the world laugh all day long, and they're trying to do the same for you. Then, if you're lucky enough to be on a show that can cut through all the other noise, you get to see that stuff ripple through the popular culture a little bit. That's exciting. But very rare. I guess the biggest reward is just doing what you like to do.

Do you have any advice for up and coming comedy writers?

Patience. Keep working no matter what. Find like-minded people and make things. Don't wait for someone to give you a break. Especially with this new world of the Internet, there's just no excuse to not keep doing things yourself and putting them out there.

Take at least one improv class. Shut up, listen, stop trying to be funny, and approach it with a serious, open mind. If you learn something and/or have fun, stick with it. Improv isn't for every writer, but the ones who do get something from it swear by it. Late-night comedy staffs are filled with people from the improv world for a reason. (Yes, it's a networking thing to a degree, too. But really, it's because improvisers get trained very well.) It's also tied in to that confidence to throw away material that I talked about before. Every improv performance is in a sense "thrown away" because it only exists once. It's a good thing to get used to as soon as you can.

Here's one that I didn't hear when I was starting out that I think could have helped me: Don't only care about comedy—there's more to the world. Relax and take in other things. Everything informs your work. Some of the most important things I've learned about comedy have snuck in from other interests and disciplines. Plus, you should know some things about the world you're making fun of. It's huge.

Most importantly, have fun. You'd be surprised how competitive and serious the business can become. It's easy to forget that we do this because we love to laugh and make others laugh. It's that sense that you're having fun too that really draws people into your work. It's no accident that—for the most part—the things I've done that people have responded to most favorably also happen to be the things I've had the most fun doing.

Brainstorm

Here are a few ideas for looking at the world in your own unique way:

- Take a trip to an art museum and bring your notebook. Look at the paintings and come up with interesting twists or captions that would make the paintings funny.
- Watch a movie or a soap opera that's in a language you don't understand and come up with your own plotlines and dialogue. Woody Allen started his film career this way when he was asked to do *something* with the Japanese spy thriller *International Secret Police: Key of Keys.* In his directorial debut, he overdubbed the film and it became *What's Up, Tiger Lily?*, a film about the life and death search for the world's best egg salad recipe.
- Try writing an advertisement for a product that doesn't need to be—or shouldn't be—advertised. Things like a hammer, or some personal hygiene product that would be weird to see advertised on television. If you really want a challenge, try writing a full 30-minute infomercial for something boring and ordinary like a paper clip, a toothpick, or a button.

Notebook

Start collecting photos and postcards that interest you. Look at the photos carefully and write your own original captions for the photos. Think of the photos as one-panel cartoons, and make your caption tell a complete story. It's harder than it sounds. Try turning the photos upside-down and side-ways—remember, you want to look at things differently—and see the photos as you see them, not how everyone else would see them. Paste the photos with your caption into your notebook. Can you write a sketch based upon your captions? Can the photo be used as a starting point for a sketch?

Now, start looking at life that way. Take the time to just stop and watch the world. Watch ordinary people doing ordinary things and question what you see, and pretty soon you'll start seeing your own comedy vision.

CHAPTER 8

Let's Get Sketchy

Sketch comedy has found new popularity on television and stage. It is one of the most gratifying forms of comedy writing. It has all the benefits of stand-up—visibility for yourself and your writing and immediate feedback from an audience—but instead of going it alone, you get to work with and learn from others. Sketches also let you get your ideas out there and let you experiment with different comedy styles.

What is a Sketch?

A sketch is really just a short play, usually ten minutes or less. Sketch comedy has its roots in vaudeville and burlesque. A small group of comedians would perform the same sketch over and over again from town to town. A typical sketch would be set in a classroom or doctor's office. These sketches were usually written to show off a performer's talents, whether they were funny voices, musical ability, or physical comedy.

Contemporary sketch comedy has its origins in 1950s comedy shows such as Sid Caesar's *Your Show of Shows*, and from the Chicago's Second City comedy theater, which blended improvisation with sketch. It was popularized with NBC's *Saturday Night Live* in the 1970s and is enjoying newfound popularity on television and the Internet today.

E-QUESTION

What is the difference between a sketch and a skit?
A sketch and a skit are essentially the exact same thing, but there is a vast difference in the way the terms are used in comedy terminology. A skit is usually used like this: "Oh, last night the Cub Scouts put on the cutest little skit at their meeting!" or "Your grandmother did so well in her skit in the Senior Follies." A skit is for amateurs; sketches are for professionals.

Television producers regularly scout sketch groups when looking for talent and comedy writers. Jim Carrey built a career from his versatility on *In Living Color*, and just think about the talent that came out of *Saturday Night Live*. There are even sketch television shows for kids on Nickelodeon that have spawned stars like Amanda Bynes. Writers that have come from sketch include Mel Brooks, Mike Nichols, Elaine May, Carl Reiner, and Norman Lear.

The Sketch Format

Sketch writing allows you freedoms you don't get with a longer format such as a play, sitcom, or screenplay. It allows you to explore ideas and develop characters in a very efficient way. You can explore a single idea or premise for a sketch. A sketch can be an excuse for showcasing an interesting character. You try the joke in front of the audience and see if it works, And you can immediately integrate any changes into the next show.

> Many comedy theater troupes such as Second City, the Groundlings, the Upright Citizens Brigade, Improv Asylum, and local groups in your area offer classes in improvisation and sketch. Class members have even been known to become full-fledged members of the troupe. Look for classes in your area and take the plunge into the world of improv and sketch comedy.

With a movie, you have at least ninety minutes to tell your story. With a sitcom you have around twenty-two minutes. With a sketch you have a fraction of that time, but you still need to introduce the characters, set up the joke, and have a beginning, middle, and end. It's a hit-and-run, guerilla-style form of comedy, and that's what makes it satisfying to an audience.

You need to work fast; sketches longer than ten minutes can start to drag. You need to get to the joke in the most efficient way you can. Don't be afraid to write a sketch that is thirty seconds long; it can be followed by a seven-minute sketch without a problem. But, don't make every sketch seven or eight minutes long. Variety in the material is what makes for a successful sketch show, so sketches in the same show can go from subtle to outrageous.

Every sketch, with time, can have a great, logical ending. However, when you are short on time, such as on a weekly television show, a sketch can start out with a great idea and end without a logical conclusion. It's presented as sort of a slice of life that just fades out to commercial. On TV you only have one chance to get it right, but on stage you can change a sketch until it works. A sketch can start out as one thing and morph into something completely different over time.

Production constraints are another problem with television sketch comedy. The more elaborate the set and scenery, the longer the sketch is going to be, whether the concept of the sketch can handle that time or not. It comes down to expense; if the set costs a lot, the producers want to get their money's worth, sometimes at the expense of the sketch. If there is last minute inspiration for a great joke that requires a set change, chances are you'll have to leave the sketch the way it was.

You can find the entire history of sketch comedy on DVD. Check out *Your Show of Shows*, *The Carol Burnett Show*, *Saturday Night Live*, *SCTV*, *MADtv*, *Kids in the Hall*, *Mr. Show*, *Chappelle's Show*, and *The Ben Stiller Show*. You need to know where comedy's been before you can see where it's going. Expose yourself to as much good sketch comedy as you can!

With stage sketches, the audience will suspend their disbelief and accept sets that merely suggest the situation. A simple table can be a desk, a dinner table, or a service counter in a fast food restaurant. Sometimes the lack of a budget for costumes and sets means more satisfying comedy with stronger endings. Elaborate sets, props, and costumes can distract the audience from the essence of the joke.

Improv versus Sketch

Improvisation, or improv, is basically the art of making comedy on the spot. No script, no costumes, no sets, no props, and no one to tell you what to do (although some improv groups take suggestions from the audience). Improv is hard work. You need to stand on stage with next to nothing and no idea what you're going to do. All you have are your wits, your ability, and your experience. With these skills in hand you need just one more thing—trust. Trust in your fellow performers, trust in the audience, trust in yourself, and trust in knowing that things will just fall into place, because they have to.

With sketch, you know what's going to happen next. You know when to be funny and when to hold back. You know what line will be spoken next. And, if you've done the sketch before, you even know where the laughs should be. You also need to trust the script. The worst thing you can do is to get up on stage, doubt the script, and start trying to be funny at the expense of your fellow performers. Don't decide at the last minute that your part will be a lot funnier if you use a silly voice to deliver your lines—it won't. You need to have faith in the script and trust that it's funny as written.

FACT

Many comedy troupes develop a revue show that can run for several weeks with sketches that have been developed from previous improv shows. It's a great way to work the whole process out in front of a live audience and use improv-inspired ideas more than once. It allows those great "live" moments to "live" another day.

There can be a rivalry between improv and sketch performers, but a combination of the two can yield the best of both worlds. Use improv to get the ideas and the characters for sketches that can be developed further. Write sketches that are loose enough to allow for some improvisation so the actors performing it can use their talents to make the sketch better. A sketch can also be performed by a comedy duo or a solo performer. Many stand-ups see parts of their acts as sketches within a stand-up framework.

How to Lay Out Your Script

There is no set format for writing sketches. Each television show and comedy troupe has its own preferred format. The basic format is usually simpler than a sitcom or screenplay script. The key to an effective script is clarity. You need to make the sketch as clean as possible on paper and write it so that someone can read it and still find it funny without seeing it performed. Here's an example of a basic sketch format for a sketch on video:

The Mad Doctor's Book of Home Remedies
SETTING: THE LABORATORY OF A MAD SCIENTIST. CREEPY ORGAN MUSIC IS PLAYING. A TYPICAL HORROR MOVIE **MAD DOCTOR**, WITH FLY-AWAY HAIR AND A WHITE LAB COAT, IS SEEN IN A LABORATORY WORKING ON AN EXPERIMENT. HE IS SURROUNDED BY COBWEBS, OLD BOOKS, BEAKERS, TEST TUBES, AND A GLOWING, BUBBLING BRAIN IN A JAR.

> MAD DOCTOR
> (speaking to the camera)
> Hello, I'm not a doctor, but I do on occasion like to cut people up and see what makes 'em tick. That makes me a mad doctor. Y'know, a brain-stealing, monster-sewing, take-over-the-whole-stupid-little-planet kind of doctor. Well anyway, other mad doctors and myself have gotten together and written this . . .

HE HOLDS UP DUSTY, CREEPY-LOOKING BOOK.

> MAD DOCTOR (con't)
> . . . the *Mad Doctor's Book of Home Remedies*. A collection of superstitious folklore, fringe science, and old-wives tales, guaranteed to ward off any kind of evil, from demonic possession to giant flesh-eating locusts. For example . . .

HE HOLDS UP SKULL AND POINTS AT ITS TEETH.

> MAD DOCTOR (con't)
> . . . did you know that, in a pinch, the silver fillings in your teeth can kill the common household werewolf?

HE PUTS DOWN SKULL.

> MAD DOCTOR (con't)
> Frankenstein's monster terrorizing your village?

HE HOLDS UP A BIC LIGHTER AND LIGHTS IT.

> MAD DOCTOR (con't)
> A simple fifty-nine cent Bic lighter set on "BAD!" will send the monster packing!

EXTINGUISHES AND PUTS DOWN LIGHTER.

MAD DOCTOR (con't)
Girls, not sure if your boyfriend is a vampire? Check to see if you can see his reflection in a . . . mirror!

HE HOLDS UP A MIRROR.

MAD DOCTOR (con't)
If there's no reflection, don't do any "necking" with him. Also, it's a well known fact that vampires are the only beings, natural or supernatural, who are unable to use the Clapper.

HE CLAPS HIS HANDS AND THE BRAIN LIGHT GOES OUT AND STOPS BUBBLING. HE CLAPS AGAIN AND IT TURNS BACK ON.

MAD DOCTOR (con't)
And, if you do get bitten by a vampire, try rubbing garlic bread on the wound.

HE HOLDS UP A SLICE OF GARLIC BREAD TO HIS NECK AND MAKES RUBBING MOTIONS.

MAD DOCTOR (con't)
Order today and find out how to ward off such evil forces as . . .

CUT TO A SHOT OF THE BOOK, LEANING UP AGAINST A SKULL, SURROUNDED BY FLICKERING CANDLES. A LIST SCROLLS UP THE SCREEN AS HE SPEAKS.

MAD DOCTOR (V.O.)
(excited, like a used car salesman)
banshees
harpies
the living dead
the evil dead
golems

vengeance-seeking somnambulists
jersey devils
beasts with five fingers!
beasts with ten fingers!!
beasts with NO fingers!!!
eye creatures
demons
giant leeches
killer shrews
brains that just won't die!
zombies
mutants
the Olsen twins
Jehovah's Witnesses
the "willies"
and much, much more!

CUT BACK TO MAD DOCTOR IN LAB.

MAD DOCTOR
Order today and learn how a simple mantra can help keep
an ancient Egyptian mummy away. Since I just sent one to
your house to do my evil bidding, you'll be glad you did!

FADES TO ADDRESS ON SCREEN, ANNOUNCER SPEAKS.

ANNOUNCER (V.O.)
To order the *Mad Doctor's Book of Home Remedies* just send
a check or money order for $19.95 to:
Mad Doctor's Book of Home Remedies
1313 Dementia Way,
Transylvania, 03187
or call 1-800-MAD-DOCC and leave off the last "c" for crazy!

FADE TO BLACK.

This is a broad, silly sketch that was based on a cheesy television commercial advertising a book called *The Doctor's Book of Home Remedies*. It was written for a television Halloween special that was geared toward a family audience. It has a natural, logical ending—the end of the commercial.

ALERT!

Remember to use ellipses as pauses in your dialogue. In the same way a music piece tells a musician how long to hold a specific note, an ellipse shows the actress how long to pause before continuing her dialogue. You are literally writing the comedic timing into your scripts.

As you can see, the format is pretty basic; the setting and all actions are flush left and in all caps. The character who is speaking is centered, and the dialogue is flush left but indented. When a character's dialogue is interrupted by action you write (con't) for continued after his name when he resumes his thought.

If a character is mentioned in the action, it's a good idea to highlight his name with bold type. It serves as a visual cue that the character will have something to do soon and is helpful for the actors who will be performing the sketch.

When you are setting up the scene for the reader, be as descriptive as possible. You want the reader to see the scene the way you do. In this example, the main character and setting are clichés: a mad doctor in his laboratory. You don't have to do much because most people have an idea of what you're talking about. Adding some music in the background helps set the scene as well. If the character has a line without a specific emotion or style behind it, you would just use his name as follows:

MAD DOCTOR
Frankenstein's monsters terrorizing your village?

If the line of dialogue is supposed to be read in a particular way to show a character's intent or emotion, you need to tell the reader. For example:

> MOM
> (sarcastically)
> Oh, you made me a card for my birthday. . . . How sweet.

You need to communicate everything that you can to your reader. If you don't tell the reader that Mom is being sarcastic, he would think she was being sincere, and that would completely change the line and possibly the sketch as a whole. Err on the side of caution. It's always better to over-explain than to omit valuable information.

Being crystal clear with your scripts makes you consider every choice; you don't take anything for granted. Attention to detail always leads to better material. For example, in the first draft of the Mad Doctor sketch, the joke about having vampires unable to use modern Clapper technology was shown by the doctor simply clapping to turn off a lamp. A lamp would have seemed out of place in a candle-lit laboratory, but the brain in the jar was already sitting there, waiting to be used. It's a more natural and funnier choice than a lamp that would have been included only for the sake of a joke. Also, it's a little darker because it extinguishes something living. And that thought leads to an idea that can be used for another sketch—having to pull the plug on a loved one but doing it by using the Clapper.

Profile in Comedy: David Cross

David Cross was born in Atlanta, attended Emerson College in Boston, dropped out immediately, went to Los Angeles, and got on TV. He starred in HBO's *Mr. Show* and Fox's *Arrested Development*. He currently lives in New York City with his dog.

When did you first realize that you were uniquely funny?

I'm not sure about "uniquely" but when I was a kid and moved around the country a lot, once a year at the very least, and it was the only way a freak (read: "Jew") could make friends.

Who do you think were your influences?

Andy Kaufman, Monty Python, Lou Costello, Steven Wright, Richard Pryor, and Lenny Bruce for sure in the early days.

Do you remember your first original joke?

Yes, I do! When I was about six or seven I came up with the joke, "When a baby boy is born how do you know if he's Jewish? If he's got Matzoh balls."

When did you realize that comedy was something you had to do for a living?

I don't think I ever thought of it as something that I "had" to do ever. I just knew I wanted to and that I was suited for it.

What was your first job in comedy writing or performance?

The first time I got paid to do stand-up was when I was eighteen years old and I opened for a band in Atlanta. I remember the name was Mr. Phelps at a club called The Nitery. It's now a respectable gay bar. I got like thirty bucks and a bunch of beer.

What is the biggest difficulty you've encountered being a comedy writer?

Discipline. Without a doubt, the toughest thing to defeat.

How do you define "alternative comedy?"

Well, it's a manufactured phrase, but I suppose it has to do with "nontraditional" stand-up preformed at nontraditional spaces, i.e., standing in the back of a coffee house talking about a terrible blow job you got or gave last night.

With *Mr. Show* and *Arrested Development*, how much did ad libs and improv contribute to the final product?

With *Mr. Show* it was pretty much a constant crafting of the sketch right up until taping. I don't think anyone ad libbed when the camera was rolling on tape night, though. As for *Arrested Development*, very little. The first year there was definitely more but still not as much as people think.

Are there jokes that you do "just for you?"

In the sense that there is a joke that I know rarely goes over well but I think is funny or I want to test the crowd, yes. Lots, actually.

What are the differences between writing for yourself and writing for others?

I've never specifically written for another person, only in the abstract where I'm writing a sketch and I know someone other than myself will play "waiter number two," and that doesn't change anything really.

What do you find exciting about comedy right now?

I suppose the idea that with the Internet, anybody with twenty cents can put their ideas out there. Of course this could lead to a glut of shit on TV and film when inevitably HBO or Showtime or Comedy Central decide to throw 10 million bucks at something like "Funny or Die" for an overall deal and then we're bombarded with painful crap.

Where do you think the future of comedy is headed?

Outer Space!!!!

As audiences are becoming more specific and more segmented, is that making your job easier or more difficult?

Well, I think that goes part and parcel with awareness of me. As I gain more exposure more people are going to see me and say, "awesome!" or "ugh, what an unfunny asshole," which is pretty much the way it's been since I've become a known entity out there in the comedy world. So to answer your question, both.

What is the best thing about being a comedy writer?

The perks. Free office supplies, almonds, Snapple, shit like that.

Do you have any advice for up-and-coming comedy writers?

Experience as much as you can all the time, THEN write about it.

Brainstorm

Look over your notebook for possible sketch ideas. In the next chapter you'll be learning the different kinds of sketches. If you have a list of ideas already, you'll be able to explore potential ways to develop your ideas. Also, watch sketches on television and play "armchair comedy writer" by rethinking the choices that were made in writing each sketch, paying close attention to the endings. Try coming up with your own endings and see if you can improve upon the original.

Notebook

A good sketch can be developed from pretty much anything that enters your mind. All you need is a good starting point. Try this: clip photos out of magazines, newspapers, or from websites that show people in interesting settings—playing touch football, walking the dog, on a date in a restaurant. Use these as your starting point for a sketch. That's the scene the audience sees as the stage lights turn on or the video fades up.

Let's say you have a photo of four older men sitting at a table drinking beer. Ask yourself questions like: Why are they together? Are they all brothers? Are they the last survivors of the Hindenberg disaster? Are they old army buddies meeting for a reunion? Are they the four ex-husbands of a woman whose funeral they just attended? Are they actors filming a commercial for some embarrassing medical product? It's an incredibly simple starting point, but the possibilities are endless if you ask yourself the right questions.

Brainstorm an idea using one of your photos and write a short sketch based upon the idea. Sometimes all it takes is a gentle nudge to get you started on the road to a great sketch.

CHAPTER 9

Types of Sketches

There are three types of sketches: character-based, situation-based, and premise-based. Some sketches might contain elements of two or all three. When developing ideas for sketches though, it's a good idea to approach one type at a time, then add elements from the others later.

Character-Based Sketches

Some sketches are just an excuse to get a strong character on stage. You can really show them doing just about anything—going to the bank, out on a date, or at work. Some examples of these character-driven sketches are Rob Schneider's "makin' copies!" guy, Julia Sweeny's sexually ambiguous character Pat, and Martin Short's manic misfit, Ed Grimley. You can create many sketches with strong characters, and some can even spin-off into a feature film. The more depth you give these characters, the greater their potential. A one-note character can quickly wear out his welcome if he doesn't grow from sketch to sketch.

FACT

Martin Short's Ed Grimly started out as a relatively small character in a sketch at Second City. Over the run of the show, the character evolved on stage and got funnier with each performance. That small part grew into a memorable character that was featured on *SCTV* and *Saturday Night Live*. He even starred in his own animated cartoon series, *The Completely Mental Misadventures of Ed Grimley*.

Start thinking of your characters—no matter how small—as real people. When you start writing a sketch, you may use secondary characters as a device—they can deliver a line that advances the story or set-up to a joke. You may even call a character "Man #1." However, always remember that "Man #1" has a real name!

To learn the importance of names, start by naming characters after your friends, family, and coworkers. That will add a face to the name, and will make the character seem like a real person. This will be in the back of your mind when it comes to the sketch.

Actors who play a throw-away character usually want more. Playing the role of the maitre d' is not very satisfying when your one line is: "This way, sir." It's a waste of everyone's time—including the audience's—if he isn't allowed to do more.

Essential Ingredients for Character-Based Sketches

You want real people in your sketches. When you create characters, think about who they are. Are they young or old, male or female? Do they have an accent or a distinctive way of speaking? Can they play a more important role in the sketch as a whole? Don't let any of your characters be throw-away material. Your sketch will benefit from strong characters and thinking carefully about each character might even lead you to a better idea for your sketch. Use characters to make the sketch more effective. Don't make every character so extreme that they distract the audience from the main point of the sketch.

For example, let's say you have a sketch with a young couple, Bob and Susan, out for a romantic dinner in a fancy restaurant. Bob is trying to propose, but he keeps getting interrupted by the restaurant staff, the bus boy, the wine steward, the guy with the giant pepper mill, the waiter, etc. You have a choice. All these restaurant staff characters can be one-dimensional—the guy with the giant pepper mill can just grind pepper on their salads and walk away—or you can make them real. Here's an example of the one-dimensional character:

> BOB
>
> Susan, there is a special reason why I asked you here tonight, I—
>
> BOB IS INTERRUPTED BY A WAITER CARRYING A GIANT PEPPER MILL
>
> WAITER
>
> Some fresh pepper?
>
> BOB
>
> Uh, yeah . . .
>
> THE WAITER GRINDS SOME PEPPER ONTO EACH OF THEIR SALADS. HE EXITS.
>
> BOB
> (frustrated)
>
> Where was I? I—

BOB IS INTERRUPTED AGAIN BY THEIR MAIN WAITER.

> MAIN WAITER
>
> How is everything?

> BOB
> (angry)
>
> Fine!

This little snippet of a sketch is fine. The audience gets the point: Bob's trying to propose but he keeps getting interrupted by the staff; with each interruption he gets more annoyed and frustrated.

Here's another example of the same sketch where the author has added depth to the secondary characters (the wait staff):

> BOB
>
> Susan, there is a special reason why I asked you here tonight, I—

BOB IS INTERRUPTED BY ANTONIO, AN EXTREMELY HANDSOME WAITER IN HIS MID-TWENTIES CARRYING A GIANT PEPPER MILL. HE IGNORES BOB COMPLETELY AND SPEAKS ONLY TO SUSAN

> ANTONIO
> (in a seductive Italian accent)
>
> Some fresh pepper for the pretty lady?

> SUSAN
> (enamored by him)
>
> Yes. Please.

> BOB
>
> Uh . . . yeah . . .

ANTONIO STARTS TO GRIND SOME PEPPER ONTO SUSAN'S SALAD. THEIR EYES MEET. BOB DOESN'T KNOW WHAT TO DO.

ANTONIO
Tell me when to . . . how you say? . . . stop.

SUSAN
(passionately)
Don't stop yet . . . a little more . . . that's it . . . no, wait!

BOB
(annoyed)
Stop!

ANTONIO STOPS, STILL NOT LOOKING AT BOB.

ANTONIO
(seductively)
Well, if you need some more . . . how you say? . . . spice, be sure to ask for . . . Antonio.

ANTONIO EXITS.

BOB
(frustrated)
Where was I? I—

BOB IS INTERRUPTED AGAIN BY THEIR MAIN WAITER, STEVE. HE KNEELS DOWN AT THE TABLE, PUTS HIS HAND TO HIS CHIN, AND LOOKS AT SUSAN, COMPLETELY IGNORING BOB.

STEVE
How is everything?

BOB
(angry)
Fine! Everything is FINE!

Notice the difference? By giving some thought to the characters, you can actually compound the situation and create more conflict by making the wait staff hit on Susan. The basic premise is intact, but the sketch is better because the development of the characters brought up new elements that enhanced the sketch.

It's not a comedy, but watch 1942's *Casablanca*, starring Humphrey Bogart and Ingrid Bergman. You'll see that the secondary background characters, no matter how small their role, are fully developed. They each have a story, a reason they're stuck in Casablanca. It's no wonder the movie is a classic.

Situation-Based Sketches: We Have to Stop Meeting Like This!

Sometimes the location or situation can be the starting point for a sketch. At the very least, it can help inspire an idea. A family reunion, a baby shower, or the opening of a modern art gallery can be fertile ground for a sketch.

Sometimes just thinking about the number of people in a sketch can get you started. In what situations would you find just one person? Someone surfing the Internet or talking on the phone. A prisoner in solitary confinement. A woman waiting for her date to show up. Showing someone alone can reveal her true self. Does she talk to herself, or sing in the shower? Is she insecure or overly confident?

How about two people? Are they on a first date? Are they stuck at the top of a Ferris wheel? Are they both men or both women? Are they mother and child? Father and son? A pilot and copilot? Are they identical twins or total strangers?

Why would three people be together? A couple applying for a marriage license? How about a date where the guy's mother tags along to make sure the woman is good enough for her son? A parent-teacher conference with both parents? What if it turned out that the father had been in the teacher's class when he was a kid?

Four people? A space shuttle crew or a carpool. Four bridesmaids waiting to walk down the aisle. Four members of a punk band? How about a sketch with the four presidents on Mt. Rushmore?

Do you get the idea? When you're hunting for that perfect sketch idea, sometimes you need to reverse engineer it by starting with something as basic as the number of people in the sketch.

If you find an interesting setting for a sketch it might just write itself. Think of the things that could happen in the following locations:

- An airport lounge
- A laundromat
- A barbershop
- A confessional in a church
- A minivan full of kids
- A pet shelter
- A corporate boardroom
- A greeting card writer's office
- A comic book convention
- A child's birthday party
- A group of tourists in Italy
- A courtroom
- A polling booth
- A retirement party
- A press conference

Have any ideas? As interesting settings or situations hit you, write them down in your notebook. As you go about your day and visit different places, ask yourself: Is this an interesting place for a sketch? What could happen here?

Another tip to get you started: Think of places where people are forced together and can't just get up and leave—an elevator, the subway, a long line at the post office, the space station, dinner with the in-laws. Audiences love watching actors extricate themselves from awkward situations.

Premise-Based Sketches

Sometimes you just have a funny idea, a great "What if?" that you can use as the basis of a sketch. Like a reality dating show called "Willing to Settle" or "Which One is My Cousin?" or a talk show for dogs.

The idea is strong enough to carry the sketch, and good, developed characters can only make it stronger. Premises are the hardest type of sketch to come by because they are difficult to brainstorm. Sometimes starting with characters and a situation will lead you to a premise, but it's more likely that something will just strike you as funny. It's great when that happens, although those ideas don't necessarily happen on command. It's better not to force it. Brainstorming will help; one idea always leads to another.

Combining the Types

Sketches can and should be combinations of sketch types. You can have a character-based sketch that also has an interesting premise, or a sketch in an interesting location that also has strong character elements. Following is an example of a sketch that uses all three. It takes place at Christmas time, inside a department store's Santa's Village. A man is hired to play Santa and his girlfriend is playing the part of his elf. So we have an interesting location, interesting characters, and a funny situation. For the premise, they are having an argument and on the verge of breaking up, but they have it in front of the kids while they're working.

Another Christmas Story

A DEPARTMENT STORE SANTA'S VILLAGE DURING THE BUSY HOLIDAY SEASON. FRED AND JOANNE ENTER FROM OPPOSITE SIDES, OBVIOUSLY IN A HURRY. AS THEY START TAKING OFF THEIR COATS WE SEE THAT THEY ARE WEARING THEIR COSTUMES (SANTA AND ELF) UNDERNEATH THEIR WINTER GEAR. THEY START GETTING READY FOR WORK.

FRED

Look, I can explain.

JOANNE

I don't want to talk to you anymore, you pig. We have one more day on this job and then I want you out of my life. You can pack up your things and get out—tonight!

FRED

But it's Christmas Eve! Where am I supposed to go? Look, I'm sorry. I was drunk. It was the temp agency Christmas party, there was mistletoe. Sheila means nothing to me!

STORE MANAGER **MR. JENKINS** ENTERS, INTERRUPTING THE ARGUMENT.

MR. JENKINS

Aren't you two ready yet? The doors just opened, a thousand kids will be here any minute. Hurry up!

DOZENS OF KIDS AND PARENTS ARRIVE AND START LINING UP. FRED SITS DOWN IN SANTA'S CHAIR, WHILE JOANNE APPROACHES **AMY**, THE FIRST CHILD IN LINE.

JOANNE
(with a real attitude)

I guess you want to see Santa.

AMY

Yes, please.

JOANNE WALKS AMY UP TO FRED AND AMY GETS ON HIS LAP. JOANNE STANDS BY FRED'S SIDE.

FRED

Well, little girl, what do you want for Christmas?

AMY

I want a makeup set, and a Flower Fun Factory, and most of all I want a Dream Wedding Barbie.

JOANNE ABRUPTLY TAKES AMY OFF SANTA'S LAP.

JOANNE

(bitterly)

Yeah, tell Barbie to keep dreaming.

AMY LOOKS A LITTLE SHOCKED AND EXITS AS JOANNE BRINGS THE NEXT LITTLE BOY, **BILLY**, UP TO SEE SANTA.

BILLY

I'm Billy! I want to sit on Santa's lap!

JOANNE PLACES BILLY ON FRED'S LAP.

JOANNE

(directed to Fred)

Oh, you mean the same lap that Santa paid a stripper to dance on at his loser brother's bachelor party? Sure, Billy, go right ahead. I hope you've had your booster shots.

JOANNE STANDS NEXT TO THEM.

BILLY

(nervous and a bit sad)

Santa, I want a lot of presents, but . . . I wasn't always so good this year.

FRED

(talking to Billy but directing his line sarcastically to Joanne)

That's okay, Billy. We can't always be good all the time. But as long as we're sorry people should cut us some slack and forgive us instead of sending us out into the cold!

BILLY BECOMES AFRAID OF SANTA, JUMPS OFF HIS LAP, AND RUNS TO HIS MOTHER. JOANNE APPROACHES THE NEXT CHILD, **MEGAN**.

MEGAN

I want to tell Santa what I want for Christmas.

JOANNE

(putting Megan on Santa's lap)

Well, Santa's great at making empty promises he never intends to keep, so go ahead. Ask away.

JOANNE STARTS TO GET THE NEXT KID WHEN FRED TAKES MEGAN OFF HIS LAP. HE STANDS UP, PULLS OFF HIS BEARD, AND TAKES OFF HIS HAT.

FRED

(desperate)

Look, I'm sorry. She meant nothing to me. I love you. There, I said it! you're the only woman I ever loved. I know you don't deserve a jerk like me, but I need you and if you leave me, I'll just die. . . . So what do you say?

ALL THE KIDS

(whimpering)

AD LIB: DON'T LET SANTA DIE!

JOANNE

(getting misty-eyed)

You really meant that? You love me?

FRED

You know I do!

FRED PICKS UP JOANNE IN HIS ARMS. THEY HUG EACH OTHER AS THE KIDS CHEER.

FRED
Kids, I'll be back in ten minutes. Santa has to go . . . feed the reindeer!

FRED CARRIES JOANNE OFF AS THEY KISS.

END

Profile in Comedy: Barry Crimmins

Barry Crimmins is best known as one of the country's top political comedians. He has worked as an Air America writer and columnist and is the author of *Never Shake Hands with a War Criminal*. Most comedians owe Crimmins a huge debt; he founded the Boston comedy scene, starting with the famous Ding Ho. This comedy club, produced by Barry inside a tiny Chinese food restaurant, spawned such amazing comedians such as Steven Wright, Paula Poundstone, Bobcat Goldthwait, Kevin Meaney, Jimmy Tingle, Dennis Leary, and Lenny Clarke, just to name a few. They all soared to new heights because Barry set the bar so high.

Who do you think were your influences?
My hilarious childhood friends: Mark Twain, Lenny Bruce, Tommy Smothers.

Do you remember your first original joke?
They taught us how to write a haiku in the third grade. I wrote:

Is the pot of gold
at the end of the rainbow
or in my dad's pocket

and it got published in the Syracuse newspaper.

When did you realize that comedy was something you had to do for a living?
When I realized anything else would entail working.

What was your first job in comedy writing or performance?
I won a talent contest at the Four Seasons Lounge in North Conway, New Hampshire, in 1973.

What is the biggest difficulty you've encountered being a comedy writer?
Trite expectations and demands of corporate play-it-safers.

Are there jokes that you do just for you?
Sure, but they're private.

As a political comedian, what is your biggest challenge?
The narrowness of the American political spectrum. It goes from just right of center to the far right. Of course, this is also a blessing because it is easy to be considered outrageous just for expressing views that would be considered moderate almost anywhere else in the world.

What are the differences between writing for yourself and writing for others?
That becomes very specific. In some cases, it's almost the same. In other cases, you must first cater to the enlarged ego of the personality—in those cases you must first ask the question, "Yes, but how does this international crisis revolve around the talent?"

What do you find exciting about comedy right now?
I am excited that Bush will soon be gone and . . . a lot of recently minted political humorists will realize that it isn't always so easy to write relevant material.

Where do you think the future of comedy is headed?
I think the movie *Idiocracy* covered it nicely.

As audiences become more specific and more segmented, is your job becoming easier or more difficult?
My job remains the same. I provide people with things to take to other people. Such is the lot of the subversive.

What is the best thing about being a comedy writer?
There is always hope of escape.

Do you have any advice for up-and-coming comedy writers?
Watch the movie *Idiocracy*.

Brainstorm

Here are some ways to come up with sketch ideas based on character and situation. On one side of a sheet of paper make a list of occupations or roles people have, and make a list of emotions or character traits on the other side. For example:

Occupations or roles people have			
astronaut	bounty hunter	toll booth attendant	veterinarian
driving instructor	magician	doctor	writer
father	waitress	salesman	politician
mother	teacher	movie director	football player
superhero	carnival worker	vegan	ice skater
accountant	chef	princess	repairman
Emotions or character traits			
depressed	impostor	condescending	bored
critical	guilty	lying	desperate
abrasive	anxious	pretentious	lazy
happy	overly enthusiastic	overly sensitive	sleepy
boring	frugal	elderly	incompetent
cranky	claustrophobic	obsessive compulsive	foreign

You know what to do—go up and down the list and see if there's a match that you can get some ideas from. For example, let's try "astronaut" and "guilty." A space ship or station is a very small space. What if there were only two astronauts, one was murdered and the other claimed innocence? Or try this—there are three astronauts, men and women, and one is having an affair behind the other's back. Or a flamboyant astronaut: "Houston, we have a problem . . . that tie you're wearing is hideous!" Here are some other ideas from the list:

- An incompetent driving instructor who teaches all the bad rules of the road—flipping people off, talking on his cell phone while driving, eating while driving, etc.
- A condescending superhero. He makes the bad guys feel bad about themselves until they turn themselves in.
- An obsessive-compulsive politician who's afraid to shake hands and kiss babies because of germs.
- An elderly prizefighter. (Oh wait, that was *Rocky IV*.)
- Bored toll booth operators who find ways to freak out drivers, just to make the job a little more interesting.
- A foreign doctor, whose English is only so-so, about to operate on a patient and there's a communication problem about what needs to taken out.
- A pretentious vegan who makes others feel guilty about just about everything.
- A lying dry cleaner who claims to have lost your clothes but is wearing your monogrammed shirt right in front of you.

As you can see, this is another quick way to get some ideas for sketches. Make your own list and give it a shot. Remember, you have a choice—you can either wait for ideas to just show up or you can go looking for them.

FACT

If you're stuck for ideas for interesting characters, just grab a copy of the yellow pages and browse through it. As you see interesting occupations, jot them down. This is a great way for you to jump-start the creative process, and you might find a new plumber in the process.

Notebook

This sketch writing exercise combines all three types. The premise and location of the sketch are okay, but you're going to use interesting characters and some added conflict to make it even stronger.

Here's the scenario: It's World War II and two soldiers are stuck in a foxhole with a battle raging around them. Suddenly, their walkie-talkie crackles to life and a voice tells them that there is no air cover and they have to be left behind. Although there is no way that they'll make it out alive, they will die heroes. The soldiers are devastated, but they still put up a brave front. One soldier tells the other that he needs to get something off his chest before he dies—a secret that he needs to confess. He reveals the secret to his fellow soldier. (You decide what that secret is.)

After the confession, the walkie-talkie comes back on and it's the same voice as before. A horrible mistake has been made; the coordinates were all mixed up, and they are going to be fine. In fact, a rescue party should be arriving for them any minute to take them back to safety. Now the secret is out and it won't die with them. What happens next?

At first glance it might seem limiting to have the basic plot just handed to you, but there are enough variable elements to make it interesting. The soldiers' characters and the nature of the secret are enough to give you an infinite number of possibilities, all of which can make the sketch uniquely yours.

Is one soldier, young, naïve, and sacred, and the other is a battle-hardened career soldier? Is one calm about his approaching death and the other a mess? Is one a simple country boy and the other a Harvard graduate? Is one of them an enemy spy? Is one the other's long-lost father? Is one of them just a temp and really shouldn't be there? Does one want to be a hero and die fighting, while the other wants to surrender? Is one hoping he'll be captured and tortured because he's a masochist?

What is the secret? Is one in love with the other? Has one soldier been sleeping with the other's wife? Is one of them a space alien, a robot, or a time traveler? Is one soldier confessing to a murder? Is one soldier really the other soldier's wife, who pretended to be a man and enlisted to keep tabs on her husband and make sure he didn't cheat on her?

How do they resolve the situation? Does one kill the other? Do they just act like nothing happened?

You get the idea. There are an infinite number of possibilities for comedy. It just takes some thought and a little time to come up with something great. Sketches are a great way to try many different comedy styles and one of the best ways to learn how to write for other people.

CHAPTER 10

Writing With Others

Learning to write and perform your sketches with others can be a very challenging but extremely rewarding process. Finding others who share and augment your sense of humor will help you become a better all-around writer. In this section you'll learn how to play nicely with others and come up with some great comedy in the process.

Make Your Friends Funnier

Do you know anyone you would like to write with? Someone who shares your comedy sensibilities and likes the same comedy that you like? Maybe you have a friend or acquaintance you think is hilarious, someone who makes you laugh consistently. Try writing a sketch with him. If he has absolutely no interest in becoming a comedy writer or has never written before, it might take some coaxing. You might have to ease him into the idea.

The best way is to ask him his opinion of your writing. If he likes what you write and thinks it's funny, that's great. If he makes suggestions that you agree with, that's even better. Try using the process of going over your writing to brainstorm new ideas. Start using that person as a sounding board for your ideas. If you and your friend are like-minded but there's still enough of a difference to make it interesting, ask him to write a sketch with you. Start with an idea that you've brainstormed together. Go out to lunch or dinner and throw around ideas. (Make sure you bring your notebook!) If the process goes well, you may have found yourself a writing partner; if it doesn't, try the process with someone else.

When you've found a comedy troupe you think you'd like to join, be warned that they may not be all that accepting to the idea of bringing in a new member or writer. Troupes can be very cliquish. Being too pushy will generally work against you.

Another approach is to look for an existing sketch troupe in your area. Watch their show and get a sense of the type of comedy they perform. If you feel that their style syncs with the material you've already written, ask them if you could submit some sketches for their consideration.

If the sketch troupe offers classes, take one or two. It's a great way to meet other comedians and writers, but it's also a great environment to show off not only your writing, but your personality and ability to work with others as well.

Finding others to work with can be a very frustrating experience, especially if they're used to writing with other people and you're new to comedy and don't have a reputation. If you find that you're not having any luck, you might have to take matters into your own hands.

Start Your Own Troupe

If you go to most college campuses today, you are likely to find several comedy troupes. For example, at Emerson College in Boston, there are anywhere from seven to ten active comedy troupes, and a couple of comedy magazines at any given time.

> Don't add too many members. *Saturday Night Live* has had as many as eighteen cast members at one time and as few as eight. The Upright Citizens Brigade had only four members and the comedy troupe Stella has only three. When it comes to comedy troupes, less can definitely be more if the writers and performers are talented.

Why so many? A good comedy troupe can only effectively support so many members—a dozen or so—before it becomes a case of too many cooks spoiling the comedy broth. With more than twelve people, it's just a lot harder to get everyone on the same page and have a unified group. So the "extras" may band together to form new troupes.

It's a Numbers Game

Think about it this way: If a troupe with fifteen members plans a show with ten sketches, five people didn't get their sketches into the show. That also means that there are a limited number of acting roles to be split among those fifteen performers. Every writer wants the most talented actors in their sketches, so some will have more parts than others. It all boils down to some unhappy troupe members.

In addition to the disaffected troupe members, other comedians may have auditioned for the group and were rejected for some reason. You may have a solid troupe, but you're leaving out some talented writers and performers who can seize the opportunity to start their own troupe with their own unique brand of comedy.

This is the best thing that can happen to comedy. It's what helps comedy grow and keeps it from getting stagnant. One troupe is formed from the dynamics of another, and another will eventually spring from that. Each finds its own identity, and that identity in turn is challenged by others seeking to be unique. If you're having trouble with the existing comedy powers, become your own force to be reckoned with.

The Power is Yours

Look for others who will complement what you write, both in their writing suggestions and their comedic acting ability on stage. You also want a well-rounded troupe that will support a wide variety of sketches. If you're a man and you form a troupe of all men, you had better get used to wearing a dress on stage or you'll be limited to sketches with all men, which can be constraining. You need some variety: men, women, different ethnicities, and different views. If everyone in your troupe is exactly like you, you won't learn very much. And learning from others is the most valuable thing you can get out of the group writing experience. It helps you stretch your talents, which makes you a better writer and more flexible working with others. It also pushes you to write sketches you probably wouldn't have written, and roles and characters that you probably would never have performed. Once you find others that you feel comfortable writing with, it's time to start getting your sketches in front of an audience.

Drag is funny. It just is. It's funny when either gender impersonates the other. But don't be afraid to work with the real thing. A good balance of gender improves the comedy make-up and voice of the troupe. If men and women write the comedy, it will speak to both the men and women in the audience and will have more depth.

Finding a place to perform can be tough. Look for existing venues that might work well for sketch comedy performances—comedy clubs, small theater spaces, restaurants, or nightclubs that have open-mic nights. Don't necessarily look for venues that only have comedy. If there's a small coffee house that that has poetry readings on Monday nights, suggest sketch comedy on Tuesday nights. If you make it easy for the venue, you might just have a nice home to help you build your career as a writer.

Keep a No-Frills Attitude

When you're starting out with your troupe, keep your expectations reasonable. Expect a lot from your comedy. Expect to become a better writer with every show in which you perform your material in front of an appreciative audience. But don't expect any of the show business niceties you might have heard about.

The talented ventriloquist Jay Johnson, star of the television series *Soap*, once appeared on a talk show without a dummy, just a guitar. He said he wouldn't be performing ventriloquism; instead he would be showing his talents as a singer. He was interrupted by a fly buzzing around him, a little man who lived inside the guitar, and Mickey Mouse speaking to him from his watch. The audience accepted the perfect illusion of a four-person conversation with four distinct characters.

Don't expect to make any money from your endeavors—at least at first. Don't expect a big fancy stage with curtains and a full professional sound and lighting system. Don't expect a dressing room, or even wings that you can make an entrance or exit from. Don't expect that you'll have access to elaborate costumes, props, music, and sound effects. But take heart—you don't need them.

All you need is a space, a script, some actors, and an audience. If you keep that in mind when you're writing your scripts, you'll be all set.

Look at a troupe that does improvisation. They don't have anything but themselves and their talent; they don't even have the luxury of a script. If two actors are playing airplane pilots, all they need to do is suggest to the audience that they are sitting behind the controls of an airplane wearing uniforms and headsets.

You need to keep that simplicity in mind when you write your sketches. It's amazing how much the audience will accept—how willing they are to suspend their disbelief, how willing they are to go along for the ride—as long as the script is strong, the actors are competent, and the comedy is funny.

By asking for and expecting more from the venue, you'll become a burden to them. They can easily find someone else to fill your place. Work within your limitations and make up for those limitations by making your sketches so funny that no one notices.

Group Dynamics

One of the most difficult problems in staging sketches is character management—bringing characters in and out of the scene flawlessly. Avoid having too many unnecessary characters on stage at once, especially when you're working in a small space. Look for natural excuses for characters to enter and exit, and condense characters and lines when you can.

Be especially careful of characters who just stand around. They come on stage to deliver a line, but you neglect to give them a logical, natural, or funny reason to leave. If you do that a lot, the bodies will pile up on stage, distracting the audience, who will find it difficult to focus on what's important in the sketch.

Two's Company, Three's a Crowd

Sometimes you might find it best to work with one other person, both in writing and performing. It's incredible what two performers can do together. In vaudeville, the comedy team was a staple. In film, Laurel and Hardy, Abbott and Costello, and Martin and Lewis dominated their respective eras.

On radio and television, we had Stiller and Meara, Nichols and May, and the incomparable Bob and Ray, who had a forty-year career.

Finding a good comedy partner is like finding the perfect spouse. It's a marriage of creativity and trust in each other's talents. You also have each other for support. The beauty of a two-person sketch is that it actually works better without any frills. Two characters just standing on stage can play an infinite number of believable characters and can leap from character to character without any costume changes or much voice alteration. The team's success stems from establishing likable personas and forming a connection with their audience.

A good team isn't two people; it's one entity. If you want to work with someone as a team, be careful. If the audience always associates you with your partner, it can be very difficult for them to adjust to either of you as a solo performer. Consider working with a partner or a larger sketch troupe as just part of your overall comedy career, and make sure to work on solo projects as well. That way, if there is a personal or professional falling-out between you and your fellow performers, you'll have the skills and contacts you need to make it on your own. Often a team of two talented performers has broken up and been unable individually to achieve even a fraction of the success they had previously. Always make sure to nurture yourself as an individual solo performer or writer.

Who Gets The Dog?

The biggest downside to writing and working with others is the question of who owns the material when the relationship goes sour. If a writing partnership is a marriage, the break-up is the divorce. And with that divorce comes the division of property—your sketches. All the sketches, jokes, and characters you created together is up for grabs when the team is dissolved. Usually this isn't a problem until you both go up for the same writing job— with the same material. This can be more awkward than running into your ex with your new girlfriend.

There is no easy solution. Perhaps you can come up with an agreement, a prenuptial if you will, that whoever had the initial idea owns the sketch. But the origins of a sketch can be very unclear; one idea comes out of all the ideas that came before it. If you've worked on an idea or a character that means a lot to you, make the case for it before a problem develops and agree that it's your baby. The written version of the sketch should indicate that you wrote it with additional material by your partner. This might avoid a potential problem down the road. It may be best to move on. You can always write more material, and having the specter of your ex-partner hovering over your shoulder can only prevent your progress.

Profile in Comedy: Tony V

Tony V is a hilarious stand-up comedian and actor who has appeared on *Late Night with Conan O'Brien*, *Seinfeld*, and *Dr. Katz: Professional Therapist*. He can currently be seen on Showtime's *The Brotherhood*. He has also appeared in lots of national television commercials and even did a stint as the American Tourister gorilla. He just finished a film with Robin Williams.

When did you first realize that you were uniquely funny?

Yesterday morning at 3:51 A.M. . . . . Woke up feeling kind of odd . . . that feeling turned into strange and that in turn morphed into funny with a capital F-U. I've been plying my trade since 1982—I have been fascinated by comedy and comics since my youth, when I would peek through a sliver of opened door late at night to glimpse *The Tonight Show* when I was supposed to be very asleep. Sometimes I wouldn't even notice my parents "doing it" on the couch I was so wrapped up in what was on the TV screen.

Who do you think were your influences?

Being a bit older than a lot of folks when I started, my influences go way back to the Marx Brothers. Much of their word play, I believe, still holds up. W. C. Fields—his attitude and outlook have been mimicked ever since. And I truly believe that if Lenny Bruce had not suffered and endured what he did there would be no comedy as we know now! Or ever! He kicked the door wide open and used his head to do it!

Do you remember your first original joke?

"I was driving down a country road, I saw a sign that read: Pony Rides $5, so I pulled up handed the guy five bucks, he put a little horse in the back of my car and said, 'Have him back by six!' We had a nice day, the pony and me. I'm going back tomorrow."

When did you realize that comedy was something you had to do for a living?

When it started paying me more than I was making as a social worker. I love the hours, have always been intrigued by working opposite hours of everyone else, and I love the idea of confronting the night. The whole idea of swimming upstream gives me a jolt! It always just seemed like a natural fit, still does.

What was your first job in comedy writing or performance?

I wrote locally for a short-lived Boston show called *Local Heroes*. I worked on an early draft of a movie named *Celtic Pride*. (I am uncredited but do have a bit part as a cabbie in the film.) I also wrote, produced, and performed on the F/X network's first-ever original show called *Bobcat's Bigass Show* starring Bobcat Goldthwait (who I believe to be one great comedian and one truly amazing friend). We really plowed some very silly, funny, out-there kind of ground. It's worth a look if it can be found anywhere. It might be out on "Viewmaster," I'm not sure!

What is the biggest difficulty you've encountered being a comedy writer?

Getting people who can get things done to look at what you wrote and understand it. My experience has shown me that many people in positions of power are dopes. It's a struggle but one worth it if you are passionate about your work. In many cases a thick skin and perseverance will triumph. I envy the young creative people of today because of all the outlets they have to have their stuff viewed. Even if you're not young, you should take advantage of everything the "ether" has to offer. Get on your computing witchcraft machines and get your stuff looked at!

Are there jokes that you do just for you?

You have to do jokes just for you or you'll go mad. Mad I tells ya—MAD! I do a bit where I ask the audience how come there are no famous tuba players. I have a standing offer of twenty dollars (when I have it, I throw it around!) to anyone who can name a tuba player that someone else in the crowd would say: "Oh yeah, he's good!" I think it's terrific, not so much with all audiences.

You co-wrote the screenplay for *Celtic Pride*. How did the movie change from your original script?

The drafts I worked on were actually funny! The finished product was nothing like I envisioned it. The idea was mine. Colin Quinn and his brother did the first draft. Then I did some punch-up on some of the gags and the three of us met several times to finalize the draft Disney bought. Once Disney bought it and ran it through their sanitation device, it was a shadow of the original. From what I remember, and it's been a while since I've seen it, the film became a whole lot of premises with no punch lines. It really seemed like they paid for the title and threw away the humor. No heart, no soul, just sap. The original script had Larry Bird (the legendary Celtic) being kidnapped in kind of a combination hero-worship/bad-bet-gone wrong scenario. It was much richer and had more places to go than the "Ultimate fan/losers" angle that they took. Of course now I will probably be hunted down and killed by Disney Black Ops . . . wait, I think I hear someone coming. . . . Quick! Call the Coen brothers! They're the only ones who can stand up for what's right.

What are the differences between writing for yourself and writing for others?

If you write for others it's theirs. If you write for yourself it's yours.

What do you find exciting about comedy right now?

Comedy is a living, breathing, ever-evolving entity. It is ageless, timeless, and defies logic and common sense. In this regard, comedy can be truly unique and wondrous all the time. Every generation has a comedy genius and most of them are people you've never heard of. That's the best thing ever.

Where do you think the future of comedy is headed?

I think there is no future in comedy. It's always in the now and what happens in the now is always happening and that's the best part. The future is now and it can happen at any time. I think people in the future will only laugh at pictures of dogs' asses . . . believe me, it's heading that way!

As audiences are becoming more specific and more segmented, is that making your job easier or more difficult?

Eventually I hope to only perform to middle-aged, out of shape guys named Tony. It's like what's happened to television, only live. I predict that very soon everybody will have their own comedian who travels with them to keep 'em laughing. "This is my lawyer, Mr. Scmegowitzbergstein, and I believe you know my comedian, Eddie!"

What is the best thing about being a comedy writer?
Being self employed and self-reliant. Who would have thought that at this time in history being a self-employed writer/comedian/actor would be as stable as any other business choice?

Do you have any advice for up-and-coming comedy writers?
"Don't let the bastards get you down." (Bono) "It's a complex world." (Rudy Cheeks) "Listen." (Tony V)

Brainstorm

Think long and hard about whether you have the desire, ability, and temperament to write with other people. If it's clear that it's not for you, that's fine. But if you're on the fence about it, give it a try. Make a list of the people you might consider writing with. Make sure to consider writers you can learn from—and who can learn from you.

Make the initial attempt casual—maybe one sketch for a specific show. You could invite another comic to be an actor in a sketch you've already written and give him the freedom to add his comedy into the part. If things go well, try it again with another sketch.

Don't focus on just one person; don't "go steady" with anyone just yet. Play the field until you find the chemistry that seems to work best.

Notebook

Try writing a sketch for two people in which you play one of the characters. When brainstorming the characters, location, situation, or premise, look for things that are natural for two people. For example:

- A job interview
- A date

- A parent trying to discuss the facts of life with a teenager
- A doctor and patient
- A talk show interview with an author
- A sales meeting pitch where the audience is the company
- A telephone conversation with a telemarketer
- A political debate
- A comedy team that doesn't like each other
- A speaker from a foreign land and her interpreter
- Two Western gunfighters at a sundown showdown

Write the sketch and rehearse it with a potential partner and see if anything comes from it. If it starts to feel good, try it out in front of an audience. That's the only way you'll know if working on a team is for you.

CHAPTER 11

Styles of Stand-Up

Performing stand-up comedy can be the ultimate form of comedy expression. What usually looks spontaneous and improvised is actually, in most cases, carefully written. Although every stand-up comedian is different, they can be categorized into several basic types.

The Observational Comic

"Did you ever notice . . . ?" or "What's the deal with . . . ?" are the stereotypical lines of the observational comic, but there is much more to this style. The observational comic picks up on all the quirks and minute details of everyday life.

This is probably the most common and popular form of stand-up comedy, and for good reason. It is the easiest for the audience to connect with—but that doesn't mean it's easy to perform. This style is much more than just making things that everyone notices funny. It's all about making the audiences see these commonplace things from a fresh perspective—yours. Observational comedians communicate the inconsistencies of everyday life to the audience. When they ask, "Did you ever notice . . . ?", the audience answers "Yes!" with their laughter. It's as if the comic is inside the audience members' heads, commenting on some of the basic truths of life—and hey, the truth is funny.

For a great example of the observational style, check out Jerry Seinfeld's 1998 CD *I'm Telling You For the Last Time.* This album is a recording of shows where Seinfeld retired the routines that made him famous. The names of the cuts sound like every other comedian's set list, but in the master's hands they are still original and fresh.

This style was popularized in the 1960s with groundbreaking comedians like Bill Cosby, who could tell a story so vividly that you were sure it was happening to you; George Carlin, who spoke truth to power and was a critic of hypocrisy wherever he found it; and Richard Pryor, who dared talk about society's ills and made people laugh at themselves. Other comics who are known for advancing this style are Jay Leno, David Letterman, Brian Regan, Patton Oswalt, and the ultimate observational comic, Jerry Seinfeld, who became one of the most successful comedians ever by talking about—nothing.

With observational comedy it's hard to feel that you're bringing something new to the table, because so much ground has already been covered.

You know the topics—dating, airline travel, dogs and cats, the differences between men and women—but don't despair. You can breathe life into even the most common topics with your unique perspective. You'll see something no one has ever seen before, a fresh take on an old subject. There's a reason this type of comedy is so successful—it works.

The Political or Topical Comedian

Topical comedy can be one of the hardest types of stand-up to master. The two biggest subjects here are the ones you were always told to avoid—politics and religion. Lenny Bruce was one of the first comedians to talk about the unspeakable on stage, and he paid the price for it with jail time and constant harassment.

FACT

You've seen Lenny Bruce's influence on so many comedians that the original may seem a little washed out. To capture the comedian who changed everything, listen to the 1992 re-release *The Lenny Bruce Original Volume 1 & 2*. Another must for political humor is Bill Hick's 1990 album *Dangerous*—it was and still is dangerously funny.

Mort Sahl wasn't the first comedian who talked about politics, but he was the first political comedian. He and Dick Gregory advanced the style, making it more acceptable for a wider audience. Bill Hicks, Dennis Miller, Bill Maher, Lewis Black, Kate Clinton, Barry Crimmins, Jimmy Tingle, Will Durst, Al Franken, Janeane Garofalo, and impressionist Jim Morris have been masters of the art in recent times.

On television, politics is the staple subject of late night talk shows. Johnny Carson, David Letterman, Jay Leno, and Conan O'Brien have been the nation's go-to sources for comedically sane interpretations of the day's news. Comedy Central's *The Daily Show* and *The Colbert Report* have redefined the genre by providing an intelligent, cutting-edge twist to the day's events. In addition, they actually educate as well as entertain. Some political comedians just tell the audience what they should think, but good ones challenge the audience by making them think about subjects from the comedian's point of view.

The Ethnic or Regional Comedian

Comedy that deals with race relations or regional material dates back to minstrel shows and vaudeville of the late nineteenth and early twentieth centuries. This area of comedy has undergone a complete revolution since the first minstrel shows became popular in the wake of the Civil War. In those days, a white performer put on blackface and presented a derogatory characterization of an African American, or a comic from the city played a country hick. Today, these topics are addressed with a sense of pride in one's heritage, race, or background.

Comedy fans are lucky that Richard Pryor gave us so much great material. If you want a sample of his creative genius check out the 2002 CD *Richard Pryor: The Anthology 1968-1992*. Listen to how his career and routines evolved as society changed, and you'll realize how much his brilliant comic voice helped change society.

In modern times, comedians like Richard Pryor, Flip Wilson, Dave Chappelle, Margaret Cho, George Lopez, and Carlos Mencia have addressed the sensitive topics of race relations and ethnic diversity with humor and a sense of self-empowerment.

Comedians like Jeff Foxworthy, Bill Engvall, Ron White, and Larry the Cable Guy have turned their regional *Blue Collar TV* style of comedy into a huge franchise. They have fans from all over the country, not just the southern states.

The Hipster Comic

Have you heard the expression that someone is "too hip for the room?" Well, that's what hipster comics strive for. Their act is meant to be for a select audience; they avoid the mainstream. But if they're good, the mainstream wants to be let in to see what all the cool people are laughing about. Everyone wants to be "hip," right?

Demetri Martin is the essential hipster comedian. His 2006 album, *These Are The Jokes*, is a great compilation of his inventive and original comedy. Another great example of the hipster style is the late Mitch Hedberg's 2003's album *Mitch All Together.*

Lenny Bruce was probably the first hipster comedian; his style was more like a jazz musician than the other comics of the time. Today, Demetri Martin is a great example of the hipster comedian. He avoids the typical references of his contemporaries and instead presents his own tilted look at the world, using stand-up and multimedia in a unique way.

The Aggressive Comedian

Loud and confrontational, aggressive comedians run on pure confidence. They are so sure of themselves and their opinions that they actually intimidate the audience into laughing at them. Some comedians have been very successful with this style. Don Rickles, Andrew Dice Clay, Sam Kinison, Dane Cook, Lisa Lampanelli, and Carlos Mencia have all benefited from this commando, take-no-prisoners approach to comedy.

The original aggressive comedian, and one of the funniest is Don Rickles, who recently scored a big hit in the 2007 film *Mr. Warmth: The Don Rickles Project.* One of the most successful comedians of recent times is Dane Cook, whose 2006 DVD *Dane Cook: Vicious Circle* shows his comedy rock star status.

Some comedians who adopt this style do it very well; they have a strong, confident persona on stage backed up by great jokes and routines. Others only have a loud voice, a big ego, and nothing else. Many comedy club owners place a premium on this type of act, and it will fill the seats for the short term. For the long term, it's the acts with jokes that have the potential to build a loyal following.

ALERT!

When you are developing your material and your stage persona, remember that there is a big difference between loud and funny. Anyone can be loud and dirty, but it's a lot harder to be genuinely funny. It's up to you to come up with material that isn't just noise.

This type of act can also be really dirty, substituting vulgar words for jokes with crowds that don't know the difference. Having this type of act can help you get work and fast money, but in terms of building a successful career, it will be much more difficult to make it onto television and into the premium comedy clubs.

The Alternative Comedian

This term is a catch-all category for acts that defy description. These are the acts that truly stand out from the pack. Their jokes are nontransferable; they will only work for the person who wrote them and would completely fall flat in the hands of others.

Ernie Kovacs, Woody Allen, Steve Martin, Robin Williams, and Steven Wright are examples of alternative comics who have been embraced by the mainstream. But the godfather of all alternative comedy, Andy Kaufman, was either loved or hated by his audience. Andy constantly strived to do things that were different. He wrestled women, had an alter ego called Tony Clifton, starred on the hit series *Taxi*, and did an uncanny impersonation of Elvis. On his television performance on the premiere episode of *Saturday Night Live*, he never uttered a word. He would only lip-sync selected parts of the Mighty Mouse theme that played on a record player beside him. He never called himself a comedian, just an entertainer who liked to play with peoples' heads.

Today the alternative comedy scene is thriving. Comedians like David Cross, Eugene Mirman, and Sarah Silverman are some of the biggest acts on the comedy scene.

Comedy has always been "alternative." The current resurgence of alternative might just be a rediscovery of stand-up, which had fallen out of favor in the early 1990s. In a way, it's a reaction or a correction to the generic nature of comedy that came with an overexposure of the market. Every generation invents its own comedy, but is always influenced by and stands on the shoulders of those who came before.

There are many examples of alternative comedy today, but three stand out as great examples of the genre: David Cross's 2004 CD *It's Not Funny,* Eugene Mirman's 2004 CD *The Absurd Nightclub Comedy of Eugene Mirman,* and Sarah Silverman's 2006 CD *Jesus is Magic.*

Another term for alternative comedy is "anti-comedy." Be careful, though—a lot of acts that try not to be "funny" end up not being funny. They can alienate a crowd by being too weird. There's a difference between weird and funny. The two can coexist, but don't substitute weird for funny; doing so can be a form of self-sabotage. It can also come off as elitist if the audience is never let in on the joke. If you're only playing to the other comics in the back of the room, you're doing a disservice to yourself and—more importantly—your audience.

The Character Comedian

Every comedian has a unique personality. To some extent, all comedians play a character, a version of themselves, every time they take the stage. But some comedians invent a whole new persona for their comedy.

Emo Phillips, Judy Tenuta, Andy Kaufman, Bobcat Goldthwait, and Larry the Cable Guy are all comics who made a name for themselves by not being themselves. The ultimate stand-up character was Paul Reubens as Pee-Wee Herman. In the late 1970s and early 1980s, Reubens created the character of Pee-Wee Herman as part of a show put on by the Groundlings in Los Angeles. His manic man-child creation was a staple of late-night talk show, host of his own award-winning children's television show *Pee-Wee's Playhouse*, and star of Tim Burton's *Pee-Wee's Big Adventure*, one of the funniest movies ever made.

> If you want to see one of the best character comedians at his roots, you must watch the DVD of 1982's *The Pee-Wee Heman Show: Live at the Roxy Theater.* This DVD shows the ultimate man-child long before his playhouse or his big adventure and offers a hilarious take on every kid show of the 1950s.

Playing a character can be a lot of fun. It gives you the opportunity to create a whole new world of material to work with, but it can be limiting as well. If you are associated only with your character, it can be difficult for the industry and your audience to see you as something else when you feel it's time to move on and try different things.

Acts With Special Skills

Often unpopular with other comedians, acts that augment their comedy with a special skill or talent are immensely popular with audiences. Traditional stand-up comics look at these kinds of acts as being "easy" and are cheating somehow to gain an unfair advantage with their comedy. They couldn't be more wrong. A joke is a joke. If an act is funny and original, that's all that matters. The fact that someone takes a different path to the joke shouldn't make any difference. The creative process for these kinds of acts is the same as a traditional monologist; there's nothing "easy" about it. In fact, it can be more difficult than traditional stand-up, and its audience appeal can't be denied.

Magicians

These are acts that combine comedy with magic. Acts like Harry Anderson, Penn & Teller, the Amazing Jonathan, and Mac King are well-known to audiences and draw huge crowds at their live shows. They have achieved this success by redefining the audience's perception of what a magician is, just as a good comic redefines comedy.

FACT

There must be something magical about magic. Johnny Carson, Steve Martin, Andy Kaufman, Woody Allen, Orson Welles, Arsenio Hall, Dick Cavett, and Jimmy Stewart were all magicians—and good ones! In *Arrested Development*, Will Arnett's character Gob took his illusions seriously, but they provided some of the show's funniest moments.

Music Acts

These acts mix music with comedy by including original songs and song parodies. Jack Benny, Henny Youngman, Tom Lehrer, Victor Borge, the Smothers Brothers, Steve Martin, "Weird Al" Yankovic, Zach Galifianakis, Sarah Silverman, Flight of the Conchords, and Jimmy Fallon have all mixed these two art forms with hilarious results.

Impressionists

Comedians who make a career out of mimicking famous people are in short supply these days. The act is very popular on television sketch shows, and the occasional comic might perform one or two impressions. Rich Little, Fred Travalena, Jim Morris, Elon Gold, Darrell Hammond, and Frank Caliendo are masters of this difficult art, but a comedy act that consists solely of impressions in stand-up is a rarity these days.

A lot of impressionists make the mistake of relying on traditional subjects to impersonate. Does a young audience really care about John Wayne or Richard Nixon? Not enough to feature in your act. Also, many talented impressionists are good at their technique; they perfectly capture the voice and characteristics of their subject, but they lack the comedy skill to put that subject in an interesting situation.

Ventriloquists

What was considered a dead art form has found new life. In the past, Edger Bergen, with his sidekick Charlie McCarthy, was one of the most popular entertainers in the country. Ventriloquists such as Senor Wences, Shari Lewis, and Paul Winchell appeared frequently on variety shows like the *Ed*

Sullivan Show, but fell out of favor with audiences in the 1970s and 1980s. Today Jay Johnson, Jeff Dunham, Ronn Lucas, and Terry Fator are immensely popular with a whole new audience and are bringing this ancient art form back into the pop culture limelight.

E-QUESTION

Why do traditional comedians have a problem with acts that use a special skill?
It's because it's different from what they do, and people are usually afraid of things that are different. There are good and bad specialty acts, just like there are good and bad traditional stand-ups. Every act should be judged by its jokes, originality, and ability to connect with an audience.

Prop Comedians

These are acts that use weird inventions or sight gags with their comedy. The term "prop" is short for "stage property." And that's all it is; it's something used on stage. While many comedians are quick to call a prop act a lesser act, they are slow to criticize their own use of a prop when the need arises. A funny object that a prop comedian uses is exactly the same as the beer bottle that a comedian takes sips from to help with his timing. A good prop comedian isn't defined by her props but by her jokes and talent.

Writing is writing. Comedy is comedy. Everyone is different and thinks differently. If everyone did the same things the same way it would be boring. Comedians should be encouraged to express themselves as they see fit. In fact, the more a comedian does to make their voice unique, the better. Being funny, talented, and original are the most important things. That's the bottom line. How an individual performer gets there is irrelevant.

Profile in Comedy: Wendy Liebman

Wendy Liebman is one of the funniest comedians and best joke writers out there. She has appeared on *The Late Late Show* with Craig Ferguson, Comedy Central's *Pulp Comics*, HBO's *Half Hour Comedy Special*, *The Tonight Show* with Johnny Carson, and *The Late Show with David Letterman*.

When did you first realize that you were uniquely funny?

I was seven or eight. I was doing a skit in our basement with my sister, and I was playing the part of a stereotypical Jewish mother. The audience was howling. I couldn't catch my breath. It was a flashbulb moment. I was wearing a lime green dress.

Who do you think were your influences?

Woody Allen, Lily Tomlin, Cher, Steve Martin, David Letterman, Garry Shandling, Johnny Carson, Lucille Ball, Joan Rivers, Elayne Boosler, Rita Rudner, Jonathan Katz, Bill Braudis, Kevin Meaney.

Do you remember your first original joke?

I was trying to enroll in a creative writing class in college, but the teacher didn't accept me. Someone asked me if I was going to write anyway, and I said I wasn't even going to write checks. That became the joke: "I'm a writer. I write checks. They're mostly fiction."

When did you realize that comedy was something you had to do for a living?

When I started making more money doing comedy than I was making at my day job (administrative assistant).

What was your first job in comedy writing or performance?

I was hired to do five minutes at the International Pub in Revere, Massachusetts, in 1985, a year after I started performing. The other comedians on the show were Zito and Bean. There were like eight people in the pub, and they were playing pool. But it was the first time I was paid to tell jokes that I had made up. The promoter, Joe Amagrasso, handed me an envelope with twenty-five singles in it, and it felt like (I imagine) a drug deal going down.

What is the biggest difficulty you've encountered being a comedy writer?

I'm not as prolific as I wish I were. Also, sometimes I'll have a really funny thought but I'm too lazy to write it down, and then the thought is lost forever.

Are there jokes that you do "just for you?"

Not as much anymore. But I do remember dropping a joke that didn't quite work ("I gave up drinking for rent"), and then starting it again after another comedian said he missed it. So I guess I do that joke just for him.

What are the differences between writing for yourself and writing for others?

I've been hired by two people to write jokes (one comedian and one singer—but I signed contracts so I can't say who), and I have to say it's easier. I don't know why. The singer asked me to "make up a true story." I'm not kidding you.

What would be your "dream job" as a comedy writer?

I would love to do punch-up on movies.

Were there difficulties being a woman in a predominately male industry? How did you overcome that?

This is my opinion. People are happy when they find a funny woman, because it is rarer. If you're a woman in comedy, you have a great career ahead of you.

What do you find exciting about comedy right now?

It's a way to talk about hypocrisy and pain without bumming someone out.

Where do you think the future of comedy is headed?

The sky is the limit. (Did I just use a cliché?)

What is the best thing about being a comedy writer?

I am paid to make things up. I can make someone laugh.

Do you have any advice for up-and-coming comedy writers?

Nothing replaces experience. So just write. All the time. You'll be amazed what comes out of your head.

Brainstorm

As you watch comedians on stage or on television, look for acts that use a special skill—any skill. It could be a ventriloquist, a magician, or a traditional stand-up that uses an impression, song, or visual aid in the act. Watch how these comics incorporate these devices into their acts and ask yourself: Do they add to the overall comedy or distract from it? Are there any skills you have that you might be able to add to your comedy?

Notebook

Look over the different stand-up styles and try to figure out where you might fit. Is your material so weird that it might be more plausible coming from a different character? What are the acts that influence you? Do you want to work in the same style as them?

If you're having trouble seeing where you fit, don't worry. Many comedians mix the various styles until they find a combination that works for them. Just let your material take you there and don't concern yourself with labels.

Try taking some of the jokes you have written and rewrite them in the different styles described in this chapter. The changes don't have to be permanent, but try it as an experiment to see what you come up with.

CHAPTER 12

Writing for Stand-Up

Stand-up comedy can be one of the best ways to show off your writing, and explore different types of comedy to help you find your voice. Stand-up can also be a great testing ground for concepts and ideas that can be used for sketches, sitcoms, and movies. It takes a lot of confidence and performance skills to become a pro, but the things you need most are good writing and knowing who you are on stage.

Look in the Mirror

Take a look at yourself in a full-length mirror. Don't worry, you can keep your clothes on. Ask yourself: What would an audience see when I walk on stage? Would they see a young sexy woman? Do I look like a slacker? A computer nerd? A grandmother? Would they see a guy who looks like an accountant? A former athlete who has let himself go? Do I have an accent?

Consider your impression on the audience when it comes to writing your material. That doesn't mean you should be defined by your look, but you do need to take it into account.

Let's say you're overweight. Don't make all of your jokes about your weight. A lot of comedians make that mistake, and it's severely limiting. However, you do have to address it somehow, because the audience will not relax until you acknowledge it. They will be distracted if you don't. Right or wrong, that's just the way it is.

You can address your look any way you like. Let's say you are very thin and look like a computer geek. You can embrace it: "I'm proud to be a geek." Or you can deny it: "So, I've been working out . . . next week my personal trainer says I can add weights to the bar." But you need to address it—somehow.

If you are average looking and there's nothing about you that sticks out, make sure to tell the audience something personal about yourself at the beginning of your set: "I just broke up with my girlfriend" or "I just moved into a new apartment." The audience wants to know something about you whether it's true or not.

Develop Your Character

It sounds like a cliché, but it's true with stand-up—in order to be successful, you need to find yourself and know who you are on stage. In the beginning of their careers, comedians can struggle to find their voice and stage persona. It takes a while, and there's no easy way to do it. Mostly you'll learn from mistakes: you'll try a joke or a style that doesn't work, and that helps steer you toward something that does. You might also make the mistake of sounding too much like the comedians you admire—more on that later.

Here's the good news: once you figure out who you are and what you're supposed to do on stage, it gets easy—*really* easy. It can take a while before you get there, but once you do you're all set. Once you define your own individual comedy universe, you have an unlimited amount of material at your disposal. It's only when you're grasping at different paths that you are truly limited.

Let the Material Guide You

When you first start performing, you should put more emphasis on your material than your character. Your jokes will help you define your character. Work hard and write good jokes, and the rest will fall into place. Look at where the material that works is taking you. If you get a good laugh with a particular joke, ask yourself some questions. Why is that working for me? What does that joke say about me? Would that joke work for anyone, or is it funnier because it's coming from me?

FACT

Once you know what you're supposed to do, you'll stop pulling material out of the same pool as everyone else. You'll have your own unlimited source at your disposal. You'll know what you can and can't do on stage, what works and what doesn't.

Don't let your mistakes distract you from your successes. The mistakes happen for a reason. If a joke doesn't work, try to fix it. Flip it around; try a different phrasing or word choice; make it longer or shorter—anything that might help it work. If your attempts to fix it fail, put it aside and move onto the next joke. But remember to keep it in your notebook. You will probably be able to use it eventually.

Just because a joke doesn't work doesn't mean it's not funny. It might be that you don't have the performing skill to make it work. This may sound weird, but the joke might be too good for you right now, and you just need to improve to make it work. Once you gain some experience, you'll be able to look over your notebook with a new perspective and take on all those old ideas that didn't have a place in your act. Remember, if it's in the notebook, it's not going anywhere. You'll only get frustrated spending too much time on one joke. It will keep you from finding all the other jokes that are out there, waiting to be discovered.

Set Your Standards

Before you attempt to get your first gig, go to shows and observe. Go to lots of shows as often as you can and watch every comedian carefully to see what you can learn. If you see a novice, watch for his performance mistakes to help you avoid making the same mistakes yourself. Watch the good comedians and take note of what you like about them. More importantly, watch the comedians you don't like because you can learn a lot more from them.

Never sit in the audience and take notes during a show; it will look like you are stealing jokes. Only take mental notes. Comedians get very paranoid (and rightfully so) when seeing an audience member with a notebook or a voice recorder. You don't want to get a bad reputation before you've even started your stand-up career!

Watch comedians with a hyper-critical eye. When you see something you don't like, remember it. It could be that the comedian picks on an audience member for no reason, or his sense of humor is really dirty and he makes the audience so uncomfortable that they only laugh from nervousness or shock. Tell yourself, "I never want to do that. I never want to have someone else see me doing what I am watching right now." Even if the comic is popular, successful, and experienced, that doesn't mean you have to like what he does. It certainly doesn't mean you have to do the same things to be successful.

Let someone else make mistakes for you. The more you discover through a critical eye, the faster you set your own standards. Having a clear set of personal standards will help make you a good comic. Other comics might have completely different standards that work for them, but you need to find what works best for you. Setting your standards also acts as a filter for material that you know is beneath you.

When you watch other acts, be polite and professional. Keep your opinions to yourself and remember that you have a lot to learn. When you go to a club, be prepared to see someone who is very good. Just be warned: watching a really good act—someone who knows exactly what he's doing, has great jokes, connects with the audience, and makes it all look absolutely effortless—can be depressing for the aspiring comic.

Don't get discouraged; seeing someone really good makes even seasoned comics feel like amateurs. Instead, have faith that with time and work, you will be just as good someday, depressing and encouraging a whole new generation of comedians yourself.

Learn From Your Influences, But Know When to Say Goodbye

Many comedians struggle with their influences. They truly admire a particular stand-up and imitate her style, wanting to be like her. This never works because at best they'll just end up being a faded second-generation copy of the original.

The faster you can shed your influences, the better. That doesn't mean you can't learn from them, but you shouldn't try to be just like them. Watch the acts you admire, and study them. Learn from your observations how the comics interact with the audience, dress, establish their character, organize their set, and make transitions. Look at all the choices they have made. Those are the things that will help you be yourself.

If you don't shed your influences, you'll never improve on them. That sounds almost blasphemous, doesn't it? But shouldn't that be your goal? Or, at the very least, shouldn't you want to be just as good, and get to a point where they admire what you do? You don't want to spend your career living in someone else's shadow, and unless you step out and away from that shadow, you'll never achieve your ultimate goal—being an original.

Take Advice With a Grain of Salt

Once you start performing and getting stage time, you'll receive advice from comics and club owners. In the beginning, listen and take their advice, especially when it comes from club owners and bookers. They know their room best and they've seen what will work and what won't. Listen to them and make changes accordingly.

Take advice from other comics with a grain of salt. Most will just tell you how they would do the joke, and that might not be particularly useful to you. Others will give you advice just for the sake of hearing themselves talk. However, if you get advice from a comic that you truly respect and admire, listen to what she has to say and follow her advice. This type of advice can really help you with your act and your career. You want good comics on your side. They can help you by introducing you to other comics and club owners and they might be helpful in getting you stage time.

If you want to know exactly how Steve Martin became a star, read his 2007 autobiography *Born Standing Up: A Comic's Life*. In this honest account of how Martin went from working at a magic shop at Disneyland to selling out stadiums and making movies, he doesn't hold back or gloss over the details of how hard he worked to develop his own unique voice.

Once you start doing well consistently and begin to get a sense on your unique persona, trust your own instincts over the advice of others. At some point you have to start trusting your gut, even when it means going against the advice that others might give you. When you know you're right, that you're onto something good, you need to defend your choices and stick to your guns—even if you meet some resistance. After all, it's your career; don't let others run it for you. If you fall out of favor with a club owner for not taking his advice, maybe you and that club weren't such a good match to begin with.

Do Your Homework

When you're writing your first sets, be careful not to accidentally use someone else's material. You're walking a weird line here: you want to watch and listen to lots of comedians, but you also want your own voice, which can get clouded if other comedians' voices are in your head as well. If you have friends who are already performing, run your jokes by them first and ask them if anything sounds too familiar. If a line comes too quickly to you and seems too good to be true, it probably is. If a line just enters your head and you can't backtrack through the thought process to see how you came up with it, it is suspect. Leave doubtful lines out of your sets until you can confide in others and run lines by them.

It's better to find out early that a line you thought of belongs to someone else. You don't want to get to the point where you have grown to really like or need the joke. Once you're in that position, it's a lot harder to give it up.

You can also try doing a simple web search using keywords within the joke. This might not be very accurate because many comedians are reluctant to put their jokes online, but keywords might be mentioned in a review of a show or on a comic's blog or fan site. You don't want to get off on the wrong foot by doing someone else's joke, even unintentionally. If it turns out that you independently thought of the same joke as someone else, it's still theirs if they did it first. Get used to it; it will happen a lot. But look at it on the bright side—you're writing professional level jokes!

Profile in Comedy: Jon Rineman

Jon Rineman is a 2005 Emerson College graduate, and has been a regular at the Comedy Studio in Harvard Square since 2004. He is a freelance monologue writer for Jay Leno and was published in the 2005 humor edition of the *Improper Bostonian*. His weekly blog *www.rinemania.com* features news jokes and his signature comedy bit, Cause & Effect.

When did you first realize that you were uniquely funny?

Honestly, I'm still not sure that I am. As someone who's only twenty-five and still trying to break in as a writer, it's tough to claim unique funniness. I think I realized I had a unique ability when I started having my jokes published in the weekly *Comedy Studio* newsletter and stand-ups I look up to told me they could never write good, tight topical jokes on a daily basis—which makes us even, since I come up with about three usable stand-up bits a year.

Who do you think were your influences?

Jay Leno's the major influence. He's been the torchbearer of monologue jokes since Johnny Carson—the original monologue pioneer—hung 'em up. I can't imagine a better duty than standing on stage night after night at 11:30 and telling twenty-five or thirty jokes written that very day. I was a big Kevin Nealon and Norm MacDonald fan when they did Weekend Update on *Saturday Night Live*, and also admire Conan O'Brien, as he essentially taught himself—a born improv comic—how to do a good monologue. I've known one of his writers, Brian Kiley, since I was in college, and he has always been very supportive and influential.

Do you remember your first original joke?

My freshman year of college, I came up with this observation about living in downtown Boston: "In my neighborhood, nobody calls an ambulance—it just runs on a shuttle schedule." I actually still use this joke when I perform, and it holds up. Thanks, Mayor Menino!

When did you realize that comedy was something that you had to do for a living?

When I left my job at a local news station and soon discovered there was nothing else for which I was qualified.

What was your first job in comedy writing or performance?

After I graduated from Emerson, I was back living at home with my parents. After a few months, nothing was working out and I was desperate, so I called my parents' friend Barry. He had grown up with Jay Leno and remained good friends with him. I asked if he could put in a word. Of course, this was a favor he was asked on a regular basis, so he was a bit reluctant (for my own good), but I told him that I had been writing monologue jokes all summer and he wound up writing a very, very helpful and positive recommendation that he mailed on a Saturday morning to Mr. Leno. That Monday night, at 11 P.M., I'm up in my bedroom—writing jokes, seriously—and my Dad comes into the room with the phone: "It's Jay Leno." We had a really great talk, and a couple weeks later, I sold my first jokes.

What is the biggest difficulty you've encountered being a comedy writer?

Still, just selling jokes, getting stuff seen. It's a weird situation for me because what I do is so specific, and there's a lot of uncertainty in the late-night genre right now as far as hiring goes. A year from now, I could be a staffer, or I could be screwed. Who knows? The toughest thing is that there are a lot—a ton—of other comics who would kill to get a job as a staff writer, many with better credentials in comedy as stand-ups and performers. My challenge is to just try to be better at writing jokes. Just work as hard as I can to be better. It means a great deal of frustration, and a lot of sleepless/thankless days and nights, and a lot of confusion by others as to what the hell I'm doing with my life—but, it's all about getting better and making the jokes stronger.

Are there jokes that you do just for you?

I don't do any topical stuff when I do standup, so basically anything I think up that's an original, personal thought, I keep. I came up with a joke that went, "If Hillary gets elected; she'll refer to her husband Bill as her First Gentleman; meanwhile, Bill will continue to refer to Hillary as his Last Resort." Nobody wanted it, so I kept it, and it wound up working pretty well for "older" crowds.

What is the most frustrating part about getting "known" in the industry?

Ask me once I am.

What are the differences between writing for yourself and writing for others?

Honestly, it's just the type of joke. To me, a monologue joke is a monologue joke—yes, you may shape it to fit the host, but a premise is a premise. You write a real setup, and follow it with a made-up punch line. Whereas in writing for myself, I tend to be more observational and conversational, as opposed to set-up/punch line. The news is great and it's what I spend most of my time writing jokes about, but as far as "writing" for myself, it's more a matter of collecting and organizing genuine, original personal thoughts into something cohesive.

What do you find exciting about comedy right now?

It's a great time for late night. You have guys switching shows, switching coasts, even switching networks. And clips from each show are popping up all around the Internet. What you're seeing is a really great fraternity of comics collectively carrying on where the likes of Carson (Johnny, not Daly) and Steve Allen left off. And, you're also seeing some great sitcoms like *The Office*, *30 Rock*, and *Family Guy* sort of reinvent comedy much the way *Seinfeld* did when I was growing up. And how can you not be in awe of *The Simpsons*?

Where do you think the future of comedy is headed?

Who knows? I think people are starting to appreciate different kinds of comedy, and the thought process that goes into it. But it's all a cycle. After a while, people get tired of down-to-earth comedy and go for zany. After that gets old, they go for down-to-earth. The main thing is the growing incorporation of the news. Jon Stewart really got the ball rolling, along with Stephen Colbert, and I think that's allowed other late nighters to be a little more political and cultural instead of just making fun of Amy Winehouse. Though Winehouse is always funny.

As audiences are becoming more specific and more segmented, is that making your job easier or more difficult?

It makes it more difficult on the inside, I think. Writers are pretty hard on themselves and each other these days to be original. But it's never a bad thing to have open-minded audiences who can catch obscure stuff as well as the old standards.

What is the best thing about being a comedy writer?

Being a comedy writer has always appealed to me since you're basically being told to be a wise-ass. I was always that kid in school who wanted so badly to make fun of whatever the teacher was telling us. It was almost like being dissatisfied with what actually happened and wanting to improve it to make it funnier. When you write jokes, that's what you get to do.

Do you have any advice for other up-and-coming comedy writers?
Being that I am one, I'd rather just ask if they'd like to sublet my apartment.

Brainstorm

When you watch other comedians, notice how they define themselves. Look at the acts that are truly unique, and others whose material is interchangeable, could be done by anyone, and doesn't reflect a unique point of view.

Then look at your own material and consider the same thing. In the beginning, it's okay if others could easily do some of your jokes. That's only natural. But start looking for glimpses of your personality shining through in certain jokes, and start cultivating that type of material. Look for ways to expand those special jokes, and weed out the generic stuff or adapt it to fit your personality a little better.

Notebook

Look through your notebook and the previous exercises for jokes that can work in a stand-up environment. When you're working on your first set, it might be a good idea to just stick to one or two topics, unless your style dictates otherwise.

You don't want to be all over the place, trying to cram all your ideas and all your jokes into a short set. You'll end up with a big mess that doesn't do you or your jokes justice. The clearer you are, the better. Your goal should be to get some laughs, gain some confidence on stage, and learn from your mistakes. You want to build on your successes from set to set; don't think you can do it all on your first shot.

Look at the lists you've made. Let's say that you have a line about your dog. It's just a funny one-liner that doesn't really go anywhere else. If you say a line and it just hangs there, it might get a laugh, but it might leave the audience asking themselves "and . . . ?" That can be a speed bump in your set. Things are going well and then you just hit a wall with a joke that leaves the audience expecting more.

This is where your lists can come in handy. Make a list of every fact you can think of about dogs and do what you did before, use those facts as set-ups for punch lines. Do this with your original dog line in mind. Hopefully, you'll come up with one or two more dog jokes or a segue that naturally leads to another topic. For example, after your dog line you could say, "My parents never let me have a dog when I was a kid, they were very strict . . . " or "My girlfriend is afraid of dogs. . . ."

Another good place to look for material is the list of daily activities and annoyances that you came up with in Chapter 4. Look for small topics the audience can relate to or things about yourself that will draw the audience in.

CHAPTER 13

Performing Stand-Up Comedy

Okay, you've written some jokes and you're starting to get a sense of who you want to be and what you want to say on stage. Now it's time to get out there and start being funny. You can write in a vacuum all you want, but you'll never know what's funny until you get it in front of an audience. This is the only way to see what works and what doesn't, and it's your chance to make all the changes necessary to begin your stand-up career.

Getting Your First Gig

A gig is a job, but in the beginning it will be more like an internship—an internship without pay, benefits, or anything. All you'll get is stage time, which is invaluable and necessary to perfect your craft. At first glance, it may seem like an unfair situation—the comedy club charges a cover to its audience, you provide the comedy the audience came to see, and the club makes all the money. That doesn't quite seem right does it?

But look at it this way. The club has to pay its rent, advertising, waitstaff, and everything else. There wouldn't be a stage, a microphone, or an audience if it weren't for them. In the beginning, you need that more than you need the money.

Open-Mic Night

So how do you get your first gig? Scout out the comedy clubs in your area and see if they have an open-mic night. An open-mic is basically a first-come first-served list. If you sign up early enough you might get five minutes on stage. In the early 1980s, this was the standard way for talent to break into comedy clubs, but today it's a rarity. You will find comedy open-mic nights in smaller clubs that may only feature comedy one night a week.

Use the web to look for comedy showcase nights in your area. Check out the website *www.openmikes.org* to see it there are any clubs listed in your area. Some cities even have online forums where comics share a lot of great information on where to get stage time. They also tell you what clubs to avoid, which can be just as important.

These clubs are your best option for a couple of reasons. First, they are probably organized by a comic who is trying to get more stage time himself. The owner of the club lets you use the stage but usually has no interest in the show other than selling more drinks on a night when business is usually slow anyway. This is a good thing, because you are only dealing with other comics, most of whom are just starting out themselves. It's a great way to meet and network with others in the comedy community and find more opportunities for stage time.

The other benefit to these smaller shows is that they are a safe place to be bad. Look at it this way: Do you really want to be seen by someone who can help or hurt your career before you are ready? Probably not. You want to fly beneath the comedy club radar until you have gained enough experience to get to the point where you *want* to be noticed.

Bringer Shows

Unfortunately, sometimes the only way to get stage time at an established comedy club is to perform at a "bringer show." A bringer show is just what the name implies. You bring paying customers to the show and the club will give you stage time. Many clubs are very specific with their bringer policies. Most will give you five minutes of stage time if you provide them with at least two paying customers. Some will give you one minute for each customer you provide. Sounds pretty horrible, doesn't it?

If you feel you're getting something out of the experience of working the club, go for it. Just don't let yourself be taken advantage of. If you live in an area where there aren't a lot of clubs, you might have no choice but to do bringer shows.

It's worse than it sounds. This highly exploitive practice boils down to making you pay for stage time. So not only are you not making any money, you are paying to be the show. If you want to get on stage this way, you'd better have a lot of friends who want to see you and don't mind paying for high cover charges and overpriced, watered-down drinks.

This might be fine if you always want to have friends in the audience, but do you really want your friends and family to see all your shows? There's a lot to be said for the anonymity that stand-up can provide. How far are you going if you have to experiment in front of people who know you? One thing is for sure—you can't talk about them. You don't want to have to watch what you say in front of your friends, family, and coworkers. You also don't want to feel uncomfortable saying lines you know aren't true, because your friends in the audience know they're not true. Also, you don't want to wonder if they are only laughing because they know you. Finding your comedy voice is much easier in a room full of strangers.

Quality suffers in bringer shows. Pretty much anyone can get stage time if they bring an audience. You might find yourself working with lesser quality acts or for audiences that feel they have a loyalty to only the comic they came to see. How would you feel about following someone who brought twenty people who get up to leave just as you start? It happens all the time.

You'll need to decide what works best for you. The bottom-line is to get as much stage time as you can. If there are no clubs in your area, start one. Go to a local bar, restaurant, or nightclub and talk the manager into having comedy one night a week. As long as it doesn't cost them anything, and they can make some money from it, it might be worth their while. And you'll have an audience to try your comedy on.

Your Set List

Now that you have a gig, you need to figure out your set list, the material you're going to perform. The set list is just a list of the jokes you're going to perform in the order you're going to perform them. This list will change constantly as you add new jokes and discard the stuff that doesn't work.

A set list might look like this:

- Opening line
- Airplanes
- Dogs and cats
- Working out
- Closing bit

Of course, you want to write out your material and know what you're going to say, but don't memorize it word for word. No one speaks exactly the same way they write. If you are bound to a script, word for word, you will tend to sound like you are reciting rather than natural and spontaneous. Stand-up is writing, but it's also a craft. A joke is like a piece of art. You are constantly adding a little here and taking away some there until you have a really good joke. If you are bound by a script with no room to maneuver, your jokes will remain stationary and frozen in time.

When you make your set list, start with a joke you know is going to work. Be sure it makes some sense as an opener. Try using a line that introduces you and lets the audience know what to expect from you.

You also want to protect fragile lines—jokes that are subtle or that you are unsure of—with stronger material or material that the audience is more likely to connect to. If you are inserting a new line, make sure to cushion it between two jokes that you know will work. That way, if the joke doesn't work, you can get right back on track and move on. End with something strong.

Avoid puns, at least when you're starting out. They're clever and intelligent and they can be a sign of good writing and clever connection, but no matter how clever the pun, the usual audience reaction is a groan. If you start the audience groaning, they will groan at everything, and you—and the other comics—don't want that!

Think about whether you want to perform a string of one-liners or stick to a single topic. Both approaches have their pros and cons. If you choose the one-liner approach, you get instant feedback from the audience, but you run the risk that the audience will judge you from line to line—laugh at one joke, not at the next. You won't be able to get the audience on a roll and you won't be able to get a picture of your performance as a whole.

If you stick to a single topic, you get a better sense of the set as a whole, but if the audience isn't into your topic, they might not give your jokes the chance they deserve. If their attention is diverted, they might not feel that they can get back up to speed and will just wait for the next comic.

Perhaps the best approach, at least in the beginning, is a mix of the two, some quick one-liners followed by a few lines based on a single topic. Of course, this will be different for every comic. There is no absolute right or wrong way to make a set list. Just try different ways and see what works best for you and your style. Give it a lot of thought before you hit the stage, and even more thought after you leave the stage.

Testing and Revising Your Material

The best way to test your material is to perform it. You can't create comedy in a vacuum. You need real-world feedback to see if it's funny or not. See what works and what doesn't, then make changes accordingly. The more you get out there, the faster you'll improve; it's that simple. Woody Allen once said, "Eighty percent of success is showing up" and it's true.

If you perform an entirely new set every time you go on stage, you'll have a lot of jokes, but you won't have strong jokes. Never look at a joke as "done." It can always get better. Each time you perform it you'll come up with distinctions that will improve your material.

You can ask friends whose opinions you value to look over your writing or be a sounding board for jokes. Be careful trying out material on other comics, though. Sometimes your styles won't mesh, or they might see your material through their filter. If they wouldn't do the joke, it's hard for them to see if it would work for you.

Lots of people will try to give you advice. If you respect someone, listen carefully to what he has to say. If you don't know the person or don't have a lot of respect for his opinion, just take it with a grain of salt. A lot of people will tell you how they would perform the joke, but that's not necessarily useful for you. Ultimately, you are your own best sounding board. Trust your instincts over the opinions of others.

Comedy Club Etiquette

Remember that as a performer you're a guest in someone else's house—the comedy booker's. In order to get asked back, you need to be a good guest.

Following are some tips to make sure that you are a welcome presence in any comedy club.

Stick to Your Time

If you are given five minutes, do five minutes. Don't do three; the host of the show might not be ready for your early departure. Definitely don't do more than five minutes, or you'll have the booker and every comic in the room on your bad side. Most clubs have a system that uses a lighting cue to tell you it's time to wrap up. Make sure you know the club's system and stick to it. "I didn't see the light" is not an excuse; it's a sign that you're being unprofessional and selfish.

If sticking to your time is continually problematic for you, invest in a small countdown timer that has a vibrate function. Some cell phones have this option; if yours doesn't, try the Invisible Clock II, available from *www.invisibleclock.com*. This will be especially useful when you are starting to audition for television, where you *really* need to stick to your time.

Be a Good Audience Member

Help make the show better. Laugh at other comedians' jokes and start applause breaks where the audience should be clapping. Don't talk to your friends or other comics during the show. Give every act the respect you would expect from your fellow comics.

Know Your Place

If you are new at this, keep your opinions to yourself unless you're asked, and even then be conservative with your comments. In general, keep your critiques to yourself. Do what you do and don't worry about trying to fix anyone else's act. If you see someone doing something you don't agree with, learn from it but keep it to yourself. If everyone is doing things you don't agree with, that room might not be for you.

Don't be High Maintenance

Don't ask the booker for a review of your act or for more dates during the show. Wait until after the show—even better, the day after the show—to get his attention. As a newbie, don't demand special lighting or music cues and don't leave props on the stage. Don't bait the audience and then leave it to the host or the next act to clean up your mess.

Show Respect

Tip the waitstaff and encourage the audience to do the same. If they are on your side, they can do wonders for your career. If they don't like you, you're in big trouble. Respect the club and the audience. You wouldn't walk into someone's house and make fun of the wallpaper, so don't make fun of the leaky toilet in the club's bathroom. If there is a small crowd, don't make them feel bad for being your audience. Remember, they are the good guys because they came to the club. If it's a small crowd, work just as hard for them as you would a full house.

Protecting Your Material From Theft

You might think you're alone in stand-up, but you're not—if you have friends. You want friends in the comedy community who know you and know your act. If you have a good reputation for being an original act who does your own material, you'll get support from other comics, who will watch your back and let you know if someone is taking your material.

FACT

If you look on YouTube, you'll see tons of video where comedians, including some that are very well known, are "outed" by videos showing them stealing material word-for-word. Comics who see a joke getting stolen will tape it and post it for the world to see before the offending comic has even left the stage.

If another comic does take one of your jokes, you probably won't have to do anything. Peer pressure from the other comics is usually enough to make them drop it. If that doesn't work, talk to that comic and ask her to stop. Sometimes you can help the situation along by letting comics and club owners know the situation.

Before you take action, you also have to consider the fact that someone else might have come up with the same idea independently of you. This happens all the time. Comics get their material out of the same comedy pool and it's inevitable that some will think of the same joke. It's especially true with observational or topical jokes. The more generic your material, the more likely it is that you'll come up with jokes similar to others. As you develop your persona and focus on your own comedy voice, it will happen less and less. You want to get to the point where your act is so well defined that you basically become steal-proof. The jokes you do are so uniquely yours that they simply won't work for anyone else.

Profile in Comedy: Harry Anderson

Harry Anderson starred in two highly successful sitcoms, *Night Court* and *Dave's World,* and he is also one of the top comedy magicians of all time. He has appeared on *Cheers, Saturday Night Live, The Tonight Show,* and in the made-for-TV movies *Stephen King's It, Harvey,* and *The Absent-Minded Professor.* He has also written for his own series and other episodic shows such as *Tales From the Crypt* and *Tales From The Darkside.* As a stand-up comic, he also starred in several television specials and has worked on projects with Apple computers.

Who do you think were your influences?

Early influences: Bob and Ray, Carl Ballantine, Johnny Carson, the Firesign Theater. My introduction to comedy as a profession came as a response to realizing that I was not equipped to make a living as a gambler, which was my first dream. I played cards and hustled a shell game on the street, but after receiving a broken jaw back around 1970, I decided to translate the work into a magician/con man character, which, though it dragged in less cash, was a safer play from the angles of law and health.

When did you first realize that you were uniquely funny?

I guess I've always tried to be considered engaging and bright. I suppose that comes from being itinerant—as a kid I moved around a lot and had to make friends and influence people quickly and effectively.

Do you remember your first original joke?

The first joke I took real pride in was pretending a gun made the sound "Peckinpah—Peckinpah—Sam—Sam—Sam!" (It played very big in the 1970s).

How did you deal with other comedians who look down on "acts with special skills" like prop comedians, magicians, and ventriloquists?

I would love to feel comfortable performing without props, and I do on occasion when I have the appropriate material. For example, I recently did a one man show, "Drowned and Quartered: How Hope, History, and Alcohol Failed to Save New Orleans," based on my post-Quatrain experiences. It was funny, dark, and informative. Very funny.

How important is it to create a character or stage persona?

Character is the thing. The only thing. There are no jokes. There are only funny stories. And there is no funny story without a person acting like an animal or an animal acting like a person.

How would you describe your writing?

Everything I write and perform has a comic angle, as life has one.

In stand-up, how important is the "script" versus ad libbing?

I'm the kind of performer who can only ad lib once there is a script to ignore.

What is the best thing about being a comedian?

Hanging out with funny people. Worst: bad club food served in group dressing rooms. And airports.

What do you find exciting about comedy right now?

I don't watch stand-ups, even on TV. Never have. Don't go to clubs unless I'm working. Maybe to the Magic Castle, but only to socialize. I am not a big fan of the kind of thing I do. The comedy I enjoy: *The Daily Show*, *The Colbert Report*, *Saturday Night Live* (when it doesn't suck), *30 Rock*, *My Name is Earl*, and *It's Always Sunny in Philadelphia*.

Where do you think the future of comedy is headed?
Future of comedy? Come on. What's the future of anything?

Do you have any advice for up-and-coming comedy writers?
Wake up early, work hard, and have two successful sitcoms.

Brainstorm

Start looking for comedy clubs and clubs that feature comedy in your area and start to make contact with the people who run those rooms. Approach them and express your interest in performing at their clubs. It will be easier if they've seen you watching shows. They might not think that you are serious about comedy if you walk into a room for the first time and expect to get a date. The more you hang out, the better your chances will be.

Notebook

Once you have a booking, start looking through your notebook for bits you want to perform. Also start to plan for all the things that could go wrong, like getting heckled or having an inattentive audience, and try to figure out how you would handle the situation. Chances are that you won't encounter any on your first set, but you might as well be prepared.

Organize your jokes into a set list and start practicing—but not memorizing—your act. Time yourself, factoring in time for laughs, so you don't go over your time.

Make sure to videotape or audiotape your set and record your observations in your notebook. You'll see where you need to fix things, but focus on your successes and build on them!

CHAPTER 14

Parody and Satire: "It's a Floor Wax—and a Dessert Topping!"

Two of the most popular forms of comedy are parody and satire, which can go hand in hand yet be totally different. Parody makes fun of something by imitating it. It can range from silly to subtle and its point is just to make people laugh. Satire tries to make a point with what it says. It can hold a mirror up to society or make you look at yourself. A work can be pure parody or pure satire or a thousand different shades in between.

Parody

Parody can be a lot of fun to write. You can use it to make fun of something that you hate and show the world how stupid it is, or you can make fun of something that you love and show the world how stupid you are for loving it.

Parody in Film

Some of the most popular movie comedies are parodies, including:

- *Young Frankenstein*, the classic 1974 send-up of Universal Studio's great monster movies, written by Gene Wilder and Mel Brooks, mimics the original films by perfectly recreating the original black and white filming style and gothic mood; most of the lightning-harnessing lab equipment was used in the original *Frankenstein*. But under Mel Brooks' direction it became as advertised: "The scariest comedy of all time!"
- In 1980, Jim Abrahams, David Zucker, and Jerry Zucker unleashed *Airplane!* upon the world, and disaster movies haven't been the same since. Their blink-and-you'll-miss-a-joke style was augmented by casting actors who weren't known for comedy in roles that lampooned their previous ones. The success of *Airplane!* created a whole new genre of parodies where everything is up for grabs and everything is taken literally. It spawned such movies as the same team's *Top Secret!* and *The Naked Gun*. Other movies that have attempted to mimic the style like *Scary Movie*, *Epic Movie*, *Meet the Spartans*, and *Superhero Movie* have never come close the goofiness and earnestness of the original.
- In 1997's *Austin Powers: International Man of Mystery*, Mike Meyers pays affectionate homage to the original James Bond movies and all things groovy. It's more a parody of an era, the swinging sixties, not a direct parody of a specific film.

Television Parodies

Some television series have been parodies of a specific genre: *Get Smart* was a send-up of the spy shows that dominated the early Cold War era; *Reno 911* is a parody of *COPS* and reality shows in general; and *Police Squad!* is a parody of all things Quinn Martin. But television sketch shows like *Saturday Night Live* and *MADtv* are the kings of parody on the small screen.

Saturday Night Live in particular has done hundreds of commercial parodies, including "The Norman Bates School of Motel Management," "Bathroom Monkey," "The Love Toilet," "Colon Blow," "Woomba," and "Happy Fun Ball." Their ability to quickly produce these parodies allows them to be right on the cutting edge of pop culture at all times.

Books

There are lots of clever parodies of classic books and genres. The Harvard Lampoon's *Bored of the Rings* is a parody of J.R.R. Tolkien's *Lord of the Rings*, and there are dozens of parodies of *The Da Vinci Code* and the *Harry Potter* series. Even Margaret Wise Brown and Clement Hurd's children's classic *Goodnight Moon* hasn't escaped parody. *Goodnight Bush: A Parody* by Gan Golan cleverly lampoons the last days of the George W. Bush administration.

Satire

Writing satire takes a skillful hand. You don't want the audience to feel as if they are being preached to; you want them to figure out your point for themselves. A satire doesn't have to be political, but it does have to have purpose. You want to shine a light on an issue that is important to you. You want that light to illuminate the flaws of society and make people think.

FACT

There can't be a serious discussion of satire without mentioning *MAD Magazine*. Started by Harvey Kurtzman and William Gaines in 1952, *MAD* has be a constant and clever source of satire on every aspect of American culture, making fun of everything from politics and religion to television and pop culture.

Satire in Film

There have been some amazing film satires that have made a real difference in the way people see things, including:

- Charlie Chaplin's 1940 indictment of Adolph Hitler, *The Great Dictator*, satirized the Nazi leader at a time when many Americans were against being drawn into the war in Europe. It was Chaplin's most commercially successful film.
- Stanley Kubrick's *Dr. Strangelove or: How I Learned to Stop Worrying and Love the Bomb* (1964) called out the Cold War mentality of the time.
- *Network* (1976) was director Sidney Lumet's prophetic vision of the corporatization of network news.
- Jason Reitman's *Thank You For Smoking* (2006) is a darkly comedic expose on the practices and politics of big tobacco.

Television Satire

In recent years, satire on television has been dominated by two genres: animation and fake news. Some notable examples include:

- *The Simpsons* began in 1989 and has never stopped being a perfect satire of every aspect of modern life—and of television itself. The residents of Springfield have never been afraid to deal with the touchy subjects of religion and politics, with hilarious results every time.
- When *South Park* debuted in 1997, some critics and the press quickly dismissed it as having nothing but shock value, but it has grown into one of the most biting satires in the history of television. Nothing is safe from the wrath of four foul-mouthed third graders and highly reactive townsfolk from the fictional town of South Park, Colorado.
- *The Daily Show* premiered in 1996, but didn't hit its stride until Jon Stewart took the reins in 1999. The show has evolved into a true force to be reckoned with. More than just a comedy show, it is a thoughtful and carefully researched news show—with an attitude. Lots of people (mostly students and twentysomethings) get the bulk of their

news from *The Daily Show*. Politicians take the show very seriously and make regular appearances. While it is not a total satire, it does have satirical segments. Some of the most successful involve just letting guests talk, showing how foolish their arguments can be.

- *The Colbert Report*, a spin-off of *The Daily Show*, is satire at its best. Its host, Stephen Colbert, plays an ultraconservative personality who doesn't let the facts get in the way of an uneducated opinion. The writing on this show is sharp, funny, and devastating to anyone who's "on notice" or "dead to Stephen."

The Easiest Kind of Comedy to Write and the Hardest to Write Well

Parody and satire can look easy, but they take a lot of work to do well. Anyone can take some words and switch them around and turn *Harry Potter and the Sorcerer's Stone* into *Hairy Potty and the Dirty Diaper*. That's easy. But the premise can't sustain itself. It's just a one-joke idea, and not a great one at that. A good parody takes a lot of time and careful work. Parodies have to be clever to be funny, not stupid. Stupid is easy; clever takes work.

To hear the master of the musical mash-up, take a listen to 1991's *Weird Al Yankovic—Greatest Hits, Volume 1* and 1994's *Weird Al Yankovic—Greatest Hits, Volume 2*. Also check out his newer albums *Poodle Hat* (2003) and *Straight Outta Lynwood* (2006).

Take a look at song parodies. There are a lot of song parodies that are really forced, and not all that funny. They key to a good song parody is clever writing and musical skill. "Weird Al" Yankovic has both as well as a great ear, and he knows what songs and genres need to be skewered. He has built a very successful career by parodying the right songs at the right time in the right way. His songs are so close to the real thing that if you aren't listening carefully you'd swear you're listening to the original.

Essential Ingredients

Some of the elements necessary for great parody and satire are:

- **Passion.** If you are going to write this type of comedy you need lots of passion for your subject. You can passionately love your subject or be just as passionate about how much you hate it. If you don't really care either way about the subject, you'll find that there's not a lot to sink your comedy teeth into.
- **Timing.** If you are writing a parody of a commercial that is two and a half minutes long, make your sketch two and a half minutes long. Don't make it five or six minutes long. Watch some commercial parodies and you'll notice when the idea has worn out its welcome. That's the point at which the parody should naturally end. It's better to sacrifice some jokes than let the sketch go on too long.
- **Mirroring.** You want to make your parody so close to the original that it's hard to tell them apart. In the early days on *Saturday Night Live*, a commercial parody generally followed the opening monologue's final line: "Stick around. We have a great show. We'll be right back!" The audience expected a commercial break; instead they got a parody. However, the beginning of the parody seemed so real that they bought it hook, line, and sinker. They were misdirected and ultimately fooled. If you're writing a commercial parody, you want to mirror the original almost line for line, shot for shot. You really want to make the audience think it's the real deal. The more realistic it is, the more impact it will have.

To get a look at some of the best commercial parodies ever made, check out the DVD *Saturday Night Live: The Best of Commercial Parodies*. Watch the ones that are dead on and the ones that are a little off the mark, and use them as inspiration to tackle ads that are currently in the public eye.

Parody and Satire Examples

Here are two commercial parodies. The first is just a silly parody of breakfast cereals that are marketed to kids.

Toaster Kitties

SETTING: TYPICAL FAMILY KITCHEN, MORNING. TWO KIDS, **BILLY** AND **SUSIE**, ABOUT EIGHT OR NINE YEARS OLD, ARE SITTING AT THE BREAKFAST TABLE LOOKING EXTREMELY BORED. THEIR **DAD** IS SITTING WITH THEM, READING A NEWSPAPER.

BILLY

I'm bored.

SUSIE

Me too.

MOM ENTERS. SHE IS HOLDING A SURPRISE BEHIND HER BACK.

MOM
(brightly)

Guess what I have!

BILLY AND **SUSIE** BEGIN TO PERK UP.

MOM (con't)

Kellogg's new Toaster Kitties!

BILLY AND SUSIE
(in unison, confused)

Toaster Kitties?!

MOM

That's right.

SHE HANDS EACH CHILD A FOIL POUCH THE SIZE OF A POP TART.

BILLY AND SUSIE
(in unison)

Wow!

THE KIDS EXCITEDLY RIP OPEN THEIR FOIL POUCHES. **SUSIE** HOLDS UP A BROWN STRIPED FUR RECTANGLE THAT LOOKS LIKE A POP TART.

SUSIE

I got Tabby!

BILLY HOLDS UP A WHITE FUR RECTANGLE, HOLDS IT TO HIS CHEEK AND PETS IT GENTLY.

Billy
(sweetly)

I got Persian!

BILLY CONTINUES TO TENDERLY STROKE THE FUR.

CLOSE-UP OF **DAD** LOOKING AT BOY, CONCERNED ABOUT WHERE HIS SON'S SEXUAL TENDENCIES MIGHT LIE.

MOM TAKES THE FUR FROM EACH OF THE KIDS AND POPS IT INTO THE TOASTER. **BILLY** AND **SUSIE** ARE VERY EXCITED. A FEW SECONDS PASS BEFORE THE TOASTER DINGS AND TWO CUTE LITTLE KITTENS—A TABBY AND A PERSIAN—CLIMB OUT OF THE TOASTER. EACH CHILD TAKES A KITTEN AND STARTS PETTING IT.

BILLY AND SUSIE

We love our new toaster kitties!

MOM

So do I, so do I.

> ANNOUNCER
> (V.O.)
> Make Kellogg's new Toaster Kitties a special part of your day.
> (quickly)
> Not available where prohibited by law. Sorry, Tennessee.

So there it is, just a silly and funny idea. One could make the argument that it is a satire of the commercialization of society and the way products are marketed to children, but that would be a thin argument. It's just a fun sketch; it's not meant to be more that that.

Here is another sketch, but this commercial parody has a more satirical bent.

"Up and Atoms!" Cereal Commercial

INT. TYPICAL 1950S KITCHEN, MORNING. A TYPICAL 1950S **DAD** IS SITTING AT KITCHEN TABLE DRINKING COFFEE AND READING HIS NEWSPAPER. **DAD** PUTS DOWN HIS CUP AND A TYPICAL 1950S **MOM** APPROACHES FROM THE STOVE AND POURS HIM ANOTHER CUP OF COFFEE. THEIR EIGHT-YEAR-OLD SON, **JOHNNY**, ENTERS SLOWLY, LOOKING TIRED AND BORED.

> MOM
> Why, there's my little sleepyhead! Sit right down, young man, breakfast is ready!

> SON
> (sitting at table, elbow on table, hand under chin)
> Thanks, Mom, but I'm not really hungry. I think I'll skip breakfast today.

> DAD
> (looking up from paper)
> No breakfast! How are you going to fight the red menace without a good balanced breakfast! That's just the kind of talk the Russkies want to hear.

SON
(whining)
But Dad! Breakfast is boring!

MOM
(brightly)
Not anymore. I bought new Up and Atoms!

MOM PUTS BOWL ON TABLE IN FRONT OF **JOHNNY.**

DAD
Up and Atoms? Isn't that the great tasting breakfast cereal that's made from atoms?

MOM POURS CEREAL INTO BOWL. EACH CEREAL PIECE IS SHAPED LIKE AN ATOMIC SYMBOL.

MOM
Why, yes, and it's good for you. Each delicious bowl is chock full of radioactive fluorocarbons.

SON
Radioactive fluorocarbons? What's that?

DAD RUBS **JOHNNY'S** HEAD.

DAD
(laughing)
That's what makes it crunchy!

AS **DAD** FINISHES RUBBING SON'S HEAD, CLUMPS OF HAIR STICK TO HIS HAND AS HE PULLS IT AWAY. **DAD** REACTS NERVOUSLY. MOM HANDS EVERYONE A PAIR OF DARK GOGGLES.

MOM
(brightly)
Everyone put on your safety goggles!

EVERYONE PUTS ON THEIR GOGGLES. **MOM** POURS SOME MILK INTO THE BOWL. THERE'S A WHITE FLASH—AND THEN A SMALL MUSH-ROOM CLOUD EMERGES FROM THE BOWL.

SON
(excited)
Wow!

DAD
(acknowledging SON'S excitement)
I had a feeling it would get that reaction!

SCENE TWO: A SET WITH A BOX OF UP AND ATOMS, A BOWL FULL OF CEREAL, AND A PITCHER OF MILK.

ANNOUNCER
Wow is right, Johnny. Kids love new Up and Atoms!, the cereal that's made from atoms. Now with new radioactive fluorocarbons, for a taste that's fusiontastic! And, inside each specially marked box, blueprints for building your own kid-sized fallout shelter and . . .

A HAND APPEARS, TURNS THE BOX OVER, AND DUMPS OUT TWO BRICKS ALONG WITH THE REMNANTS OF THE CEREAL

ANNOUNCER (con't)
. . . two free bricks to get you started! Collect all nine hundred and twenty eight. Mix and mortar not included.

SCENE THREE: A DAY IN THE FUTURE. THE SKY IS ON FIRE. A SMALL FALLOUT SHELTER WITH A SIGN SAYING "NO GIRLS ALLOWED" IS

SHOWN IN THE BACK YARD, WITH MOM AND DAD, ADULTS, KIDS, DOG, ETC. ALL BEGGING TO BE LET IN.

SCENE FOUR: CONTINUOUS. WE SEE THE INTERIOR OF THE FALL-OUT SHELTER. SON IS QUIETLY READING A COMIC BOOK TO HIM-SELF, SNACKING FROM A BOX OF UP AND ATOMS. HE IS TOTALLY IGNORING THE HORRIBLE CARNAGE OUTSIDE.

> ANNOUNCER
> (V.O.)
> And when the bombs go off, you'll be the most popular kid on the block!

SCENE FIVE: INT. KITCHEN BACK DOOR, TEN MINUTES AFTER SCENE ONE. THE DOOR IS OPEN AND THE SUN IS POURING IN. **JOHNNY** IS STANDING IN THE DOORWAY, CASTING HIS SHADOW ON THE REFRIG-ERATOR. **MOM** AND **DAD** ARE FACING HIM. **JOHNNY** IS DRESSED, HAS HIS BOOKS, AND IS ALL READY FOR SCHOOL.

> DAD
> Well, son, don't you feel better now that you've had a good breakfast?

> SON
> (happily)
> I sure do, Dad! I feel like I'm . . . I'm . . . bursting with energy! Uh oh, it's getting late. I better make like an atom and split!

JOHNNY RUNS OUTSIDE, LEAVING HIS SHADOW ON THE REFRIG-ERATOR. **MOM** AND **DAD** LOOK AT EACH OTHER, SURPRISED. THEY PAUSE, THEN POINT AT THE SHADOW AND LAUGH. A LOGO (A FARMHOUSE NEXT TO A NUCLEAR REACTOR) APPEARS SUPERIM-POSED OVER THE SCENE.

> ANNOUNCER
> From Oppenheimer Farms.

This sketch is still silly, but it has a lightly satirical point of view. It makes fun of "the atom is our friend!" mentality of '50s culture.

Profile in Comedy: Eugene Mirman

Eugene Mirman is one of the most inventive comedians of his generation. He has appeared on *Late Night with Conan O'Brien*, Comedy Central's *Premium Blend*, *Carson Daly*, *Aqua Teen Hunger Force*, *Home Movies*, *Third Watch*, and HBO's *Flight of the Conchords*. He has released two comedy CDs: *The Absurd Nightclub Comedy of Eugene Mirman* and *En Garde, Society!*

When did you first realize that you were uniquely funny?
About an hour and a half ago. As a kid I might have been more weird than funny, or maybe people didn't get that I was kidding around.

Who do you think were your influences?
I listened to tons of stand-up as a kid. I loved Emo Philips. I listened to lots of Bill Cosby, Steve Martin, and Woody Allen also. Later I listened to Lenny Bruce, Coyle and Sharpe, Daniel Kharms. But I also really loved music, like Lou Reed, Robyn Hitchcock, and Jethro Tull, and I think the sensibilities of musicians and artists influenced me, as well as comic books and generally nerdy pop culture.

Do you remember your first original joke?
The first joke I ever wrote and did as part of my stand-up was, "What profession has the highest suicide rate? Most people think its dentists. But it's kamikaze pilots."

When did you realize that comedy was something that you had to do for a living?
At the end of high school when I realized it was a profession someone could do.

What was your first job in comedy writing or performance?
I got paid $10 at a comedy club when I was nineteen. After college I worked on a newspaper that I started with some friends in Boston called the *Weekly Week*, so that was my first real-ish comedy job.

What is the biggest difficulty you've encountered being a comedy writer?

Probably getting the first initial work and then in general the stress of being a freelancer and not knowing where you'll get money from month to month.

Are the lines between sketch and stand-up getting blurred?

I know lots of people who have been doing characters or more elaborate bits as stand-up for many, many years. I don't know if it's becoming blurred, but I do think it's more commonplace.

How has the Internet helped your career?

The Internet is a great way to get exposure and a great medium to get your work out there. The first big exposure for my career was my website traveling around virally and being passed from person to person. I used to get recognized more for my site than appearances on television and realized how powerful of a medium it was. Also, like radio, print, and television, you can get paid to do stuff online. It's not a means to an end, it is an end.

Are there jokes that you do just for you?

I'll sometimes have a joke that's part of a bigger bit that only some people will laugh at that I think is really funny. But I don't really have a lot of stuff that I do that is for me at the exclusion of the audience. I'll try things that I think are funny and don't always work. And then I'll try to figure out how to convey what I think is so funny about it to an audience, but if I can't get the joke to work after a while I'll generally drop it. Sometimes I'll revisit it a year later.

What are the differences between writing for yourself and writing for others?

I've only really written for myself, so I don't know. I imagine you have to understand their voice and rhythm and what their strengths are.

What do you find exciting about comedy right now?

A lot of people are doing very funny, very innovative things. Shows like *Mr. Show*, *30 Rock*, *The Colbert Report*, and *The Daily Show* are genuinely great television. There's a lot of fantastic stand-up comedians doing very creative work. In general, it feels like there's a renaissance of sorts.

Where do you think the future of comedy is headed?

Comedy is always headed to a great place and a terrible place. I think there has been a rebirth of a lot of great comedy over the last ten years, but at the same time there's lots of terrible stuff out there.

As audiences become more specific and more segmented, is your job becoming easier or more difficult?

Easier probably. You can find your own niche, and with growing technology, it's becoming easier to produce work and get it to audiences in ways you couldn't twenty years ago.

What is the best thing about being a comedy writer?

You get to stay up late drinking and making jokes. That's also true for someone who is unemployed.

Do you have any advice for up-and-coming comedy writers?

My advice is probably like anyone else's—to write a lot. Do it for at least ten years. Everyone has to be talented, but more important is working hard consistently for a long time.

Brainstorm

Look at and listen to parodies with a critical eye and ear. See which ones have a more satirical attitude and which ones are just comedy for comedy's sake. Look at the difference between the two and examine the choices their writers made. Look at which ones follow the original very closely and which ones stray off course. If you feel a piece is satirical, ask yourself what points the writer was trying to get across and whether or not she hit her mark.

Notebook

Exercise #1: Pop a tape into the VCR or set your DVR and watch television for an evening, recording everything you see. As you watch, make a note of every commercial you see. Now take a closer look at the ads that you think are really stupid or annoying. Pick the commercial that bugs you the most and rewind your recording to that commercial. Watch it, write down the dialogue, and briefly outline the commercial. Now make a line-by-line study of the offending commercial and write a line-by-line parody that closely mirrors the original.

Exercise #2: Make a list of topics, important to you, that you feel are politically or socially relevant. Next, write down the key point that truly expresses your feeling toward each subject. Now try to write a funny, satirical piece that will make your point absolutely clear, but in a way that doesn't force your point of view down the audience's throat.

CHAPTER 15

Writing Sitcoms

This is an exciting time for sitcoms because things are changing rapidly, with no clear direction in sight. That's a good thing because you can help define the genre for the future. You'll be rewriting all the rules of what a sitcom should be. But before you can see the future, you need to look at the past.

What Defines a Sitcom

A sitcom is a situation comedy and, unlike a movie, has no real ending. Episodes contain small stories that are wrapped up every week, but the situation itself never ends. Shows that run for a long time can keep going even after they are cancelled. *M*A*S*H*, which had a powerful series finale, had a spin-off called *AfterMASH* that picked up and continued the stories of some of the characters from the original show.

The situation itself can be vital or incidental to the show. Take *Bewitched*—a man marries a witch and it turns his life upside down. But the situation is unimportant in a show like *Friends*—friends live in apartments across from each other. In that case, the situation was really just a device to put a group of interesting characters together.

The 1940s to the 1950s

The television sitcom, an American original, was born in the 1940s and 1950s. It had existed on radio with shows like *Amos 'n Andy*, *The Jack Benny Program*, and *My Favorite Husband*. Listeners would tune in every week to spend some time with familiar characters they grew to love.

Repetition of gags, catchphrases, and character quirks in radio shows thrilled a loyal following who still laughed even though they knew exactly what was going to happen. Sometimes, these shows would also have a continuing story line, like a soap opera that guaranteed that the audience would tune in to see what happened in the next episode.

When television arrived in the late 1940s, many of these familiar shows made the transition successfully, although others lost something in translation. One of the most successful shows of the 1950s was a reworking of *My Favorite Husband* into the classic comedy *I Love Lucy*. Starring Lucille Ball and her real husband Desi Arnaz, this show pioneered the way sitcoms would be filmed for the next forty years. Shows were filmed in running order in front of a live studio audience, with three cameras recording everything for later editing.

The shows of this era, such as *Leave it to Beaver*, *The Honeymooners*, and *Father Knows Best*, were big on laughs but avoided controversy. They reflected the ideals of the time: The man was the head of the household, and the children were respectful of their parents and took their advice whenever they made a mistake.

The 1960s

Some 1960s sitcoms were still family comedies but had a more modern sensibility, like *The Andy Griffith Show* and *The Dick Van Dyke Show*. But the shows that dominated the decade redefined the situation in situation comedy. A hillbilly family strikes it rich and moves to Beverly Hills (*The Beverly Hillbillies*). An astronaut finds a bottle complete with a beautiful genie (*I Dream of Jeannie*). A man meets a space visitor who poses as his uncle (*My Favorite Martian*). A talking horse (*Mr. Ed*). Two hilariously creepy families (*The Addams Family* and *The Munsters*). These high-concept shows blended fantasy with comedy at a time when the nation was going through major social upheavals. Most of the shows of the era used a laugh track instead of a live studio audience.

The 1970s

While some of the shows of the 1970s were still light-hearted family fare like *The Brady Bunch*, *Happy Days*, and *The Partridge Family*, three elements crept in and changed the medium forever: sex, social issues, and controversy. Shows like *One Day at a Time*, *Three's Company*, and *Maude* broke the long-held taboo of discussing sex on television. Groundbreaking shows like *All in the Family*, *Good Times*, and *Soap* dealt with social issues and showed a less-than-perfect side of the perfect American family. Kids started to be seen as smarter than their parents.

The 1980s

Shows in the 1980s tended to steer away from controversy and social issues (except for "very special" episodes), but sex was here to stay. There was also a return to the high-concept shows of the 1960s with shows like *Alf*, *Bosom Buddies*, and *Diff'rent Strokes*. Shows like the *Mary Tyler Moore Show* and *M*A*S*H* in the 1970s started to redefine what a family was, but these types of sitcoms flourished in the 1980s. The nuclear family was replaced by the family of choice. The new family was the workplace in shows like *Taxi*, *Cheers*, and *Night Court*.

FACT

Early on, every sitcom husband and wife slept in separate beds, including Lucille Ball and Desi Arnaz. The first couple from a popular series to slip past the network standards and practices department and slide into a shared bed was Herman and Lily Munster. The censors were too distracted by the fact that they were monsters to think there might be anything going on under the sheets.

A sense of family is the most important factor behind the success of every sitcom. The family can be traditional, or a workplace or situational family. Each character in a show fills a role in that family unit. When actors leave a show, they were replaced by a similar character filling the same role. When Col. Blake left *M*A*S*H*, he was replaced by a similarly fatherly character, Col. Potter. When Trapper John left the show, B.J. Hunnicutt filled the role of Hawkeye's best friend. When Major Burns left the show, he was replaced by Major Winchester, who served as comic foil.

The 1990s

Many of the sitcoms of the 1980s and 1990s were family friendly. *The Cosby Show*, *A Different World*, and *The Fresh Prince of Bel-Air* were big hits. In the 1990s a large number of sitcoms were made especially for children, such as *Boy Meets World*, *Blossom*, *Family Matters*, *The Adventures of Pete and Pete*, *Sabrina, the Teenage Witch*, and *Clarissa Explains It All*.

The 1990s also saw the return of a show dealing with social issues, *The Simpsons*, which has gone on to become the longest-running sitcom in history. Another trend in the 1990s was the sitcom based on stand-up. The success of *Roseanne*, *Home Improvement*, *Grace Under Fire*, *Everybody Loves Raymond*, *The Drew Carey Show*, *Seinfeld*, *The Jeff Foxworthy Show*, *Norm*, and *Ellen* made comedy clubs the place to look for the next big sitcom. In this decade, shows like *The Larry Sanders Show*, *The Wonder Years*, *Get a Life*, and *Dream On* started to experiment with the form.

The First Decade of the Twenty-First Century and Beyond

This is when things really changed with the American sitcom. Shows started being filmed with a single camera, shot on location or on studio sets with no laugh track or studio audience. *Malcom in the Middle*, *Arrested Development*, *30 Rock*, and *The Office* have set the standard for sitcoms of the future. Shows like these co-exist with traditional sitcoms, which are starting to look old-fashioned by comparison.

The way people watch television has also changed. There is no such thing as appointment television anymore. The Internet provides fans with the ability to download favorite shows and watch them anytime, leaving the networks scrambling to figure out what happens next. That's where you come into the picture. You will be the writer who helps them figure it out.

The Planning Process

A treatment, the story told in paragraph form, is the first step in writing a script. It may take only one page, and it should be written in a casual way. It should read as if you were telling the story to your best friend.

FACT

Most shows tell more than just one story in an episode. The main story is your "A" story, a smaller plot is your "B" story, and the smallest plot is the "C" story. Watch the show you are using as a model to see how it weaves its stories together, and mimic that technique as closely as possible.

The next step in the process is an outline. An outline is the script in skeleton form. It's an act-by-act, scene-by-scene breakdown of how you want the final script to play out. The entire story and scene transitions get worked out at this phase. The outline is also written in paragraph form, but it includes much more detail and even key lines of dialogue. The more detailed the outline is, the easier it will be to write your final script. When you have a solid, finished outline, your job is to just start adding meat (the jokes) onto the bones of the skeleton.

How to Lay Out a Sitcom Script

Every sitcom has its own format, but there is a basic format you can use to get started. Here is a spec script for *The Simpsons*:

ACT ONE
Scene One, Int. Simpson Living Room—Morning
(Day 1)
(Homer, Bart)

HOMER WALKS INTO THE LIVING ROOM WEARING HIS BATHROBE AND NOTICES SOMETHING ON THE FLOOR. AS HE BENDS DOWN TO PICK IT UP WE SEE THAT IT IS A SHINY LOTTERY TICKET. HE SCRATCHES IT. ONE MONEYBAG APPEARS, THEN TWO, AND FINALLY A THIRD.

HOMER
(excited)
Woo hoo! I won! I'm a millionaire!

HE RUSHES OUT THE DOOR, LOSING HIS BATHROBE IN THE PROCESS. AS WE HEAR HIS EXCITED YELLS FADE INTO THE DISTANCE, BART EMERGES FROM THE KITCHEN, SNICKERING. HE HOLDS UP A BRIGHTLY COLORED PACKAGE WITH THE LABEL: FUNCO NOVELTIES: "LOTTO-LAUGHS PHONY LOTTERY TICKETS."

BART
Ahhhh Funco, you never let me down.
Scene Two, Ext. Springfield Nuclear Plant—Five Minutes Later
(Homer)

HOMER IS RUNNING TOWARD THE PLANT IN HIS UNDERWEAR, SCREAMING. HE ENTERS THE PLANT.

<u>Scene Three, Int. Springfield Nuclear Plant Hallway—Continuous</u>
(Homer, Lenny, Carl)

HOMER RUNS BY LENNY AND CARL. HE'S SO EXCITED THAT HE HAS LOST THE ABILITY TO ACTUALLY FORM WORDS. HE SAYS SOMETHING TO THEM IN GIBBERISH AS HE SPEEDS PAST.

CARL

Boy, that Homer sure loves casual Fridays.

<u>Scene Four, Int. Mr. Burns's Office—Continuous</u>
(Burns, Smithers)

MR. BURNS AND SMITHERS ARE LOOKING AT PAPERS AS HOMER RUSHES INTO THE ROOM, CLUTCHING THE FAKE LOTTERY TICKET.

HOMER

I quit, and you, Mr. Burns, can kiss my hairy yellow butt.

HOMER EXITS.

MR. BURNS

Make a note to cancel casual Fridays.

SMITHERS

Will do, sir.

<u>END OF ACT ONE</u>

It's pretty basic and not too different from a sketch layout. The acts are broken up by the commercial breaks and a scene is broken up by a change in location or time.

Writing a Spec Script for an Existing Show

One good way to get your feet wet in the world of sitcom writing is to write a spec script for an existing show. It should be a show that you are very familiar with, is currently airing, and is likely to continue airing for a few years. No agent or producer wants to see your spec script for *Gilligan's Island*, no matter how funny it is.

FACT

Does the sitcom of the future need to be twenty-two minutes and fit into a thirty-minute timeframe? If someone was watching a show that was exclusively on the web, that might be too long. Maybe the perfect time for a "webisode" is fifteen minutes, or ten, or even five.

Here are a few things to take into consideration when developing a plot for your episode:

- **Work within the limits of the show.** Use existing sets and avoid location shots that would be expensive to shoot. Writing a spec script that uses an elaborate set, no matter how funny it is, will show the producers that you can't fit your ideas into the show's basic framework. If the show is animated, however, it's just as easy to draw any location, so go for it.
- **Don't introduce any new main characters.** That's a decision for the producers and the head writer. Also avoid bringing in a character like a main lead's sister or father. It might not jive with the character's backstory. You can have a new secondary character in your script as long as he is out of the picture at the conclusion of the episode.
- **Avoid any references to a continuing story line.** Your episode must work by itself, even if the show has an ongoing story line. By the time someone reads it, that story line may have changed. Also, remember that the producers are the only ones who know what's in store for the characters.

- **Don't rock the boat!** If two characters on a show are involved in a "will they or won't they" romantic tension, you can't put them together. Those are major decisions made by the producers.
- **Look online for sample scripts of the show to see how they are laid out.** If you're using screenwriting software like Final Draft, you can download templates for pretty much every show on television.
- **Watch out for character entrances and exits.** You don't want someone in a scene standing around with nothing to do. Find funny ways to bring characters on and off.

FACT

There are several alternatives to Final Draft, including other software and free applications that can be downloaded from the Internet. You can also find templates that can be used with almost any word processing program. But Final Draft is the industry standard, and it gets better with every new release. If you are serious about scriptwriting, it is worth the investment.

Writing an Original Pilot

If you have an original idea for a show don't rush it. Take your time and really make it something special. Look to a similar show as a model and lay out your script in a similar way. Consider to whom you might want to sell the script. Are you thinking network? Maybe the Disney Channel or Nickelodeon for a show geared to kids? Do you have an idea for a weird and quirky cartoon that you could sell to Comedy Central or the Cartoon Network's Adult Swim block? Or maybe you want to write something edgier for HBO.

Knowing your market will help you focus your show in the right direction. If you try to write a generic script for any market, you may end up with something no one wants.

A typical show runs about twenty-two minutes; that's roughly a minute a page. A typical show has two or three acts, with three of four scenes per act. Some have a teaser scene that is basically a quick joke before the credits or a tag scene that follows the last act. These are becoming a thing of the past as networks now try to blend from one show to the next. If your script does have a teaser or a tag, make sure they are independent from the body of the show and don't contain any major plot points, because these scenes are frequently cut when the show runs in syndication. Animated shows can have a lot more scene changes and can run twice as many pages for the same twenty-two minute script.

If you are pitching an original series, you'll want to have a pilot script along with two or three additional episodes, and a show bible. The show bible tells the prospective producers everything they need to know about the show: descriptions of the characters and locations, the overall story arc that tells them where the series is going, and a general synopsis of your vision of your show. This should be as complete as possible and should contain all the information you want to communicate about your show.

Existing shows have very specific bibles that contain information on every previous episode and miscellaneous trivia that has been released about the show. Everything from characters' middle names to phone numbers and addresses are included.

Protecting Your Work

It is very hard to prove in a court of law that someone has stolen your idea for a script. Theft does happen, but usually it's just a case of two people thinking of the same idea at the same time. But there are ways to help protect your ideas, and you should take advantage of them.

E-QUESTION

Is it true that mailing myself a copy of a script is all I need to protect my copyright?
The "poor man's" copyright, a sealed and postmarked envelope containing a script, is not that reliable. It does prove that the script was written by a certain date, but it's not the same as making a public claim to the material.

To protect your work, contact the Writer's Guild of America, West at *www .wga.org* or Writer's Guild of America, East at *www.wgaeast.org* and you'll find information to easily register your script with the Guild. At this writing, the fee is just $22, and it's good for five years with the option to renew. You can register by mail, online, or directly through Final Draft. It is not necessary to be a member of the Guild. This is convenient peace of mind at a low cost, so take advantage of it!

Selling Your Script

You can go about selling your script in a few different ways, but it really comes down to a combination of luck and who you know, just like any other business. The best way is to be a visible force in the comedy world, like a stand-up or a part of a popular sketch troupe, and be asked to submit a script.

The second way is through networking. The more friends that you have in the business, the easier it will be to get your script on a producer's desk.

Remember to register your script with the Writer's Guild before you send it to anyone! While you're on their websites, check out their updated lists of Guild-approved agents. You should definitely take advantage of this great resource.

The third way is through a writing agent or a manager. The best way to find an agent is by networking with friends who have agents they like and trust and will help you set up a meeting. If you don't have a connection, you might run into the classic Catch-22: You can't get anything sold because you don't have an agent, and you can't get an agent because you haven't sold anything. Beware of fly-by-night agents who will take your money, string you along, and produce no results for you. Beware of anyone that asks you for money up front. Check with the other clients they have worked with to see if they are legit.

The fourth way of selling your script should be avoided if possible. There are websites that, for a fee, will post your script. The chances are slim that producers will be looking at that site.

Profile in Comedy: Rick Jenkins

In addition to being an excellent stand-up comedian and writer, Rick Jenkins founded the Comedy Studio in Cambridge, Massachusetts, in 1996. Since then it has become one of the hottest comedy rooms in the country. It is the go-to place for industry producers seeking the next big thing.

When did you first realize that you were uniquely funny?
When you asked me that question.

Who do you think were your influences?
At first it was Woody Allen. He showed me that you could write about anything you wanted and make it funny. Then I got the chance to open for Jay Leno. He showed me you could deliver anything you wanted to say and make it funny.

Do you remember your first original joke?
"A female archeologist is a woman who digs early men." Remember, I was seven, and it was 1968.

When did you realize that comedy was something that you had to do for a living?
After my first time on stage, the MC gave me $5 for the five minute set. I remember arrogantly telling my Dad, "Find me another job that pays a dollar a minute and I'll consider it!"

What was your first job in comedy writing or performance?
It starts with a couple dollars here and there—$15 for writing a joke, then a couple hundred for performing a week at a club. It's really a matter of putting together enough freelance work to make it add up to a job.

What is the biggest difficulty you've encountered being a comedy writer?
By far, it's the discipline. I always want something brilliant to just come to me, but it takes a lot of work to get lucky.

Are there jokes that you do just for you?

Jokes are like children; I think they're all beautiful. But there are a couple you should leave in the attic when company comes over.

What do you look for when you see a comic for the first time?

Obviously, we like laughs, but professionalism and potential are what I really look for.

What makes the Comedy Studio unique?

I want to be able to take credit for how good a comedian becomes . . . not how good they are.

How does the live comedy experience differ from TV and film?

It's the difference between a date and an online profile. It's the difference between hearing someone and connecting with someone.

What are the differences between writing for yourself and writing for others?

It's the difference between hearing a voice and having a voice. Any time I'm stuck, I loosen up by writing a couple jokes for a famous comedian.

What do you find exciting about comedy right now?

Comedy is now about doing it yourself. Waiting around for a big producer to give you a break has become quaint and retro.

Where do you think the future of comedy is headed?

Again, it's about doing it yourself. Getting your stuff to an audience, finding that audience, doing your shows. Good stuff is always in demand.

As audiences are becoming more specific and more segmented, is that making your job easier or more difficult?

We do a showcase format, so our audiences come in expecting to see variety. Other places have funny people; we have interesting people who happen to see the world in a funny way.

What is the best thing about being a comedy writer?
Being able to think of something and get it exactly right. When the audience laughs, you're right.

Do you have any advice for up-and-coming comedy writers?
Comedy writing is like every other kind of writing . . . but more so. It needs to be clearer, tighter, and have a more pointed point of view. And the way to get better at writing is to write. Just do it.

Brainstorm

Make a list of all the elements that make a particular sitcom your favorite. Is it the quirky characters, the snappy dialogue, or the interesting plots? Next, break the show down to its simplest elements and write a two- or three-sentence description of your favorite episodes. Pick a few episodes, try to find scripts online for those episodes, and look carefully at how they are written. This helps you work backward to get down to the bare bones of the ideas. Look at how the individual characters' lines are written and try to envision the characters actually saying their lines. This will help you understand the power of the script and the scriptwriter's ability to write for existing characters.

Notebook

Write down a list of places that would be an interesting setting for a sitcom. For example:

- A hairdressing salon
- A bike messenger service
- Behind the scenes of a reality show
- A small group of twentysomething friends that have an Internet company that has recently made them millions
- A group of celebrity paparazzi
- A rock band trying to hit the big time

Start to picture the scene in your mind. Ask yourself: Who would be the natural group of characters in this setting (a boss, a parent, a kid, etc.)? Start to imagine what those characters and their relationships are like.

Next, start working on your show bible and potential story lines for episodes. What is the best story to introduce the characters and the situation in a natural, unforced way? That is your pilot.

Write a pilot, put it away for a while, and come back to it after you have thought about the characters some more. Keep revising the script and putting it aside until you feel happy with the final product.

Read the script to some friends, listen to their feedback, and then revise some more. Once you like your pilot, start writing treatments—synopses of episodes in paragraph form—until you have a good idea for a second script, then start the whole process over again.

CHAPTER 16

Movies

Lights, camera, action! Writing screenplays can be a lucrative but highly competitive form of comedy writing. Before you write that script that turns into a multimillion dollar blockbuster, you might want to get your feet wet with short films. These might make the studios and Hollywood insiders want to see more of you.

A Sketch on Steroids

Good sketches have a beginning, a middle, and an end. They should tell a story. However, you don't have a lot of time to really set up characters or the plot. You have to work fast and just go for the essence of the concept that makes the sketch funny.

Short comedy films work the same way. They are all about the story. You can have lots of jokes or a great surprise ending that wraps up the story in a powerful way, but you need to tell a complete story.

Feature-length comedy movies tell a story, but you have the luxury of time. You can slowly introduce the characters and give the audience a lot of detail about them, as much as they need to know. You can also take your time getting into and resolving the plot.

So, you can look at a short film as a sketch on film and a feature-length film as a big sketch that is made up of a lot of little sketches. You aren't telling just one story over a longer period, but you also need to tell little stories along the way.

FACT

If you want to attend expensive film school-quality lectures from the comfort of your own home, check out your favorite comedies on DVD and listen to the commentaries that feature the writers, actors, and directors talking about the film. You'll get an insight into the movie that will show you why decisions were made and how the film ended up funny.

Take a look at Mel Brooks and Gene Wilder's 1974 comedy classic *Young Frankenstein*. What is the plot? The grandson of the infamous Dr. Frankenstein, after years to trying to clear the family name, inherits his grandfather's castle—and old habits. He creates a monster who terrorizes Transylvania. As a plot goes, it's not very exciting.

Now look at the movie as a series of sketches that advance the plot but work on their own as well. For example:

- Dr. Frankenstein and his assistant find a secret revolving bookcase triggered by removing a candle from a holder. The secret door hides a secret passageway that leads to his grandfather's laboratory. However, getting the timing of the mechanism correct causes a lot of problems and ultimately leads to the doctor getting crushed between the bookcase and the wall. ("Put . . . the candle . . . back!")

- The Monster meets a kindly blind hermit while he's on the run. The hermit offers him some hot soup but misses the bowl and pours boiling soup onto the Monster's lap. Later, he gives the Monster a cigar, but accidentally lights his thumb on fire, causing the Monster to flee. ("Wait . . . where are you going? I was gonna make espresso.")

- After trying to refine the Monster, Dr. Frankenstein introduces his "experiment" to a group of doctors and scientists. He and the Monster, dressed in top hats and tails, sing and dance to "Puttin' on the Ritz" (or as the Monster says— "PUDDINN ON DAA RIZZZZZZSHH!").

- The doctor is "nonchalantly" playing darts while being questioned by the one-armed police inspector. His nervousness causes him to misfire every shot with hilarious timing.

These scenes all have a purpose—they are necessary exposition—but they are hilarious. They are classic sketches within a classic film. Each scene is a mini masterpiece.

What makes the movie is the journey, all the scenes and characters we meet along the way. They can be more important than the ending. You need a logical and satisfying ending, but half the time the audience already knows how the movie is going to end: the guy gets the girl, they save the orphanage, etc.

Instant Movie: Just Add Jokes

Try brainstorming a movie on your own. Here's a plot that has become a cliché in movies. Bob inherits a fortune from a distant relative, but there is a catch—he has to be married to collect the inheritance. So he has twenty-four hours to find a bride. Break down the plot to its simplest elements:

1. Bob is introduced as the main character.
2. He gets a letter asking him to attend a reading of the will.
3. He finds out about the money and the catch.
4. He tries many different ways to find someone who will marry him.
5. He either succeeds or fails.

This is the skeleton of the script. Now add some meat on the bones by asking questions:

- How do we meet Bob? Should you show that he is in need of money? Did he just lose his job? Is he being evicted?
- What is Bob like? Does he have trouble meeting women? Has he just been dumped? Is his ex his one true love?
- How does Bob get the letter and what is his reaction to it? How much information does it reveal? Does he think he's being sued? Should we meet the lawyer and know about the inheritance before or after Bob does?
- How does Bob get to the meeting? Is it across town or across the country? Does he walk, drive, or take the bus?
- At the meeting, how does Bob react to the news? Are there any other relatives who might have been left out of the will? What are they like?
- If Bob fails to get married, what happens to the money? Does the lawyer get it? Does it go to other relatives?
- How does Bob try to meet women? Can he tell them about the inheritance or does that violate the terms of the will? How is his ex involved? Is she engaged to someone else?
- Does he finally find a bride? Do other relatives complicate things?
- If he does get married, are there still complications in getting the marriage license to the lawyer in time? Does he find true love? Does he get the girl of his dreams and the money or does he have to choose between the two?

Those are just a fraction of the questions you should ask yourself. Each answer should lead to more questions, and remember—good questions lead to great comedy. It's all about making the journey to the ending filled with funny and interesting scenes. Look at it this way: you have many choices to make along the way, and every choice is an opportunity to make the movie even funnier.

Squeeze Those Scenes!

Once you've figured out your story, write an outline with a scene-by-scene breakdown. Once you have the outline and a story that makes sense—relax.

Now concentrate of getting as much out of a scene as you can. You want to get all the needed information and exposition into each scene, but you want to do it in an efficient and funny way.

It's the economy, stupid! In all comedy, but especially film, you need to get to the joke in an economic and efficient way. You need to cut any superfluous dialogue—every word in the script has to help you get to the joke without the distraction of unnecessary dialogue.

Look at each scene and ask yourself: Does this need to be a really funny scene, a serious scene, or something in between? If it's a serious scene, can a joke ruin the moment or make it stronger and more emotional? How can you give each comedic scene a funny beginning, middle, and end? How can you make a scene work almost as a sketch by itself?

Have you ever seen an actor on a talk show promoting his new comedy and show a clip from the film that isn't funny or doesn't make any sense out of context? Wouldn't it be great if every scene in your movie had clips that were funny and told a story? Wouldn't it be great if each and every scene could stand on its own?

A great example of a movie where every single scene is funny and works on its own as a perfect 'mini-sketch' is Paul Reubens's and Tim Burton's 1985 film *Pee-Wee's Big Adventure*. The plot couldn't be simpler: Pee-Wee Herman's beloved bike is stolen and he travels across the country to find it. But the film takes you on an amazingly funny trip.

How to Lay Out Your Script

You should start by writing a treatment just like a sitcom. A treatment simply tells the story in paragraph form. Then you should expand your treatment by turning it into an outline, a scene-by-scene breakdown of the main story and any smaller stories within it. Once you're happy with your outline, you're ready to move on to the actual screenplay.

If you are going to be writing a lot of scripts, buy a copy of Final Draft software (*www.finaldraft.com*). It takes care of all the formatting for you and intuitively helps you move the script along without interrupting the creative process. It will even read the script back to you with different voices for each character!

Here is the basic formatting to use when writing your script:

- The scene header should tell the reader who is in the scene, where it is, and when it is taking place. It should be flush left, written in all caps and bold, with abbreviations for interior (INT.) and exterior (EXT.) For example: **INT. BOB'S APARTMENT—DAY**
- The scene description tells us what is happening in the scene in paragraph form, with each thought clearly separated from the others. The names of characters that are in each scene are written in all caps. It should be written in a simple, conversational style in the present tense. Don't be afraid to show a little attitude. For example:

We see a small, messy two-room apartment that looks like it has never been cleaned.

A cheap black–and-white television is showing an infomercial for some kind of self-improvement product.

We see BOB lying face down on the bed, snoring and creating a nice little puddle of drool that he is oblivious to.

The radio alarm clock clicks on and loudly plays mariachi music.

BOB is startled into consciousness and stumbles out of bed. As soon as he gets his footing, he steps onto a pizza that is lying on the floor in a box.

Dialogue is written under the character who is speaking and if there is a certain tone or attitude that you want to express, it should be written in parentheses below the name and above the dialogue. Final Draft intuitively auto-fills character names as you are writing your script, which comes in handy if your main character's name is long and difficult to type.

FACT

Your movie might be a romantic "chick flick," a college sex romp, or a family film that works on one level for the kids and another for their parents. If you keep your audience in mind for every joke you write, you'll have a successful script. You also need to respect your audience.

If a character's dialogue is interrupted by an action, (con't) should follow the character's name when he picks up the thought. Both the character's name and the dialogue should be centered as a flush left paragraph, indented about one and a half inches from the scene description or action.

BOB
(angrily)
Dammit! There goes my breakfast.

The phone rings. BOB Answers.

> BOB (con't.
Hello?

An automated recording is heard.

> VOICE ON PHONE
> This is just a friendly reminder that you phone service will be cut off unless we receive payment by twelve noon tod—

The phone goes dead as BOB looks at the clock. It is exactly twelve o'clock. BOB freaks, realizing that he is late for work.

> BOB (con't)
I'm late! Not again!

A script is laid out this way for clarity. You want the reader to understand every line and every thought at first reading. The screenplay also leaves a lot of white space to make room for written corrections, improvements, and production notes as each version of the script is revised.

Profile in Comedy: Dwayne Perkins

A native of Brooklyn, New York, Dwayne Perkins is a very funny stand-up comedian who has appeared on *Late Night with Conan O'Brien*; *The Late, Late Show*; and *Premium Blend*. He recently starred in his own comedy special on Comedy Central. In 2008 he was named one of the top five comics to watch in *Rolling Stone*.

When did you first realize that you were uniquely funny?

I still don't know if I'm uniquely funny. I'm kidding; I think when you begin to realize the times when you're not being intentionally funny and people are laughing, that's when you begin to get insight into your real funny. My first moment was in fourth grade when in a bodega in Brooklyn someone said, "You have such white teeth." And I said without skipping a beat or trying to be funny, "but my gums are black." The grown ups in the store started cracking up and I made a mental note.

Who do you think were your influences?

The more I live, the more I realize how influential my mother has been to my comedy. She is one of the funniest people I know and her humor isn't mean or cynical. Always good-natured but somehow she really cracks me and my siblings up.

Do you remember your first original joke?

I think my first unofficial stand-up joke/observation was the problem I had with a Head & Shoulders commercial in third grade. In the commercial a person would scratch their head and all their friends would flee in disgust and fear because of dandruff. I thought if people don't run out of your life when you scratch your butt surely they will stay when you scratch your head. Maybe the irony of the ad was lost on me.

When did you realize that comedy was something you had to do for a living?

Probably in college. I just felt 9-5 wasn't for me. Not that I couldn't hack it or take orders. I just felt that for me the curtain has been pulled back on the wizard for quite some time.

What was your first job in comedy writing or performance?

My first paid gig was in Gloucester, Massachusetts. Up until that point I had done a bunch of free shows in New York and then in Boston. But I was to do many free shows after that as well.

What is the biggest difficulty you've encountered being a comedy writer?

Two things. One is getting people to accept me as a writer of scripts and screenplays. The weird thing is people used to always assume I wrote screenplays back when I didn't. And now that I do write screenplays and develop show ideas, it seems people want to think of me as a pure stand-up. Hopefully that reflects positively on my stand-up and the impact it has. The second thing for me is forcing myself to be original has actually hurt me. I will skip over entire subjects if I think they're overdone. But that robs me and my supporters of a possible fresh take on an old concept. I'm working on focusing on being real first and original throughout.

How long does it take to write your own comedy special?

Hard to say. I had been doing comedy about ten years when I taped it, so maybe that long. But I probably could have done one six years in. For me, the writing and performing ebbs and flows and progress isn't always noticeably linear. A comic's comedy progress is like the stock market. It goes up and down but over time, if they stick to it, goes up. Although that example may not work in our current times.

How do you prepare for a short TV appearance?

First you pluck out about seven minutes of material you haven't done on said show that you think would really work well. Next, you get the set approved by the show. Finally, you do the set as many times as possible but never forgetting that each show is different and you always have to remain in the moment. Even doing jokes to the point of monotony, you have to make them relatable and "new" every time.

Are there jokes that you do just for you?

Definitely. You would go crazy if you didn't have a few of those in your arsenal. It's also a way of seeing if a good crowd is great and of finding core fans who even like·the jokes more suited for the comic mind.

What are the differences between writing for yourself and writing for others?

Sometimes it's easier to write for others because you're a bit detached and more able to see all the angles. Also, another performer may get away with something or be able to pull something off that you couldn't. So it's great to see another comic make your words come to life . . . provided they had permission to do so.

What do you find exciting about comedy right now?

The Internet and all these satellite sites are making it exciting. It's allowing guys who are not industry darlings to carve out a piece for themselves.

Where do you think the future of comedy is headed?

It's hard to say because there are so many factors and people trying to steer the ship in their favor. I hope the field levels and the general public comes to realize that fame and funny don't always come hand in hand. Basically, I hope we get to a point where the consumer is a tad bit more informed. We have comedy fans and they are great, but then you have the people who have never been to a comedy show or only go if it's a bigger name.

As audiences are becoming more specific and more segmented, is that making your job easier or more difficult?

For me, it's way more difficult. I have always geared my act to be universal and now everything is customized. But as in other things, I don't think separate is equal. It's like people don't want to challenged in the slightest, but why pay top dollar to hear what you could hear at a family barbecue for free? The other tough thing is it seems that the industry wants you to deliver a segment. They reward you for it. I'm not sure what happened that made people feel their comedians have to look and sound exclusively like them. That's not what comedy is about. I'm trying to find my audience, but as my audience cuts across race, gender, socioeconomic, and age lines—no one is going to cut me a fat check and say, "Here, Dwayne. Bring in a cross-section of the population." I think that's where the Internet comes in.

What is the best thing about being a comedy writer?

Having everything at your disposal for potential material—every experience, every crazy idea you have, every piece of news. Comedy is almost like high-level sampling. And like with music, great sampling becomes its own music. But also like music, bad sampling is borderline thievery and stale and rehashed at best.

Do you have any advice for up-and-coming comedy writers?

Start writing ASAP. I wished I had started sooner. Also, find some discipline. No matter how hectic things are, try to carve out some semblance of a routine that you can stick to. Don't make it so hard that you can't stick to it and get discouraged, but try to have some challenge in there for yourself. Also, you have to read. For me, catching up on the classics I had skipped really helped awaken my mind and my imagination.

Brainstorm

Take one of your favorite comedies and reverse engineer it. Break the story down and dissect it into its most basic elements. Work backward and break every scene into an outline. Look at how the characters are introduced and how the action is moved along. Look at the movie scene by scene and see which ones work by themselves as a comedy sketch and which ones don't. Look at how locations are used to help tell the story. Also look at how serious scenes and moments are integrated with the comedy.

Study all the choices that were made in the movie and try to imagine what it might be like if different choices had been made.

Notebook

Look at sketches you've written and try to rewrite them as short films. See which ones would be better as films, and turn them into screenplays, reexamining all your choices—the setting, the characters, the background action, etc. With modern editing equipment, you can experiment with making short films quickly and inexpensively.

FACT

If you don't think you can make a film on the cheap, read and get inspiration from director Robert Rodriguez's 1995 book *Rebel without a Crew: Or How a 23-Year-Old Filmmaker with $7,000 Became a Hollywood Player*. It's Rodriguez's diary of the making of the low budget but critically acclaimed film *El Mariachi*.

Turning your sketches into short films and getting positive feedback will help you build the confidence to tackle larger projects. It will also help you acquire material for your reel—a visual resume with samples of your work.

CHAPTER 17

Making "Sense" of Comedy

Comedy can be so much more than just words on a page. To get great reactions from the audience, take all their senses into consideration when you write. Sight and sound are the most common, but all the senses can come into play, even smell (well, sort of).

, Not Heard: Writing Material That is rely Visual

In the days of silent movies, the era's finest comedians—Charlie Chaplin, Buster Keaton, and Harold Lloyd—used the restrictions of the technology to their advantage by creating some of the finest visual comedy ever made. Chaplin even continued to successfully make silent comedies well into the sound era.

Why? It worked. Even though silent movie-era comedians didn't speak, their actions spoke volumes, and their films are still considered to be some of the most expressive and human movies ever made. And because they had no dialogue, they could be appreciated all over the world.

Would silent films work today? Yes and no. A long film without words might be a difficult sell to a mainstream audience, but to a targeted audience it might be a success. Short films, especially animated ones can work very well. 2008 was a great year for visual comedy. Pixar released the popular family film *Wall-E*, about a robot that falls in love. It used very little dialogue and relied on visual images, music, and sound effects to create a funny and touching film. Screenings of *Wall-E* were also preceded by a short called *Presto*, which shows an amazing battle of wills between a pompous magician and his hungry rabbit. It also had audiences in hysterics without a single word of dialogue. But the lack of dialogue doesn't mean there's no need for writers. All those visuals are scripted.

In the 1950s, the eccentric and inventive comedian Ernie Kovacs used television to beam his weird, funny, and sometimes surreal comedic vision into the homes of audiences who were used to "safer" comedies like *Father Knows Best*. Kovacs was television's master of visual comedy. He presented powerful images. Imagine the effect these images had at the time:

- An old rotary dial phone sits on a table. Suddenly, a finger pops through the center dial and starts dialing the phone.
- You see a bathtub and hear the water draining. The camera pans into the tub to reveal a hand coming up through the drain, desperately trying to cling onto the tub to avoid going down the hole.
- A group of gorillas perform the ballet *Swan Lake*—very well.

Kovacs was the first to understand that people weren't watching television. They were watching a lit-up box in the middle of their living rooms. Kovacs knew that audience could only see what they saw through the window in the box. He controlled when the images were revealed, and what images the audience could and couldn't see. He could pan up or down to show the comedy at his own pace—and he had impeccable timing. He played tricks with people's assumptions of what was in that box. He would show an orchestra playing a serious classical piece, and he would keep cutting to a kettle drum playing. On the third cut to the kettle drum, plop! The mallets sank into what was really a kettle drum filled with thick white paint. Because you control what the audience sees and when they see it, you have complete power to surprise them.

Many of Ernie Kovacs's shows were lost, but you can see a great collection of some of his classic bits on the DVD *The Best of Ernie Kovacs*. Kovacs influenced a whole generation of comedians and changed late-night TV forever. When Chevy Chase accepted his Emmy Award for *Saturday Night Live*, he thanked Ernie Kovacs.

Visual comedy can add depth and humor even to projects with dialogue. For example: Consider a scene with a businessman who has to give a big speech desperately trying to find a men's room. He finally finds one that's available, uses it, then has to rush back to the auditorium with little time to spare. He has a moment to calmly collect himself, straighten his tie, and walk on stage for his big presentations before the bigwigs. After he delivers his speech, the camera slowly pans down to show that his fly is open and his shirt is sticking through it. The scene is funny because his fly was open the whole time he was talking. His audience could see it, but we couldn't. And that's why it's funny—we couldn't see it until just the right moment. Without a word being spoken, we learn that his career is over.

Remember the "I'll have what she's having" scene from 1989's *When Harry Met Sally*? In this hilarious scene, Meg Ryan fakes an orgasm in the middle of a crowded delicatessen. Would that scene have been nearly as funny if all you saw were Meg Ryan and Billy Crystal sitting in a booth up against the wall? Absolutely not. It works because you see that they are sitting in the middle of Katz's Delicatessen. Watch it again and look at the background characters. At first, they are completely unimportant and the audience barely notices them. Now watch as the scene develops. Every character becomes important, and finally one previously incidental background character delivers one of the funniest lines in movie history.

Don't forget that you can use visual elements to really mess with an audience. In 2000, the pest control company Orkin produced a very clever ad. What started out as a commercial for a fabric softener became much more when the shadow of a very realistic-looking cockroach crawled across the television screen. Viewers' initially thought it was a real bug until they saw the Orkin Man calmly come into the scene and spray the bug. It shocked some viewers so much that they actually broke their television sets by throwing objects at the bug. Most viewers found the ad to be funny and appreciated the practical joke that had been played on them. And you can be sure that the commercial generated a lot of water cooler talk.

FACT

The Simpsons, the longest running sitcom, has tons of jokes that are hidden in the background. Watch some episodes and study how they are used. Notice how a funny gag on the message board in front of the church enhances what would normally be just a simple, boring establishing shot. If you can add a quick laugh, why not?

Imagine you're writing a script that has a long scene with two characters deep in conversation. You have a choice: you can have a static scene of the two characters talking, or you can add some simple visual elements to make the scene more interesting—without sacrificing the importance of the dialogue. You can do this by having something interesting in the background or set the scene in an interesting place. What are the characters doing while they are talking? Is one eating a sloppy burger? Are they at a Japanese hibachi restaurant with a chef cooking at their table, doing all his fancy knife tricks? Are they in the park feeding pigeons? Are the two characters playing a video game while they talk? Do you see the power that visuals can have on an audience? Many writers write their scripts and only concentrate on clever dialogue. Make sure to always keep in mind what the audience is seeing and come up with ways to make your comedy even stronger.

A Cast of Thousands: Writing Comedy that is Meant to be Heard

From the late 1920s to the late 1940s, most Americans got their entertainment from the radio. Audiences got big laughs during tough times from popular radio comedians like Jack Benny, Edgar Bergen & Charlie McCarthy, and Fred Allen. Like the silent comedians of film, they used the limitations of the media to their advantage.

A great online source for quality sound effects is *http://sounddogs.com*. They have a growing library of thousands of effects. You can sample them before you buy, and the price is reasonable. Spend an hour on the site and let your imagination go wild.

You can do anything just using audio. With the help of a talented sound effects crew, four people standing around some microphones can easily convince an audience that they are trapped inside the hull of a submarine, doctors and nurses performing a delicate operation, or the crew of a pirate ship with a fierce battle raging all around them.

But that's the past, right? Wrong! Most people think of radio as music, talk shows, and news, but it's much more. With the exploding markets of satellite and Internet radio, audio comedy is enjoying a resurgence. Today, more CDs of stand-up are being made than at any other time. Comedy stations have to supply their audiences with comedy twenty-four hours a day, seven days a week. And they have to compete with other stations that are doing the same thing. For stand-ups, that means it's easier than ever to get your voice heard. Comics benefit from the exposure and begin building a following. It's a win-win situation. Contact the stations to see what their submission policy is.

But stand-up isn't the only kind of comedy on the radio. Sketch comedy works just as well, and more comedians are adding sketch to their CDs. Sketch troupes can also benefit. Podcasts are another use of comedy; there are hundreds of comedy podcasts available that let you target practically any niche market.

FACT

Podcasts are not just for adults. In fact, one of the longest-running podcasts is *The Radio Adventures of Dr. Floyd*. Created by Grant Baciocco and Doug Price in 1994, this family-friendly podcast has featured some of the biggest names in comedy as guest stars, and it's still going strong.

What does it take to write great audio comedy? Unlimited imagination and the ability to think big. You can make the audience "see" anything with audio, and just like visual comedy, you control when they "see" it. But timing, the ability to wait just long enough before delivering the joke, is the most important thing you need with audio. Learn to trust that pauses can deliver big laughs. Just like visual comedy can be all about what you don't see, audio comedy can be all about what you aren't hearing.

For a great example of pauses and what you don't hear, check out *Something Like This . . . The Bob Newhart Anthology*. This CD is a compilation of the best of Bob Newhart's 1960s record albums. Essential listening: "Abe Lincoln versus Madison Avenue," "Driving Instructor," and "King Kong." Bob Newhart is the master of the pause. Audio doesn't get better than this.

Another great thing about audio is that sound effects are cheaper than visual effects, and often just as effective. You can use sound to create any environment that you need, from the stands of a crowded baseball stadium to a campfire in the middle of the woods. With audio, your imagination doesn't have to be limited by your budget.

Combining Audio and Visual

Your audio comedy doesn't have to be just for audio outlets. Adding audio to your visuals can punch up a scene as well. Here's a simple scenario that might be part of a movie:

- A detective is driving his car when his cell phone rings. An anonymous caller gives him the telephone number 555-496-7325, which will help him solve a case. As the detective is listening, he's looking unsuccessfully for a pen to write down the number. The caller abruptly hangs up, leaving the detective with no way to ask her to repeat the number.
- The detective starts repeating the number to himself so that he won't forget it. As he's fumbling to dial the number, he drops the phone. He keeps repeating the number while he looks for the phone and continues to drive.
- Meanwhile, the radio DJ comes on the air to announce that it's time to call in for the big cash prize of the day. He gives the number of the toll-free contest line, 1-800-569-4326, and the amount of the big cash prize, $472.96, and repeats the information over and over.
- One-hit wonder Tommy Tutone's '80s hit *867-5309* starts playing. The detective has to fight to block out the radio station numbers as he finally locates his phone.
- As the detective starts to dial, his GPS chimes in to tell him to take a left in 1.5 miles onto route 495 and travel 16.8 miles to the 5th Street cutoff, which is exit 27. Of course, with this barrage of numbers the detective forgets the phone number, and he's back to square one.

In this scene, audio elements are used to barrage the character with common, everyday sounds involving numbers fatefully piling up at the same time. Now here's the cool part: If you can make the audience forget the telephone number as well, they will empathize with the detective and be drawn into the scene.

Smelly Comedy?

How can you make the audience taste, touch, and smell comedy? By using descriptive language, you can make the audience actually experience these senses. What would make the audience cringe more: "You have bad breath" or "Your breath smells like sour milk mixed with puke"? Probably the latter. The average audience member can't help but imagine what that repulsive odor would smell like no matter how hard he tries not to.

Your imagery certainly doesn't have to be disgusting for it to work; it can be used for any kind of story. To get a sample of comedy's master story-teller using imagery to provoke emotions in his audience, check out Bill Cosby's 1966 album *Wonderfulness* and listen to the classic routine "The Chicken Heart." It will make you feel like a kid who is frightened to death after seeing a scary movie.

It's like someone instructing you not to think of the color blue. You can't help yourself, you absolutely have to think of the color blue. In the same way, you can use taste, touch, and smell to make the audience feel as if they are experiencing what you are writing about.

Look to your own experience. Have you ever heard someone describe something disgusting? Something that tasted, felt, or smelled awful? As they described it, what did the listeners do? They probably cut the story short because they couldn't take it anymore. It's a visceral reaction. The brain is a powerful thing. Use your brain to mess with your audience's.

The Sixth Sense

Hopefully, you won't see dead people in your audience. Scientists call the sixth sense social intelligence, but it's really just about being able to read your audience. Honing your sixth sense means becoming a good judge of human nature and anticipating how people will react. To develop this skill, you need to watch people.

It's a very powerful moment when you deliver a punch line at exactly the instant the audience arrives at the same conclusion. It's almost as if you're sending them the joke telepathically. Audiences love anyone who can connect with them in such a magical way. It takes a joke from being a passive experience to a deeply personal experience.

Profile in Comedy: Henriette Mantel

Henriette Mantel is an Emmy award-winning writer. She is also a director, actress, and former stand-up comic and has extensive experience in documentary and reality television as a writer, director, and producer. In 2007, *An Unreasonable Man*, a critically acclaimed documentary about Ralph Nader that she co-wrote and directed with fellow-comedy writer Steve Skrovan, was released in theaters across the country and later shown on PBS. She has had four of her comedy plays professionally produced. All four are directed by Michael Patrick King. Her favorite project, *Midge and Buck*, an expose on the life of her longtime feline companions, was originally produced on stage and is now a series on *www.icebox.com*. Her critically acclaimed *Girl Talk*, a play about one woman's journey in New York City after September 11, was featured at the 2002 Aspen Comedy Festival. She won her first Emmy for writing on *Win Ben Stein's Money*. As an actress, Henriette has appeared in many television comedies and feature films, including *The Brady Bunch* movies, in which she portrayed Alice, the maid. She currently lives in New York City.

When did you first realize that you were uniquely funny?

Kindergarten, growing up in Vermont. I made everyone laugh by being an insane Baby Bear in our play about Goldilocks and the three bears. Things would have been so different if I had been cast as Goldilocks.

Who do you think were your influences?

My dad, my brother, my best grade school friend Tommy Dahlin, and later, Phyllis Diller, Abbott and Costello, Pat Paulson, Paula Poundstone, and anyone else whose name begins with "p."

Do you remember your first original joke?

I used to imitate my eighth-grade teacher. I would draw a crowd with jokes on the playground when I imitated her doing our daily reading.

When did you realize that comedy was something that you had to do for a living?

When my closest brother died in an accident, I knew if I was going to stay on earth I had to make people laugh because I personally was never going to laugh again. Prior to that I had been working for Ralph Nader and it never entered my mind to get into comedy as a career. I was twenty-four years old.

What was your first job in comedy writing or performance?

[I made] $5 at the Holy City Zoo in San Francisco as a stand-up.

For you was stand-up an end in itself or a platform to move on to other projects?

At the time it was an end in itself but after about ten years I got tired so I guess it led me to other things.

What is the biggest difficulty you've encountered being a comedy writer?

Misogynist male writers who hate women but make you laugh so hard that you think it's not affecting you but it is. Also, male comics, due to their strong personalities and ability to convince a crowd that they are funny, also make you try to believe that the penis is funnier than the vagina, but I beg to differ. And by the way, some of my best friends are male comics.

What are the differences between writing for yourself and writing for others?

I love writing for people who can truly, truly deliver a joke, i.e. Teri Garr, but it's rewarding in a different way. I like writing for myself because I feel guilty if I write for someone else and it's not funny. I guess I like specific character writing that is from a specific point of view that I can lock into and work with like actresses Jennifer Cox, Jennifer Coolidge, and once again, Oscar-nominated actress Sister Mary Teresa Garr.

What do you find exciting about comedy right now?

I guess Tina Fey and *30 Rock*. She is the frickin' Lucy of our time.

Where do you think the future of comedy is headed?

Now that Obama has won, everything is going to be fine, so there might not be any comedy ever again. Comedy depends on pain and misery and conflict and idiots leading the country.

What is the best thing about being a comedy writer?

The paychecks, and once in awhile you actually get to laugh uncontrollably. I still live for that shit.

Do you have any advice for up-and-coming comedy writers?

Write and write with unbridled abandon. Get the core of your humor and don't let anybody tell you how to do it till you find your sense of humor on paper. Then just work your butt off and by then you'll have a good pension to live off of.

Brainstorm

Ernie Kovacs was the king of the blackout gag. These were quick, visual gags, usually set to music, that lasted only a few seconds. He would show a string of these, coming back to a scene and showing a different outcome every time. It might be a woman making a grand entrance into a room or a Native American trying to shoot an arrow. Same scene, but something different and funny happened every time.

Give it a try. Here's a simple scene that's almost a cliché: A group of three or four doctors and nurses in full medical garb are working on a patient as a heart monitor beeps steadily. Keep the scene the same, but come up with multiple site gags. For example:

- The doctor makes a cut and strikes oil, with an oil gusher coming out of the patient. Then a grizzled old prospector enters the scene saying, "We're rich!"
- As the surgeon successfully removes an organ, a dog jumps onto the patient, grabs it and runs off with it.

- The surgeon reaches into the patient with his arm going in all the way up to his shoulder, and pulls out some keys and says, "That's where I left my keys!"
- In the middle of the operation, a steam whistle blows, then a ladder emerges from the open cavity and a construction worker climbs out of the patient, carrying his lunch box.
- The surgeon tries to pull an organ out but has a tug of war with it and ends up disappearing into the patient's body cavity.
- As they work on the patient, the heart monitor starts to beep out a familiar tune, *Tainted Love* by the new-wave band Soft Cell (beep . . . beep . . . tainted love) and they rock out to it.

Get the idea? This scene has been seen so many times that almost anything you come up with can be funny, and an infinite number of things could happen. Write some of your own and you'll make Ernie proud.

Notebook

Review your jokes and scripts and try adding visual, audio, and descriptive language to give your writing added depth. Try writing a purely visual scene without using a single word to tell the story. Write a scene that only uses audio. See how far you can take it by creating images for the audience to imagine.

Try writing a gag for something that happens in everyday life: a cell phone ringing at an inopportune time. Ask yourself what's a *really* inopportune time? At a funeral maybe? What could the ring tone be that makes that bad situation even worse? *Girls Just Want to Have Fun*? *Happy Days Are Here Again*? Get the idea? Great! Now get to work!

CHAPTER 18

Places to Be Funny

Sitcoms and stand-up are not the only ways to sell your comedy. Starting in secondary markets can help you discover your comedy voice, build an audience, and get some attention that can bring bigger projects, help you polish your comedy skills, and supplement your income. Here are a few markets that you might want to consider.

Virtual Hilarity

New technology has created an infinite number of places for you to high-light your sense of humor. You need very little money to get started in these areas, and they can lead to huge successes if you use them to your best advantage.

Blogging

Sure, there are more than 100 million blogs out there, but if your voice is unique, yours will get noticed. You can be very specific—blogging your own movie reviews—or you can safely hide behind an outrageous charac-ter. There are plenty of free blogging sites such as *www.blogger.com*, so give it a shot. At the very least, it's a great writing exercise that you can commit to every day. The keys to writing a successful comedy blog are:

- **Keep it short.** A blog longer than 300 words is too long. The sub-scribers to your blog want quick information. Keep your writing eco-nomical and you're more likely to have people read your stuff on a regular basis.
- **Give them somewhere to go next.** Provide links to news stories and other websites, or embed videos from YouTube and other services into your blog. For example, if you're commenting on a politician's or celebrity's statement, give your audience the chance to see that video clip, so what you're talking about will be clear.
- **Make it personal.** Don't hold back on your opinion; that's what peo-ple are looking for. Also, keep the style of your writing consistent from post to post—this will help you develop your comic voice.
- **Update your posts on a regular basis.** Whether it's every day, once a week, or once a month, don't disappoint your fans by being lazy and inconsistent. If they check out your site a couple of times, and there's nothing new—they won't come back.

One more thing—just remember that once it hits the web, it's there for-ever. So be careful what you say!

Podcasting

Most podcasts are weekly or monthly programs, usually anywhere from two to sixty minutes in length. Users subscribe to them, so if you maintain the quality, you'll quickly gain a loyal audience who wants to hear your comedy. You can do anything with a podcast—interviews (real or fake), audio sketches, soap opera parodies—the sky's the limit. If you're ambitious, you can also create video podcasts that feature your stand-up, sketches, road diaries, or pretty much anything you want. This is a low-cost option to get some valuable attention. The iTunes store offers customers more than 100,000 different podcasts to choose from. Comedies like *The Onion Radio News* and *Ask a Ninja* are some of the most popular. Lots of popular podcasts have sponsors, so it can become a profitable venture if yours catches on.

Start slow. Start out with a short podcast and increase their length as you get more confident with your podcasting skills.

It doesn't cost a lot to get started in podcasting. You can get a decent USB microphone for about $100, and many come bundled with software as well. Apple's Garage Band application comes with the basic software and allows you to easily record your podcast and add professional quality music bumpers and sound effects to make yourself sound like a pro. If you're on a PC there are lots of recording options (many for free) as well. An free, easy-to-use program to get you started is Audacity (*audacity.sourceforge.net*).

Animation

If you have a talent for animation, why not create short films? Inexpensive animation software such as Adobe Flash is simple to use for budding animators. If you are a good artist (or know someone who is) you can inexpensively create your own animated shorts that can become Internet sensations. *Charlie the Unicorn* has millions of hits on YouTube.

In 1995, Trey Parker and Matt Stone created an animated Christmas card called "Jesus versus Santa." It got passed around from person to person until it found its way into the hands of Comedy Central's president, Doug Herzog, and became *South Park*. Mike Judge, creator of *Beavis and Butthead*, *King of the Hill*, and *Office Space* started his career with just a $200 camera and a desire to be an animator. Today's technology makes animation easier and cheaper to create, and allows you to instantly upload your work for the world to see.

Traditional Media

You can break into comedy writing and earn a paycheck at the same time. You can work as a freelancer or a full-time staffer, but it takes motivation to get yourself into the market.

Speechwriting

Do you have a knack for making great toasts at weddings? Then try your hand at writing them for others. If you search the Internet for "speechwriting services," you'll find dozens of companies offering their services to CEOs, politicians, and anyone who gets tongue-tied in front of an audience. Another place you can offer your writing services is *www.guru.com*, a website for freelancers to offer their services.

Joke Writing

Are you great at writing jokes but have no interest in performing stand-up yourself? Try writing jokes for other comics. Many well-known comics have freelance writers who submit jokes to them on a regular basis. If they like the joke, they send you a check. Some television shows also accept prescreened freelancers' submissions for use in their monologues. In Los Angeles it's not unusual to see a comic read some jokes out of his notebook on stage, and then collect cash from comics eager to make those jokes their own.

Newspapers and Magazines

Being a freelance writer for newspapers and magazines is a great way to get your work noticed. It will also help you build up a body of work that could later lead to a book of comic essays—or better yet, a nationally syndicated column. The best way to get started is to submit some writing to your local newspaper and work your way up.

Greeting Cards

Greeting cards are big business. Billions are sold every year, and funny cards are a big chunk of the market. If you think that you can write a funny line that would cheer up someone's day, you might want to pursue a career as a greeting card writer. And it's not just the big companies that get all the action. About a third of the market consists of smaller companies with their own clientele in specialty stores. The quality and low cost of printing makes it an inexpensive proposition to try your luck at selling your own line of cards to smaller, independent stores that aren't beholden to the larger companies.

Light Humor Books

There is a huge market for comedy books that are purchased mostly as gifts or impulse buys. Hundreds of titles are published every year. Books like Simon Bond's *101 Uses for a Dead Cat*, Tim Berg and Tim Nyberg's *Duct Tape Book* series, and Daniel Butler, Alan Ray, and Leland Gregory's *Dumbest Criminal* series are big sellers that spawn sequels. If a topical story breaks in the news, there might just be a couple of books about it in the stores a week later. Also, new joke books and humor books on every subject from golf to parenting are published every year. While they're not exactly *Tom Sawyer*, they don't pretend to be anything more than books that provide a few laughs and brighten people's days. With the ease of self-publishing these days, you can easily write and sell your own books both online and after your stand-up shows to make extra cash.

FACT

In addition to his successful comedy column for the *Miami Herald*, Dave Barry has written dozens of best-selling books and screenplays. He even had a sitcom called *Dave's World* based on his column that ran on CBS from 1993 to 1997.

In the days before inexpensive, quality printing, vanity presses—where you paid to have your book published—left a lot of disillusioned would-be authors with a garage full of books they couldn't sell. But with services such as Lulu (*www.lulu.com*), you can upload your book or CD and sell your work yourself or let people buy directly from the site. You set the price, and you keep the profit. And your garage will be clutter-free! (Well, probably not; that would take a miracle.)

Writing for Kids

The children's market is one of the most profitable and most overlooked markets for comedy. Even if you put aside all the children's books that are published every year and just focus on actual performances for kids, the possibilities are endless. Writing and performing shows for kids is just as satisfying and difficult as it is performing for adults (if not more so). You can take your show to private parties, schools, childcare facilities, and theaters.

E-QUESTION

Is writing for kids as important as writing for adults?
Absolutely! Are kids less important than adults? If you treat the job like it's beneath you, you probably won't write anything significant. But if you put your whole self into writing for kids and write with passion, you might be a hit. Look at it this way: Who do you think has had more impact on the world—Jackie Collins or Dr. Seuss?

If you're wondering what has happened to the great American sitcom, you don't have to look very far. Just flip to Nickelodeon or the Disney Channel, and you'll find almost as many sitcoms as there are on the networks for grown-ups. And they can be just as successful when you factor in merchandising to a very loyal fan base (think *Hannah Montana*). If you want to write in the traditional sitcom format, kid's television might be for you.

From the Funnies to the Airwaves

Other forms of traditional media might not come readily to mind when you think of a career in comedy, but you should consider whether comic strips, advertising, or radio writing can be the best way to showcase your talents.

Comic Strips

It's tough to become a professional cartoonist. Of the thousands of new strips that are submitted to syndicates every year, only a handful are even given a shot, and even fewer are a success. The field is dominated by reader favorites, strips that have been around for a long time. Even though some ceased being funny decades ago, it's hard for a new one to get noticed and get syndicated into newspapers. But if you can make that breakthrough, you could have a very rewarding career.

Advertising

There was a time when humorous ads were frowned upon. But the brilliant comedian Stan Freberg came along and changed all that. He created successful ad campaigns that were hilarious and memorable but said very little about the product. In a way, consumers bought the product as a way to thank the company for a good laugh.

Rhino's *Tip of the Freberg*, a boxed set of Stan Freberg's best stuff, includes video of some of his industry-changing television commercials. Essential tracks: "John and Marsha," "Banana Boat," and "Little Blue Riding Hood."

Today, comedy and advertising go hand in hand. If you look at a successful ad campaign like the Geico cavemen ads ("so easy a caveman can do it"), it's just a simple joke. But it's a joke backed by millions of dollars and the expectation that it will work. If you can take that kind of pressure, the advertising field might be for you.

Comedy Writing Services for Radio Stations

Have you ever wondered how those crazy "Morning Zoo" type disc jockeys come up with all their jokes? And have you marveled at how quickly they produce song parodies and polished audio sketches about topical events in the news? The answer is simple; they buy them. A lot of the comedy on radio shows is bought from comedy services that stations subscribe to. Services like the American Comedy Network, Comedy Wire, and the United Stations Radio Networks have writing staffs that continually churn out topical comedy material and fully produced bits. With satellite radio fueling growth in the industry, providing comedy to these stations is certain to become a rapidly expanding field. With the proper motivation and production equipment, you can set up you own company and get your work on the air every day.

Profile in Comedy: Martin Olson

One of the founding fathers of the Boston comedy scene, Martin Olson has become the go-to guy when Hollywood needs comedy. He has sold screenplays to Dreamworks and Warner Brothers and has been a staff writer for the Screen Actors Guild Awards for three years. He was head writer for four HBO comedy concert specials and is presently head writer for Disney's *Phineas and Ferb*.

When did you first realize that you were uniquely funny?
You won't believe this. My mother just had open heart surgery when I told her I sold a comedy screenplay to Dreamworks. Soon after, on her deathbed she said, "I have something to show you." She pulled out a shirt box with two old notebooks inside. On the covers: "Joke Book 1" and "Joke Book 2" by Martin Olson. I'd forgotten about them. I wrote them when I was eight and in her mind I was destined to be a comedy writer. I thumbed through the books and couldn't break the truth to her that they were execrable. Later in life I vowed to duct-tape them to my chest when I hung myself from the Hollywood sign.

When did you realize that comedy was something you had to do for a living?
I remember the moment I wanted to be a comedy writer. I was nine years old. I was watching *The Merv Griffin Show* with my mom when Merv introduced a comedian named Brother Theodore. The screen went black and a harsh spotlight hit this weird scary-looking German guy all in black. He began ranting about life being meaningless and how we should all kill ourselves. And each rant ended with a precise paradoxical punch line. Like a Steven Wright

joke. It was the funniest thing I'd ever seen, and liberated my mind. I knew then what comedy really was, a license to fuck with people's minds and break their thought patterns, to inspire freedom of thought through satire, and show that what we consider normal is, from another perspective, insane.

Do you remember your first original joke?

My first bit was "Bachelor Baby Tips." One of them was if you open the top of the toilet tank and put the baby in, it'll not only wash the baby but save water when you flush.

Who do you think were your influences?

The writers I worshipped were Brother Theodore, Mark Twain, Samuel Beckett, and later, Bruce J. Friedman. Also the composer Charles Ives who did profound orchestral music with weird comic elements thrown in. I was of course mad about all the comedy greats from Chaplin on, all the way through Jack Benny, Spike Jones, Steve Martin, Albert Brooks, and Andy Kaufman.

What was your first job in comedy writing or performance?

I created a late night local comedy series, a half hour of original comedy every week sandwiched between a bad monster movie. I wrote it for a year with one of the funniest Boston comics, Lenny Clarke, who was also the star and my roommate.

What is the biggest difficulty you've encountered being a comedy writer?

For whatever reason, I never liked sitcoms. And aside from comedy movies, that's where the big money is. What happened was, I was spoiled by seeing Brother Theodore early on. The sitcom format was way unfunny to me compared to my initiation through free-form imaginative formats like Brother Theodore and Spike Jones, formats that threw you off-kilter and made you have to think and struggle a bit before the payoff.

What are the differences between writing for yourself and writing for others?

As a writer I never try to write for anyone other than myself. My writing process is me typing and laughing. Everyone who works with me has to put up with me laughing like a goon in my office. If they only knew after the door closed, how the laughter stops and the cutting begins.

What is the difference between writing for kids and writing for adults?

Obviously you can't write "adult humor" for children. I've never written a toddler show, which would definitely call for a different comedy sensibility. As for the kid shows I've written, I never write for kids but for myself, since I am twelve years old. If I laugh I'm pretty damn sure some version of the joke or story will make people laugh, not because I myself am funny, but because of my experience and success in writing in which I start by making myself laugh. Never fails.

What show have you worked on where you feel you had the most creative freedom?

Shows for Penn and Teller and for comics like Bobcat Goldthwait and Kevin Meaney. They specialize in satirizing comedy performance in three unique ways.

What do you find exciting about comedy right now?

Exactly what you'd expect. All the imaginative linear-thought-busting trickster weirdos: Zach Galifianakis, Sarah Silverman, Sasha Baron Cohen, Mary Lynn Rajskub, Michael Meehan, the Mighty Boosh, Demetri Martin, Paul Kozlowski, Ron Lynch, Louis CK, Dino Stamatopoulos, Brendon Small, the Lampshades, crazy Charlyne Yi, many others. There are so many either super imaginative comics or smarmy hacks performing right now comedy clubs are like taking a cool refreshing dip in a pool filled with embalming fluid. There's exciting comedy at the Fake Gallery in Los Angeles.

Where do you think the future of comedy is headed?

The new guys either build on everything that came before them or react against it. So since self-reference and put-on humor and obscenity are accepted elements now for "edgy" comedy, I predict more of the same combined with a synthesis of unlikely styles of performance juxtaposed in new ways. Bobcat Goldthwait's two new films, *Sleeping Dogs Lie* and *World's Greatest Dad* are two examples I think of synthesizing different styles of comedy and creating something new that on the surface looks normal. Sort of "put-on" films and comedy that work on several levels at once. I have no idea what I just said.

As audiences become more specific and more segmented, is your job becoming easier or more difficult?

I usually write the same kind of nonlinear or self-referential comedy that makes me laugh, so that's what they hire me for. It's always the stars or creators of shows that hire me, never the executives, who understandably are not in it for the art.

What is the best thing about being a comedy writer?

Being paid to have challenging creative fun and to work with incredibly imaginative geniuses on a daily basis.

Do you have any advice for up-and-coming comedy writers?

Write for yourself and not for an audience or for executives, try your best to be respectful to everybody, and on a personal note, if you strangle a nurse after a party, make sure you find a ravine with off-road access to dump the carcass.

Brainstorm

Look over the markets listed in this chapter and see which ones might be a match for your type of comedy. Do some research on what it takes to get started. Also, brainstorm other markets that would have a use for your skills.

Notebook

Have a friend copy some daily comic strips from the newspaper and white-out the captions or the dialogue in the talk bubbles. Now try to write your own captions for each comic strip. You can try to match something that the characters would actually be likely to say or you can be as irreverent as you like.

This exercise is harder than you think, but it's a great way to practice the Comedy Rule of Three, because the typical four panel comic strip uses this rule all the time. Just look at the four panels as set-up, set-up, set-up, and punch line. If you really want a challenge, combine panels from different days. You can also try your luck with single-panel cartoons, either adding dialogue or replacing the caption with your own.

CHAPTER 19

DIY Fame: YouTube, MySpace, and Beyond

We live in an age where it is easier than ever to show your work to the world. The Internet has revolutionized comedy and the way comedy is delivered. Start creating content, and you could literally be an Internet celebrity overnight.

Make Yourself Famous

In the old days—about ten years ago!—there was only one way to become famous as a comedian: you had to pay your dues. As a stand-up, you started at an open-mic night. In a couple of years you graduated to being an opening act. After a few more years you moved on to being a middle act. A few more years after *that*, you finally graduated to headliner. But then you had to start all over again to become a national headliner or sitcom star.

If you were a filmmaker, you had to come up with a lot of capital to make a film. Once you had a finished film, you had to enter it in countless film festivals in the hopes that it might get you noticed by people who could advance your career.

E-QUESTION

Isn't paying dues a good thing?
Yes, it is. The harder you try, the better you get. You still have to work hard and produce a good product, but right or wrong, the traditional paths to success are quite different from what they used to be. You might not have to pay your dues to others, but you still need to set your standards high and pay your dues to yourself.

Comedy writers had it even harder. You first had to get an agent, but of course you couldn't get an agent without some writing credits. Usually you had to rely on a friend in the business to get you an internship writing for a show. Eventually you convinced the writers that you might actually be funny and you got some small assignments writing for others. But if you wanted to write for your own projects, you were looking at years of waiting for an opportunity to come along.

Things are different now. The rules to success are being redefined. You don't need to look for work, producers, agents, and studios are looking for you. Because of exposure on the Internet, you can bypass paying your dues and go directly to a paying job—if your stuff is good and it gets seen.

The major television and movie studios have people who look at the Internet all day for the next big thing. So if your little YouTube movie gets a ton of hits, you might be getting a call from the studio to see if you have any projects they might be interested in developing. The beauty of this is that you start where comedians in the past hoped to end up—writing and producing your own material, the way you want.

However, before you start posting video, make sure you have material to back it up. If you post the only five minutes of stand-up you have, you might get a call from someone wishing to hire you. If you can't live up to their expectations, you might have wasted your fifteen minutes of fame. Have future projects in mind before you post.

On the Cheap

With the accessibility of inexpensive but high-quality video cameras and editing and special effects software, you can make your mini-masterpieces for next to nothing. In most cases, you don't have to pay actors and grips or deal with unions and regulations. You're on your own. You can make a decent, quality film that looks almost as good as it does on the big screen.

However, even though you can get big screen quality, remember that in most cases your video will be watched on YouTube on a tiny screen, or even a really tiny cell phone screen. Make sure your comedy is made to fit on the small screen when you produce it. Keep the important elements visible to make sure that your audience isn't missing something vital.

FACT

Judson Laipply's "Evolution of Dance" routine has been seen by more than 100 million viewers (that's around the same number of people who watched the Super Bowl) and is the top YouTube video of all time. Judson is a "motivational comedian" and he made an Internet sensation out of his energetic six-minute video showing how dance has changed since the 1950s.

Anyone can make a technically expert video, but you need great content. That's what the studios are looking for—truly original ideas they haven't seen before. That's what gets you noticed. Don't worry if your film-making skills aren't perfect. As long as your content is funny and original, you'll be just fine.

On video sites like YouTube, it's getting harder to stick out. So many videos are uploaded every day, and most of them are predictable—guys getting hit in the groin, babies laughing, or babies laughing at guys getting hit in the groin. But truly funny videos and performances still move to the top very quickly.

Another Internet advantage: You can create material quickly. As soon as a news story breaks, you can make a funny response and upload it within hours, and it can travel around the world in seconds. That can be a blessing and a curse. Uploading a ton of stuff to see if something sticks might cause your audience to think that you had only one good video in you. Take pride in what you do and work your ideas until you know they're funny. Chances are the world will agree with you.

Because your videos can get lost in the junk that fills up YouTube, you might want to consider submitting them to sites that are more selective like *www.collegehumor.com* and *www.funnyordie.com*. Your video might even get featured, guaranteeing it will be seen by thousands of people. If you're working with a troupe, you'll definitely want to work together and brand your material as one, not as individuals. In addition to YouTube, you'll also want to link to and embed video in your website.

Studios are trying to sponsor and profit from Internet media. It's possible that more outlets will start paying you for content, so you may be able to profit from your video's popularity.

Be Your Own Press Agent

Having a quality website and fan mailing list can really help your career. If you can't design a website yourself, pay someone to do it for you. Your site should list your credits, include a short bio, display quotes from the press, and even have video samples of your act or the short films you've made. You could also have short stories and a daily blog on your site to show off your writing chops.

You can use websites like *www.cafepress.com* and *www.zazzle.com* to print and sell everything from t-shirts and mugs to neckties and thongs! What's great about these services is they don't cost you a dime—you set the price and keep the profit.

Your website will show potential clients your best side, and if you have videos on YouTube, make sure you link to your site and embed those videos on your site. This helps to add a face to your work. You can also use your website to sell t-shirts, CDs, and other products.

Grow Your Fan Base

Comedian and actor Dane Cook gained popularity by using the Internet to build a huge following. He was the first person to have more than 2 million friends on MySpace. He has used the Internet to truly connect with his fans and allow his fans to connect with each other. Aside from promoting his CDs and personal appearances, he's developed an almost personal relationship with his fans. That relationship makes his audience feel closer to him and ensures that he has some of the most loyal fans around. He's like the Oprah of comedy. He loves his fans, and they love him back. On the other hand, so much attention has also led many people to dislike him, and there are a fair number of hate sites for Cook.

Extreme popularity can be followed by backlash, causing your hot career to cool down quickly. There is such a thing as being too popular. Overexposure can hurt you; that's why it's a good idea continue to evolve and keep your feelers out there for your next career step.

How can you build a fan base? Start simple. Don't expect 2 million fans overnight. The best way is to use every opportunity you can to drive people to your website. But getting them there isn't enough—remember that you have to entertain them once they're there. If they see the same old site with the same old videos and blogs, they won't come back.

Make sure you update your site at least once a week. It doesn't take much—a quick blog about recent shows and projects that you've done, or better yet, a quick, funny video "hello" that shows fans that you're happy they're checking in. It doesn't take a lot to show your fans that you respect them.

Use Facebook and Twitter to quickly pull together a list of friends and fans. You can let them know where you are performing by sending invites to your whole list at once. It's great for stand-ups with last-minute gigs, and you can also use it to let your fans know when you've posted something on YouTube by providing them with a link.

One of the major downsides of Internet exposure is that a bad performance might get more attention than a good one. You may not have control of what gets posted. In 2006, Michael Richards, who played Kramer on *Seinfeld*, was caught on a cell phone camera shouting racist remarks at a heckler. The resulting uproar damaged his career—perhaps forever.

Keep your site simple. It doesn't need to be wacky to let people know you are a comedian. Just make it fit your personality and update it consistently with comedy and information. You can also keep a schedule of upcoming appearances and link directly to a site that allows fans to buy tickets. If you are performing at a club and you help to bring in customers, the club owner will love having you back as often as possible.

Comedy Police

Another plus to having your material online is that, in a way, it's a proof of ownership. You are telling the world, "I lay claim to this joke." It's a good way to make sure that up-and-coming comics don't have their material stolen by others. In fact, there are constant battles about who stole what from whom raging on the Internet. Some of the biggest names in comedy are involved in calling others out, usually with video or audio proof.

Profile in Comedy: Bill Braudis

Bill Braudis is one of the best joke writers around. Just ask any comic. In addition to his stand-up performances (including an appearance on *The Tonight Show with Jay Leno*) Bill has written for and performed in the animated shows *Science Court*, *Home Movies*, and *Metalocalypse*.

When did you first realize that you were uniquely funny?

In retrospect, I think I realized I was "funny" at an early age. Probably at around the age of seven or eight. That's when I entertained everyone at family gatherings by imitating my father's daily ritual of coming home from work, sitting in his chair, eating supper, watching TV, falling asleep in his chair, and snoring. I remember getting big laughs. I remember knowing what would get a laugh and I remember loving it.

Who do you think were your influences?

Although my mother always encouraged me to write (because I was pretty good at it) and I used to love listening to my father's wild stories about growing up with his four brothers, I'd have to say that one of my first true leaps into the world of comedy came from Bill Cosby. I was twelve years old when a friend let me borrow some Cosby albums. I remember one bit in particular about "Old Weird Harold" that had me laughing so hard I fell off my chair. Little did I know a seed had been planted. Then, when I was about thirteen, my sister took me to see Woody Allen's movie *Take The Money And Run.* Again, I literally fell off the chair in the theater laughing. Slid right down to that dirty, sticky floor. Comedy from Bill Cosby and Woody Allen were forever imprinted on my young mind. (Reading Woody Allen's books, *Side Effects* and *Without Feathers*, didn't hurt, either, and were probably my springboards for writing humor.)

Do you remember your first original joke?

First "official" joke came about while taking a sitcom writing class at a local continuing education program. (It was taught by an ex-staff writer from the TV show *The Jeffersons*.) The first assignment was to write a joke. He told us to pick a stand-up comic, use his or her persona, and write a ten-minute monologue. For some reason, I picked Rodney Dangerfield. I guess because not only had I seen Rodney Dangerfield a bunch of times on TV, but his was an easy personality to lock into—"no respect." (I always leaned a little toward the self-deprecating stuff anyway.) So one of the jokes that I wrote in that assignment (this was in 1980) went like this . . . "I'm supposed to be going downhill skiing next weekend, but I've never gone downhill skiing before in my life. So I've been practicing. Every morning I get up, go out into the hallway and throw myself down three flights of stairs."

When did you realize that comedy was something that you had to do for a living?

Probably when I wrote that assignment, because when I read the jokes in class everyone laughed and that was the first time I had ever written a joke with the intention of getting a laugh, and then actually got the laughs. But what solidified comedy as my career was my first time on stage, in 1981, at the Comedy Connection in Boston. I, as we comics say, killed. My first time ever on stage could not have gone better. Five minutes of material and I got a bunch of laughs, several rounds of applause, and I still have the cassette tape to prove it. That single appearance on stage solidified my goal to write comedy. And even though my next time on stage, the following week, I bombed so badly I was shaking, it didn't matter. I was hooked.

What was your first job in comedy writing or performance?

First paid gig as a stand up comic was at a restaurant in a western Massachusetts town. I was supposed to do twenty minutes. I did about eight. The cruel thing is, material flies by when you're bombing—usually because you don't have those pesky laughs to slow you down. But of course, the actual time, even eight minutes, crawls painfully by when people are just staring at you. It was my first paid gig. I was actually splitting the set with another comic. It was his first paid set as well. We were supposed to split the time of forty minutes and the pay of eighty dollars—cash. Forty bucks for bombing, horribly. I felt very guilty taking the money. There would be many more nights like that to come.

What is the biggest difficulty you've encountered being a comedy writer?

Tough question. Do you mean work wise? As in getting paid work? Because that would be the biggest problem. Especially living in Boston and getting paid for writing scripts is not easy. I've been very fortunate to have the opportunities I've had. Like anything, it takes perseverance and some talent. And, every now and then, you've got to step out of your comfort zone. It's funny—I like to write, and writing for the most part is a singular experience. But to sell yourself and pursue work, you have to come out of that cocoon. As comics in the early '80s in Boston, we used to pride ourselves on being our own everything. Our own writers, performers, managers, booking agents, travel agents, etc. We had to do it all. Part of that is still true today. Especially if you're not living in New York or LA. Gotta push yourself to sell yourself.

As far as the biggest difficulty in actual writing terms, for me, would be an honest rewrite. No matter how many times one might rewrite one's own stuff, another pair of eyes is always the real test. While writing for several TV shows, I learned a lot about having your work rewritten. It can be very humbling. But, as I eventually learned—and now preach to any writer who'll listen—you shouldn't fall in love with the stuff you write, you should fall in love with your ability to write it. That way, it's not unthinkable to go back and chop up your babies. (By "babies" I of course mean your "writing," not the little things that poop.)

Sometimes you get too close to your material. You think, "This is good stuff, I don't care what they say. A zebra giving birth in an elevator is perfect for our show." There were many times while writing scripts for TV shows that I thought I'd written some really good stuff. But not everybody saw it that way. That can be jolting. I have to think there are few writers alive whose skin is thick enough to never be bothered just the teensiest, tiniest bit by what others think. It's the nature of writing. People naturally judge and critique. As a writer, what you put on paper is almost always some measure of your ability, your intelligence, your station in life.

Most people's words and thoughts and ideas are on the inside and private. They may come out in a conversation, but then they probably disappear into the ether. But the written word, oh man, it just sits there on the paper for all to see. That's why it's so scary. When writing for a living, you learn to pick your battles or swallow your pride for the good of the show, the good of the relationship, or the good of the pay check. But, as I said, it's better to fall in love with your ability to fix things—because after all, "writing is rewriting"—than to fall in love with what you've written. You can like it, just don't marry it.

Are there jokes that you do "just for you?"

I never really subscribed to the "I do that joke for me" theory, mostly because I don't think it truly exists. In other words, I don't believe a comic is really doing stuff only for themselves and the hell with the audience. The only time you usually hear a comic say this is right after a joke bombs. They're trying to dig themselves out of the hole they just made. As a stand up comic, when you're on stage, your job is to get laughs. That's hard enough. I don't go out and try to dig myself a hole by doing jokes that I like but aren't that funny. If a joke I like consistently stops getting laughs, then I stop doing the joke. Or I try to fix it.

Sometimes a new joke works on 90 percent enthusiasm and after a while you realize the joke isn't getting the laughs it used to, even though it's the exact same wording. In those instances I like to stick a "crutch" in there. Something to help the joke. Maybe a little throw-away joke, or some rhetorical line along the way to the punch line. These help to put the crowd in position to better get the final punch line. The funny thing is, I'd say that there are jokes I do just for them, the audience. Jokes that I've grown tired of over the years, but they still get laughs, so I do them. But if a joke doesn't get a laugh, even if I like it, I don't do it.

What are the differences between writing for yourself and writing for others?

The biggest difference is the personality or character of the person you're writing for. You have to be able to get inside the character's head, whether it's a character you've created in a sitcom or an established performer. You really have to know a character well before you write for them. Real or fictional. I spent one season writing for Dennis Miller and when I got the job, even though I felt I knew his comedy, I still rented a couple of his videos to watch and become more familiar with his delivery, preferences, nuances, voice, etc. As far as writing for yourself, you probably know your character better than anybody. You're probably willing to take a lot more chances than somebody else with your material. And if it bombs, you only have yourself to blame.

How do you balance educational material and comedy?

In writing educational shows for kids (*Science Court* on ABC and *Joy Learno* and *Between The Lions* for PBS) I don't really think of maintaining a balance between delivering the educational content and creating humor. Educational shows for kids have to be one thing first and foremost: entertaining. If it's not entertaining, they won't watch it. When I would sit down to write a script for *Science Court,* I was given an outline of the educational points I had to make. But I wasn't looking for a balance. I wanted humor to be pretty much everywhere, except when delivering the key educational points. Imagine you're going to paint your bedroom white and you're going to do some stenciling on it. Well, you're not going to paint a little white, then do a stencil, then paint white in another spot and then do another stencil. You'll paint the entire wall white first, then go back in and put your stencils where you need to. That's kind of the idea I had with humor and educational content. Be funny first. When the educational stuff comes along, you'll be able to hit it on the nose, without taking anything away from the story or the humor.

What do you find exciting about comedy right now?

Comedy to me is always exciting and fun. It's fun to make people laugh, whether it's performing or writing. The Internet has certainly opened up a lot of possibilities for new creative outlets.

Where do you think the future of comedy is headed?

Comedy goes where the tragedy goes. Comedy goes where the celebrities go. It goes where the politicians go. It goes where the Internet goes. Comedy goes where life goes.

As audiences become more specific and more segmented, is your job becoming easier or more difficult?

I'm not sure what you mean by "more specific and more segmented." Joke writing doesn't change. Subject matter changes. Mores change. Lines that once were never crossed are long gone and new ones are drawn. Levels of exposure and sophistication of audiences have changed, but a joke is still a joke. A joke is still the unexpected. A set up and a twist. The subject matter may be different. The audiences may be different. But, the steps needed to get a laugh—a punch line—remain the same and seems to me, always will.

What is the best thing about being a comedy writer?

I'm going to say something that might sound stupid, but it's my opinion. It's a lot easier to write drama than it is to write comedy. (I think a lot of people actually share this opinion.) Most people can't write good jokes and certainly even less can get up and perform them. That's one of the cool things about being able to write jokes—knowing that most people can't do it. Now, as a stand-up I've been lucky to perform on national television several times. I've also attended fancy dinners—no sneakers, dark socks—with my wife, who is a clinical nurse specialist in the pediatric cardiac intensive care unit of one of the most important hospitals in the world. I'm a little uncomfortable at these functions because I don't feel I have a lot in common with nurses and doctors who work on baby's hearts. I certainly can't comment on cardiac stuff. (Of course, I agree that when the heart stops, that's not good.) But the funny thing is, these dedicated and brilliant doctors and nurses pretty much say the same thing to me: "I could never do what you do. I could never get up and tell jokes." It either awes them or outright scares them, the thought of trying to be funny in front of a crowd of strangers. They're opening up a two-week-old chest to repair a hole in the heart, but telling jokes on national TV scares them. That's what I love about being a comedy writer.

Do you have any advice for up-and-coming comedy writers?

Advice for comedy writers . . . this is kind of tricky. Be funny. Be original. Study the old comics and writers, and learn the rules so you can use them or break them to your benefit. Go out on a limb as often as possible. Be honest with yourself. If you think it might be a hack joke, chances are it's a hack joke. Challenge yourself. And remember the words of the great Lenny Bruce, comedy is tragedy and a nice clock. Something like that.

Brainstorm

Check out some of your favorite comedians' websites and see how they connect to their audience. Do they have blogs? Videos? Are there places for fans to connect? Are they selling products? Do they offer free MP3 downloads of their appearances? Also, does the look of their site fit their personality?

Once you've seen how the pros do it, come up with a plan for a site that will work for you at your level. Remember keep it simple but current. It should reflect your style, look, and personality.

Notebook

Look at YouTube for videos you like and for channels you feel have consistently good material. Remember, it's a good idea to set your standards before you start. Look at the material you've written so far in your notebook and pick out ideas that might work online, either as a YouTube video or for your personal website. If you don't have fancy equipment, work within your limitations and save your epic film ideas for later. The important thing is to get started. Before you upload your videos for the world to see, let friends check them out to give you some feedback. The biggest mistake people make with their videos is keeping them too long. If they're short, simple, and funny, you should be all set.

CHAPTER 20

The Scouts Were Right— Be Prepared!

If you are really committed to making comedy writing your career, there are things you can do that will help you be prepared when your big break comes. Having a clear vision of what you want will help you make decisions that will shape your career—and your life.

Improve Yourself

If Steve Martin offers advice, take it. One of our greatest comedy minds, in seven words, sums up the key to success as a comedian: "Be so good they can't ignore you."

A lot of people disregard that simple advice. They get to a point where they think they have great material and they deserve their big break. It can be very frustrating if you're writing great stuff and getting really good responses, but no one in the industry seems to notice.

Many comedians at this point in their careers start to get bitter. They compare themselves to other performers or writers at their level. They start thinking to themselves (or worse, out loud to others), "I'm as good as she is, so how did she get that job and I didn't?" or "I'm better than her, why is she getting her own TV special?"

This kind of thinking can be very harmful and self-defeating. Instead of focusing on getting better, writing better, and improving your performance, you focus on the negative. If you focus on the negative, guess what? You're going to get stuck in a rut. You're going to get bitter, not better. You won't come up with the ideas and jokes that might advance your career, and the jokes you do have will get stale and hold you back.

The solution is to improve yourself. Never take for granted the fact that you're funny. You can always get better. If you see someone advance ahead of you, learn from it. What was she doing that got her ahead? If it's something you don't approve of, realize she took a different path to success and you'll take a better path. If you see that same comedian doing something you do like, don't copy it, but learn from it and use it to get better. Maybe the material she chose for an audition was better than the choice you made. Look at the structure of her act and see how she started and ended. Maybe you can make some simple adjustments in your set order and it will be better next time. Learn from the people you like and learn even more from the people you don't.

The Back of the Room

Be careful who your professional friends are. The back of the room is where all the comedians hang out. There tend to be two groups: the positive and the negative. The negative will make snarky comments about comedians on stage. Sometimes these comments are deserved, but in most cases they come from bitterness or jealousy. This group tends to see someone else's success and attack it, especially if the comedian on stage is doing something different. And you can be sure that when you're on stage, they are probably talking trash about you as well.

The positive group is always moving forward. They support you and offer suggestions about how you can improve your act. Their attitude is, "This a great job, and it can only get better!" This group is constantly striving to make themselves and others around them better.

If you're not a stand-up, you'll find the same personality types in writers' support groups and classes. It's your choice who you want to hang with; you just need to decide who you want to become. You can move forward or get stuck where you are. You can surround yourself with negative or positive influences; it's up to you.

Create a Body of Work

Suppose that you made a hilarious video, uploaded it to YouTube, and watched it become a hit. It gets more than a million views within the first two weeks, and people are raving about it on the Internet and at the water cooler. Now suppose that industry insiders take notice and contact you to see what else you have to offer.

FACT

In 1982, Steven Wright was discovered at a small Boston comedy club called the Ding Ho, and appeared on the *Tonight Show with Johnny Carson.* He received such an amazing response that he was asked to make another appearance just a week later, which was unheard of. If he'd only had one good set in him, he wouldn't have the career that he's had. But he had lots of jokes prepared that were just as good as the first set—if not better. He also had a notebook full of ideas for future jokes.

What position do you want to be in when you get that call? What if they ask to see what else you have or ask about your ideas for future projects?

"Uh, that's all I have right now, but I'm sure I'll come up with some more great stuff" is not going to cut it. You'll be seen as a one-shot wonder. You got lucky. You had one great idea, but that's it. They will pass you over and look for the next phenom. You will have blown a great opportunity by being unprepared.

Now suppose your answer is "I'm glad you like it. I have five more videos that I haven't posted yet, but I can send them to you. I also have a script for a sitcom that I'm developing." Now you sound like someone with potential, an undiscovered new talent with a clear vision.

Don't go for your shot too soon. Before you post that great video, wait until you have a few more to back it up. Before you try to get an audition for a stand-up television spot, make sure you have a lot more material than your great six-minute audition set. You might get the show, but you'll have nothing to back it up.

Before you say "Hey world, here I am!" you want to make sure that you are ready to have the world take more than a passing glance. You can be great, but that doesn't matter unless you're prepared.

Present Yourself in a Professional Manner

If you're getting to the point where people seek you out and ask for demo tapes, press releases, and writing samples, it's time for you to start looking like a pro in the following areas.

Your Press Kit

What is a press kit? It is a package of information about yourself. It might include a photo, press clippings and reviews, a list of clubs you have worked, TV appearances, and a bio. You can use it to send to club owners and entertainment journalists to promote club appearances. It should look nice and professional. Don't make it wacky. Avoid padding it with fake quotes like "Jeff is the funniest comedian I have ever seen!"—Jeff's mom. If you don't have a lot of experience yet, just put what you have and add to it as things come along. Don't make up fake quotes or fake credits—they will come back to haunt you.

A Demo Tape

You need two types of demo tapes, one for clubs and one for auditions. A tape for clubs just needs to show you doing well. You don't have to show a complete set, just a montage of quick lines and audience response.

If you really want a professional tape, invest in a wireless microphone system that plugs into your camcorder. Sound is usually the biggest problem you will face when making a demo tape. A wireless mic system allows you to record you and the audience separately and at different levels so that you get the best of each. Viewers watching your tape can hear you and the response perfectly.

For an audition, you need a complete set from beginning to end. You need to show consistency, not just a bunch of high spots from multiple shows. Producers want to see your start, your middle, and your closer. Tape yourself as often as you can; you never know when that perfect set might occur.

Your Website

You can use your website as a press kit that anyone can access 24/7. You can also use it to show off demo tapes of performances, link to your YouTube videos, and promote your upcoming appearances. You can also use it to promote yourself further by linking it to and from your Facebook and MySpace pages.

By cultivating your public image, you make yourself a professional, someone with whom people will want to do business. Keep your resources simple. Provide valuable information and make it easy to use, and you will look like the pro you want to be.

Know What You Want

Everyone needs to have goals, but many people's goals are short-sighted. The goal of many stand-up comedians is to appear on a late-night talk show; *The Tonight Show with Conan O'Brien, The Late Show with David Letterman, Late Night with Jimmy Fallon,* or *Jimmy Kimmel Live.* Their only focus is to get that six-minute spot on TV, and all their efforts go into that goal.

It's not a bad goal to have. An appearance like that can make a big difference in a comedian's career. But what's next? Now that you got what you want, where do you go next? What's your next goal?

You need to know why you want that spot. Is it just an ego thing? Is it just to say you were on the *Tonight Show?* For a lot of people it is just that. But that spot on TV, no matter how gratifying it is personally, is nothing if you don't know what you want next.

E-QUESTION

Do I have to be in Los Angeles or New York to have a comedy writing career?
It makes things easier, but the world is changing and technology is making it a smaller place. Because of this, you can be pretty much anywhere and still be a success. Sometimes being outside the system can actually be an asset.

You can waste a lot of time taking different paths that don't take you where you want to go. If you don't know what you want, you might end up where someone else sends you.

You might want to be a superstar with all the trimmings—lots of money, a bunch of houses, and international recognition. But on the other hand, you might want a simple life in the suburbs with a nice house, a family, and a dog. You may just want to make a living as a good comedy writer. If ultimately you don't want to live in Los Angeles or New York, why pursue jobs that will force you to live there?

If you want to travel and see the world, then you might want to hit the road and work wherever you can. If you ultimately want to become a movie star, then take acting lessons, write your own plays, and get some experience. If you want to be a stand-up comedian but are having trouble making a living as one, get a day job that you like but doesn't demand all your time. That way, you can pick and choose where and when you want to work. If you're tired of doing stand-up, figure out what you want to do next and start doing it.

If you know where you want to end up, you can look at every decision you make and weigh every offer you get with a clear goal in mind. A lot of people make it big and have a horrible life. But even more people make it on a smaller scale and have the life they want. Always look at the big picture, know your goals, and don't get distracted by things that will keep you from what you want.

Be Master of Your Domain

Comedians tend to take what they are offered. A club owner will say, "I'll give you $100 to middle for me next weekend." And most comedians will simply accept. Most areas of show business don't work this way. You need to set your price, and stick to it.

That's in a perfect world, of course. The fact is that there are other comedians that will happily take that spot if you turn it down.

When you write something great, get excited about it! Make sure that your excitement and commitment shows in your work. And when you get the chance to pitch your work, be confident in your ideas and sell it. Many comedians give very flat readings when they are pitching a script.

So what's the answer? How do you change things? You must be in control of your own career and not at the mercy of someone else. That doesn't mean that you should turn down the gig. Take it, but realize you are getting more from the experience of the stage time than the club owner knows. He thinks he's using you, but in reality you are using him—and getting paid to do so. As you develop a following and recognize that people are coming to see you, that's when you can start negotiating your price for future shows.

Profile in Comedy: Lizz Winstead

As a co-creator and former head writer of Comedy Central's *The Daily Show* and co-founder of Air America Radio, Lizz Winstead has emerged as a critically acclaimed political writer and producer. As a performer, Winstead brought her political wit to *The Daily Show* as a correspondent and later to the radio waves co-hosting *Unfiltered,* Air America Radio's mid-morning show with citizen of the world and hip hop legend Chuck D and political big brain Rachel Maddow.

Lizz's comedic talents have been recognized in *Entertainment Weekly*'s 100 Most Creative People issue and she was nominated Best Female Club Performer by The American Comedy Awards. She has appeared in HBO's *Women of the Night, The U.S. Comedy Arts Festival in Aspen, Comedy Central Presents,* and too many basic cable stand-up shows and VH-1 *50 Greatest This* and *100 Greatest That* lists to count.

Lizz is currently writing, producing, and starring in *Wake Up World,* a live theater and web show in New York that satirizes all of our beloved morning shows. For details go to *www.shootthemessengernyc.com.* To keep up to date with what's on her mind, you can read her essays at *www.plentymag.com, www.huffingtonpost.com,* and *www.myspace.com/lizzwinstead.*

When did you first realize that you were uniquely funny?

I think it was seventh grade in Catholic school, when they redid the uniform policy. Boys no longer had to wear them yet girls still had to don the hideous wool grey plaid jumper. I decided to respond by shredding it like a hula skirt. It was not received well.

Who do you think were your influences?

The Church and anyone who said no to me. As far as actual comics, Carlin, Nichols and May, *Laugh-In.*

Do you remember your first original joke?

Ugh. I think it was "They make a product called Correctol, the women's gentle laxative. As opposed to the less popular Ravage, the women's not-so-gentle laxative."

When did you realize that comedy was something you had to do for a living?

I have no other skills, so very early on.

What was your first job in comedy writing or performance?

My first comedy writing job was on a Comedy Central show called *Women Aloud*, hosted by Mo Gaffney. First performance was at Dudley Riggs Brave New Workshop in Minneapolis. December 18, 1983. Twenty-five years ago!

As a woman, was it difficult when you got started? Are things easier now for up-and-coming women comics?

I had a hard time because comedy was hard; I didn't do a lot of women-centric material so I was making both genders laugh.

Politically speaking, what is the responsibility of the comedian?

It's always the responsibility of the comedian to make people laugh. My own criteria for myself is to always target those who have power and use it unwisely or abuse it.

What are the differences between writing for yourself and writing for others?

Writing for yourself, you get to craft your own voice and opinions. Writing for others requires listening and learning the voice and the ideals of that person, helping them develop their best voice.

What do you find exciting about comedy right now?

The Internet, because it opens up the creative field in a whole new way.

Where do you think the future of comedy is headed?

The Internet. It is no longer the networks' game; it is the creatives' game, and if you utilize that box called the computer you can create your own destiny.

As audiences are becoming more specific and more segmented, is that making your job easier or more difficult?
It requires you to devote more time to finding like-minded audience members and through social networking you can do that. But a comic now is not only a performer but a publicist and a producer. It is not for the lazy!

What is the best thing about being a comedy writer?
Having your thoughts and ideas heard and validated through laughter.

Do you have any advice for up-and-coming comedy writers?
Write what you love and believe in. Never present something you haven't thought through. It's the only control you have in this business.

Final Thought

It is easier to make your own opportunities today than at any other time. Because of the Internet, you're only required to be good. It's easier to get your work seen. You can put comedy out there every day if you want, and you can write what you want. If you have an idea for a short film, make it. If you have a comment about something topical, put it on your blog. If you write a great short story, post it on your site. You can just do it cheaply and efficiently, because of technology.

You don't have to worry about opportunities passing you by; you make them for yourself. If you can't get stage time, start your own venue. If you can't get published, publish yourself and sell your own work at *www .amazon.com* or *www.lulu.com*. While you're waiting to be discovered, make yourself better by discovering your own challenges. Trust in what you do, love what you do, and respect yourself and your talent.

Oh, and one more thing—don't forget to have fun.

APPENDIX A

Preparation "H:" Being Prepared for Hecklers

If you're going to be a working comic, there is one thing you're not going to like but have to expect no matter how good you are—hecklers.

Hecklers can be a problem, but they're usually a bit more subtle than those you've seen on TV or in movies. You've seen the scene where the comedian is tortured by an obnoxious heckler, but it's different in real life. It's still annoying, but it's definitely something you can deal with if you prepare properly.

The key to handling most hecklers is not to take their behavior personally. You need to separate yourself from the problem in order to deal with it. If you do take it personally, you'll just make the problem worse. That detachment might be hard to achieve, but it is essential if you want to deal with and recover from the problem.

There are three basic kinds of hecklers, with a million variations in between. First you have the guy who thinks that he's helping you out. He thinks it's part of the show. He's probably seen hecklers portrayed on TV and believes it's something he's supposed to do. He thinks he's helping, but deep down he just wants attention—at your expense.

Next there's the most common type of heckler—the heckler who feels that the middle of a nightclub is the perfect place to have a conversation. A small pocket of the audience talking loudly while you're trying to perform is probably the number one problem comedians have. These types of hecklers aren't necessarily being malicious—they are just ignorant. They aren't aware they're causing a problem.

The third type of heckler, and the most difficult to deal with, is the drunk. This heckler has had too much to drink and you become the focus of his inebriation. Here are six possible solutions that you can use to help you deal with most forms of hecklers:

1. **Ignore the problem.** You can do this and just hope the problem goes away, but know that it probably won't. Remember that the audience is expecting you to deal with it. If you want to be the person in charge on stage, you need to take charge.
2. **Let the audience help you. Chances are, they will be on your side if someone disrupts the show.** Let them do the work for you. Encourage this by directing your responses to them, not the heckler. If you look at the heckler and deliver a clever put-down line, you might get a big laugh, but it might complicate the problem. By looking at the heckler, you are directly challenging him to a battle of wits. You're focusing your attention on one person, and leaving out the rest of the audience. Things will just escalate and it

will make the audience uncomfortable. You run the risk of not only losing the battle of wits, but the audience as well. Try this approach instead: Look at the heckler, then at the audience, and say something funny about the heckler to the audience. You do two things here. You make the heckler look foolish without challenging him directly, and you start to build an alliance with the audience against the heckler. You set it up as us against him, and the audience is on your side no matter what happens.

3. **Use the problem as an opportunity to advance your character.** A lot of comedians will break character or resort to a stock heckler response. If you do this, you are wasting a valuable opportunity to advance your persona. Use can turn this minus into a plus by showing the audience how you (your character) would deal with the problem. This will come off as an honest response and will give the audience a deeper glimpse into your personality. It will in a sense "prove" to your audience that you are who you say you are onstage. If your performing style is quiet, naïve and low key, and you respond the same way, your response will be "real." If you respond harshly, the illusion you created with your character will be shattered.

4. **Don't respond at all if you're not completely sure what the heckler said.** Suppose you are doing a show and someone yells out from the back of the room. It you don't hear it but snap back at the person because you assume it was something negative, you might be making a big mistake. What if a fan yelled out his love for you? The crowd will turn on you—and fast.

5. **Pick your battles.** A lot of the time, the audience doesn't notice there's a problem until you draw attention to it. If a small group is talking, for example, see if it works itself out before you say something about it, and only say something if you get the sense that the audience is distracted as well.

6. **If the heckler says something that was funny, acknowledge it!** It makes him a hero and makes you look like a nice guy (a comic with a sense of humor). By giving the heckler some positive attention, you might just turn a potential enemy into a valuable ally.

When you're learning to deal with problems on stage, whether it be hecklers, drunks, or noisy crowds, you mainly have to deal with it after the show. The ride home is a great opportunity to review the situation and think about how you could have handled it differently. The next time you'll be better prepared, and remember—there will always be a next time.

APPENDIX B

Comedy Clubs in the United States

Alabama

The Comedy Club at the Stardome
1818 Data Drive
Birmingham, Alabama 35244
205-444-0008
www.stardome.com

Arizona

The Comedy Spot
7117 East 3rd Ave.
Scottsdale, AZ 85251
480-945-4422
www.thecomedyspot.net

The Improv
930 E. University Drive
Tempe, AZ 85281
480-921-9877
www.symfonee.com/improv/tempe

Laff's Comedy Club
2900 E. Broadway Blvd.
Tucson, AZ 85716
520-323-8669
www.laffstucson.com

Arkansas

The Loony Bin Comedy Club
10301 North Rodney Parham Road
Little Rock, AR 72227
501-228-5555
www.loonybincomedy.com

Funnybone Comedy Club
107 E Markham St.
Little Rock, AR 72201
501-801-8881

California

The Comedy & Magic Club
1018 Hermosa Ave.
Hermosa Beach, CA 90254
310-372-1193
www.comedyandmagicclub.com

Ice House Comedy Club
24 Mentor Ave.
Pasadena, CA 91106
626-577-1894
www.icehousecomedy.com

J R's Comedy Club
27630 The Old Road
Valencia, CA 91355
661-259-2291
www.comedyinvalencia.com

Improv Comedy Club
71 Fortune Dr.
Irvine, CA 92618
949-854-5455
www.improv2.com

Cobb's Comedy Club
915 Columbus Ave.
San Francisco, CA 94133
415-928-4320
www.cobbscomedyclub.com

Fubar's Comedy Club
1150 Arnold Dr.
Martinez, CA 94553
925-295-2150

Improv Comedy Club
4555 Mills Cir.
Ontario, CA 91764
909- 484-5411
www.improv2.com

Improv Comedy Club
71 Fortune Dr.
Irvine, CA 92618
949-854-5455
www.improv2.com

Improv Comedy Club
62 S. 2nd St.
San Jose, CA 95113
408-280-7475
www.improv2.com

Punchline Comedy Club
444 Battery St.
San Francisco, CA 94111
415-397-7573
www.punchlinecomedyclub.com

**National Comedy Theatre
—Comedy Sportz**
733 Seward St.
Los Angeles, CA 90038
323-871-1193
www.comedysportzla.com

Laugh Factory
8001 W. Sunset Blvd.
West Hollywood, CA 90046
323-656-1336
www.laughfactory.com

Hollywood Improv
8162 Melrose Ave.

Los Angeles, CA 90046
323-651-2583
www.improv2.com

The Groundlings Theater
7307 Melrose Ave.
Los Angeles, CA 90046
323-934-4747
www.groundlings.com

Comedy Store
8433 Sunset Blvd.
Los Angeles, CA 90069
323-650-6268
www.thecomedystore.com

**Pepper Belly's Comedy
& Variety Theater**
849 Texas Street
Fairfield, CA 94533
707-422-7469
www.pepperbellys.com

The Comedy Union
5040 W. Pico Blvd.
Los Angeles, CA 90019
323-934-9300
www.thecomedyunion.com

Rooster T. Feathers Comedy Club
157 W. El Camino Real
Sunnyvale, CA 94087
408-736-0921
www.roostertfeathers.com

Colorado
Wits End Comedy Club
6080 92nd. Ave.

Westminster, CO 80031
303-430-4242
www.witsendcomedyclub.com

Improv Comedy Club & Dinner
8246 E 49th Ave.
Denver, CO 80238
303- 307-1777
www.improv2.com

Loonees Comedy Corner
1305 N. Academy Blvd.
Colorado Springs, CO 80909
719-591-0707
www.loonees.com

Comedy Works (Denver)
1226 15th St.
Denver, CO 80202
303 595-3637
www.comedyworks.com

Connecticut

The Hartford Funny Bone Comedy Club
194 Buckland Hills Dr.
Manchester, CT 06042
860-432-8600
www.hartfordfunnybone.com

District of Columbia

DC Improv
1140 Connecticut Ave. NW
Washington, DC 20036
202-296-7008
www.dcimprov.com

Florida

Bonkerz Comedy Club
2524 Roxbury Rd.
Winter Park, FL 32789
407-629-2665
www.bonkerzcomedy.com

Coconuts Comedy Club
105 N. Bayshore Dr.
Safety Harbor, FL 34695
727-797-5653
www.coconutscomedyclubs.com

Atlantic Theatre's Comedy Club
751 Atlantic Blvd.
Atlantic Beach, FL 32233
904-249-7529

Jokeboy's Club of Comedy
18 SW Broadway St.
Ocala, FL 34471
352-368-5653
www.jokeboys.com

Laugh In Comedy Cafe
8595 College Pkwy. # B6
Fort Myers, FL 33919
239-479-5233
www.laughincomedycafe.com

Coconuts Comedy Club
3311 US Highway 98 N
Lakeland, FL 33805
863-688-7972
www.coconutscomedyclubs.com

Improv Comedy Club
3390 Mary St. # 182
Coconut Grove, FL 33133

305-441-8200
www.miamiimprov.com

Side Splitters Comedy Club
12938 N. Dale Mabry Hwy.
Tampa, FL 33618
813-960-1197
www.sidesplitterscomedy.com

Tallahassee Comedy Zone
401 E. Tennessee St.
Tallahassee, FL 32301
850-575-4242
www.comedyzonetally.com

Sak Comedy Lab
380 W. Amelia St.
Orlando, FL 32801
407-648-0001
www.sak.com

Improv Comedy Club
550 S Rosemary Ave # 250
West Palm Beach, FL 33401
561-833-1812
www.palmbeachimprov.com

Comedy Zone
3130 Hartley Rd.
Jacksonville, FL 32257
904-292-4242
www.comedyzone.com

Coconut's Comedy Club
6000 Gulf Blvd.
St Pete Beach, FL 33706
727-360-5653
www.coconutscomedyclubs.com

Comedy Zone Cafe
7305 Wild Oak Ln.
Land O' Lakes, FL 34637
727-239-7100

The Tampa Improv Comedy Club
1600 E. 8th Ave.
Tampa, FL 33605
813-864-4000
www.improvtampa.com

Jackie Gleason Comedy Club
4270 Aloma Ave.
Winter Park, FL 32792
407-671-5653

Improv Comedy Club
5700 Seminole Way
Hollywood, FL 33314
954-981-5653
www.improvftl.com

The Gypsy Comedy Club
828 Anastasia Blvd.
St Augustine, FL 32080
904-461-8843
www.thegypsycomedyclub.com

Bonkerz Comedy Club
2500 N. Atlantic Ave.
Daytona Beach, FL 32118
386- 672-0990
www.bonkerzcomedy.com

Off the Hook Comedy Club
599 S Collier Blvd # 218
Marco Island, FL 34145
239-389-6900
www.captbriens.com

Groucho's Comedy Club
785 S Babcock St.
Melbourne, FL 32901
321-724-1220
www.grouchoscomedy.com

Mc Curdy's Comedy Theatre
3333 N. Tamiami Trail
Sarasota, FL 34234
941-925-3869
www.mccurdyscomedy.com

Visani Theater
2400 Kings Hwy.
Port Charlotte, FL 33980
941-629-9191
www.visani.net

Georgia

Comedy Club
4570 Pio Nono Ave.
Macon, GA 31206
478-785-3155
www.maconlaughs.com

Uptown Comedy Corner
800 Marietta St. NW
Atlanta, GA 30318
404-881-0200
www.uptowncomedy.net

Hawaii

Sharkey's Comedy Club
99-016 Kamehameha Hwy.
Aiea, HI 96701

808-531-4242
www.sharkeyscomedyclub.com

Illinois

Jukebox Comedy Club
3527 W. Farmington Rd.
Peoria, IL 61604
309-673-5853
www.jukeboxcomedy.com

**Mason City Limits Comedy
& Variety Club**
114 E. Chestnut St.
Mason City, IL 62664
217-482-5233
www.mclimits.com

Zanies Comedy Clubs
1548 N. Wells St.
Chicago, IL 60610
312-337-4027
www.zanies.com

Zanies Comedy Night Club
4051 E. Main St.
St. Charles, IL 60174
630-584-6342
www.zanies.com

Zanies Comedy Night Club
230 Hawthorn Village Commons
Vernon Hills, IL 60061
847-549-6030
www.zanies.com

Funny Bone Comedy Club
1407 N. Veterans Pkwy.
Bloomington, IL 61704

309-664-5653
www.funnybonebloomington.com

Second City
1616 N. Wells St.
Chicago, IL 60614
312-337-3992
www.secondcity.com

Lenny's Comedy Cafe
2466 Washington Rd.
Washington, IL 61571
309-282-4646

Improv Comedy Club
5 Woodfield Mall
Schaumburg, IL 60173
847-240-2001
www.improv.com

Improv Olympics
3541 N. Clark St.
Chicago, IL 60657
773-880-0199
www.ioimprov.com

George's Treehouse
2060 Ireland Grove Rd.
Bloomington, IL 61704
309-662-5231

Comedy Shrine
22 E. Chicago Ave. # 205
Naperville, IL 60540
630-355-2844
www.comedyshrine.com

Juz Jokkin' Comedy Club
115 N. Genesee St.
Waukegan, IL 60085

847-406-3114
www.waukegancomedy.com

Chemically Imbalanced Comedy
1420 W. Irving Park Rd.
Chicago, IL 60613
773-865-7731
www.cicomedy.com

Funny Bone
2937 W. White Oaks Dr.
Springfield, IL 62704
217-391-5653
www.funnybonecomedyclub.com

Barrel of Laughs Comedy
10345 S. Central Ave.
Oak Lawn, IL 60453
708-499-2969
www.seneseswinery.com

Chicago Comedy Company
601 N. Martingale Rd.
Schaumburg, IL 60173
847-240-0380
www.chicagocomedy.com

Jokes & Notes
4641 S. King Dr.
Chicago, IL 60653
773-373-3390
www.jokesandnotes.com

Annoyance Theatre & Bar
4830 N. Broadway
Chicago, IL 60640
773-561-4665
www.theannoyance.com

Indiana

Crackers Comedy Club
6281 N. College Ave., # 1
Indianapolis, IN 46220
317-255-4211
www.crackerscomedy.com

Crackers Comedy Club
247 S. Meridian St., #2
Indianapolis, IN 46225
317-631-3536
www.crackerscomedy.com

Morty's Comedy Joint
3625 E. 96th St.
Indianapolis, IN 46240
317-848-5500
www.mortyscomedy.com

ComedySportz Indianapolis
721 Massachusetts Ave.
Indianapolis, IN 46204
317-951-8499
www.indycomedysportz.com

Snickerz Comedy Bar
5535 Saint Joe Rd.
Fort Wayne, IN 46835
260-486-0216
www.snickerzcomedyclub.biz

Iowa

Joker's Night Club & Comedy
401 Main St.
Cedar Falls, IA 50613
319-266-1132
www.barmuda.com

Penguin's Comedy Club
525 33rd Ave.
Cedar Rapids, IA 52404
319-362-8133
www.penguinscomedyclub.com

Penguin's Comedy Club & Sports
1850 Isle Pkwy. # 105
Bettendorf, IA 52722
563-324-5233
www.penguinscomedyclub.com

Funny Bone Entertainment
560 S. Prairie View Dr.
West Des Moines, IA 50266
515-270-2100
www.funnybonedm.com

Funny Barn Comedy Club
1609 Hill Ave.
Spirit Lake, IA 51360
712-336-4888
www.funnybarn.com

Bonkerz Comedy Club
1855 Greyhound Park Dr.
Dubuque, IA 52001
800-373-3647
www.bonkerzcomedy.com

Funny Bone Comedy Club
8529 Hickman Rd.
Urbandale, IA 50322
515-270-9602

Kansas

Loony Bin Comedy Club
6140 E. 21st St N., #200

Wichita, KS 67208
316-618-4242
www.loonybincomedy.com

Famous Johnny's Comedy Club
10635 Floyd St.
Overland Park, KS 66212
913-648-5233
www.famousjohnnys.com

Stanford & Son's Comedy Club
1867 Village West Pkwy., Suite D-201
Kansas City, KS 66111
913-400-7500
www.stanfordscomedyclub.com

Funny Farm Comedy Club, Llc.
9601B Metcalf Ave.
Overland Park, KS 66212-2218
913-383-3276

Kentucky

Comedy Off Broadway
161 Lexington Green Cir.
Lexington, KY 40503
859-271-5653
www.comedyoffbroadway.com

Louisiana

Funny Bone Comedy Club
4715 Bennington Ave.
Baton Rouge, LA 70808
225-928-9996
www.funnybonebatonrouge.com

La Nuit Comedy Theater
5039 Freret St.

New Orleans, LA 70115
504-899-0336
www.nolacomedy.com

The National Comedy Company
727 St. Peter
New Orleans, LA 70118
504-523-7469
www.nationalcomedycompany.com

Funny Bone Comedy Club
Louisiana Boardwalk
130 Plaza Loop, Bossier City, LA 71111
318-549-0829
www.funnybonelouisiana.com

Maine

Comedy Connection
16 Custom House Wharf
Portland, ME 04101
207-774-5554
www.mainecomedy.com

Maryland

Baltimore Comedy Factory
32 Light St.
Baltimore, MD 21202
410-547-7798
www.baltimorecomedy.com

Bethesda Comedy Club
4735 Bethesda Ave.
Bethesda, MD 20814
301-358-5237
www.bethesdacomedy.com

Standup Comedy To Go
4608 North Park Ave.
Chevy Chase, MD 20815-4501
301-933-5648
www.standupcomedytogo.com

Magooby's Joke House
9306 Harford Rd.
Baltimore, MD 21234
410-356-1010
www.magoobys.com

Jokes On Us Comedy Club
312 Main St.
Laurel, MD 20707
240-568-5081

Headliners Comedy Club
2329 Reedie Dr.
Silver Spring, MD 20902
301-622-5494

Rascals Comedy Club
34 Market Place
Baltimore, MD 21202
410-545-0590

Massachusetts

The Comedy Studio
1238 Massachusetts Ave.
Cambridge, MA 02138
617-661-6507
www.thecomedystudio.com

Nick's Comedy Stop
100 Warrenton St
Boston, MA 02116

617-482-0930
www.nickscomedystop.com

Dick's Beantown Comedy Vault
124 Boylston St.
Boston, MA 02116
800-401-2221
www.dickdoherty.com

Improv Asylum
216 Hanover St.
Boston, MA 02113
617-263-6887
www.improvasylum.com

Improv Boston Theatre
40 Prospect St.
Cambridge, MA 02139
617-576-1253
www.improvboston.com

The Comedy Lounge
287 Iyannough Rd.
Hyannis, MA 02601
508-771-1700
www.comedylounge.com

Giggles Comedy Club
517 Broadway
Saugus, MA 01906
781-233-9950
www.gigglescomedy.com

Comedy Connection
245 Faneuil Hall Market Pl. # 2
Boston, MA 02109
617-248-9700

Michigan

Dr. Grins Comedy Club
20 Monroe Ave. NW
Grand Rapids, MI 49503
616-356-2000
www.thebob.com

Connxtions Comedy Club
2900 N. East St.
Lansing, MI 48906
517-374-4242
www.connxtionscomedyclub.com

Laughing Post Comedy Club
241 E Kalamazoo Ave.
Kalamazoo, MI 49007
269-342-7100
www.thelaughingpost.com

Joey's Comedy Club
36071 Plymouth Rd.
Livonia, MI 48150
734-261-5500
www.kickerscomplex.com

Ann Arbor Comedy Showcase
314 E Liberty St.
Ann Arbor, MI 48104
734-996-9080
www.aacomedy.com

Mark Ridley's Comedy Castle
269 E. 4th St.
Royal Oak, MI 48067
248-542-9900
www.comedycastle.com

All Star Comedy Club
4200 Allen Rd.

Allen Park, MI 48101
313-388-6020

Wise Guys Comedy Club
40380 Grand River Ave.
Novi, MI 48375
248-919-6640

Comedy Den
2845 Thornhills Ave. SE
Grand Rapids, MI 49546
616-949-9322

Chaplin's Comedy Club & Restaurant
34244 Groesbeck Hwy.
Clinton Township, MI 48035
586-792-1902
www.chaplinscomedyclub.com

Gary Fields' Comedy Club Theater
51 W. Michigan Ave.
Battle Creek, MI 49017
269-965-4646
www.garyfieldscomedyclub.com

Jackson Comedy Club
212 N Jackson St.
Jackson, MI 49201
517-789-6800

Bea's Comedy Kitchen
541 East Larned St.
Detroit, MI 48226
313-961-2581

Minnesota

Acme Comedy/Sticks
708 N. 1st St.
Minneapolis, MN 55401

612-338-6393
www.acmecomedycompany.com

Courtney's Comedy Club
600 30th Ave. S.
Moorhead, MN 56560
218-287-7100
www.courtneyscomedyclub.biz

Joke Joint Comedy Club
2300 East American Blvd.
Bloomington, MN 55425
612-327-0185
www.jokejointcomedyclub.com

The Comedy Gallery
2201 Burns Ave.
St Paul, MN 55119
612-961-4242
www.thisplaceisajoke.com

Minnesota Comedy Club
4703 Highway 10
Arden Hills, MN 55112
612-961-4242
www.minnesotacomedyclub.com

Goonie's Comedy Club
7 2nd St. SW
Rochester, MN 55902
507-288-8130
www.gooniescomedy.com

Comedysportz
3001 Hennepin Ave. S.
Minneapolis, MN 55408
612-870-1230
www.comedysportztc.com

Knuckleheads Comedy Club
406 E. Broadway
Minneapolis, MN 55425
952-854-5233

Renegade Comedy Theatre
222 E. Superior St.
Duluth, MN 55802
218-336-1414
www.renegadecomedytheatre.com

Missouri

Deja Vu Comedy Club
405 Cherry St.
Columbia, MO 65201
573-443-3216
www.dejavucomedy.com

Funny Bone Comedy Club
614 Westport Plaza
St. Louis, MO 63146
314-469-6692
www.funnyboneusa.com

Comedy Forum
4141 N. Cloverleaf Dr.
St Peters, MO 63376
636-498-1234
www.comedyforum.com

**Stanford and Sons Restaurant
and Comedy Club**
504 Westport Rd.
Kansas City, MO 64111
816-561-7454
www.standfordscomedyclub.com

Comedy City
817 Westport Rd.
Kansas City, MO 64111
816-842-2744
www.instantcomedy.com

Montana

Trails Inn Bar & Comedy Club
607 Main St.
Miles City, MT 59301
406-234-2922
www.trailsinn.com

Nebraska

Funny Bone Comedy Club
17305 Davenport St. # 201
Omaha, NE 68118
402-493-8036
www.funnyboneomaha.com

Joker's Comedy Club
1314 Jones St.
Omaha, NE 68102
402-345-4584
www.standupshop.com

Zimmy's Comedy Club
2801 N 27th St.
Lincoln, NE 68521
402-466-0068

Nevada

LA Comedy Club
Trader Vics @ Planet Hollywood
3663 Las Vegas Blvd. S.

Las Vegas, NV 89109
702-275-3877
www.lacomedyclub.com

Funny Bone Comedy Club
345 N Arlington Ave.
Reno, NV 89501
866-409-3093
www.funnybonereno.com

Catch A Rising Star Comedy Club, Reno
407 N. Virginia St.
Reno, NV 89504
775-329-4777
www.catcharisingstar.com

Comedy Zone
1 Main St.
Las Vegas, NV 89101
702-386-2444

Comedy Stop at the Tropicana
3801 Las Vegas Blvd. S.
Las Vegas, NV 89109
800-829-9034
www.tropicanalv.com

New Jersey

Stress Factory Comedy Club
90 Church St.
New Brunswick, NJ 08901
732-545-4242
www.stressfactory.com

Knuckle Heads Comedy Club
17 Washington St.
Toms River, NJ 08753

732-473-9200
www.knuckleheadstomsriver.com

Banana's Comedy Club
283 Route 17 S.
Hasbrouck Heights, NJ 07604
201-727-1090
www.bananascomedyclub.com

Catch A Rising Star
102 Carnegie Ctr.
Princeton, NJ 08540
609-987-8018
www.catcharisingstar.com

Casba Comedy Club
3810 Atlantic Ave.
Wildwood, NJ 08260
609-522-8444
www.casbacomedyclub.com

Uncle Vinnie's Comedy Club
518 Arnold Ave.
Pt. Pleasant Beach, NJ 08742
732-899-3900
www.unclevinniescomedyclub.com

Comedy Cabaret
Route 73 & Baker Blvd.
Marlton, NJ 08053
856-866-5653
www.comedycabaret.com

Pop's Comedy Club
2055 State Route 27
Edison, NJ 08817
732-287-3500

Rascal's Comedy Club
2349 Marlton Pike West

Cherry Hill, NJ 08002
856-662-9200

Rascal's Comedy Club
499 Bloomfield Ave.
Montclair, NJ 07042
973-744-3711

Rascal's Comedy Club
360 Luis Munoz Marin Blvd.
Jersey City, NJ 07302
201-217-8900

New Mexico

The Box Performance Space
1025 Lomas Blvd. NW
Albuquerque, NM 87102
505-404-1578
www.theboxabq.com

New York

Caroline's Comedy Club
1626 Broadway
New York, NY 10019
212-757-4100
www.carolines.com

Laugh Factory @ Times Square
303 West 42nd St.
New York, NY 10036
212-586-7829

Gotham Comedy Club
208 W. 23rd St.
New York, NY 10011
212-367-9000
www.gothamcomedyclub.com

Ha Comedy Club
163 W. 46th St.
New York, NY 10036
212-977-3884
www.hanyc.com

New York Comedy Club
241 E. 24th St.
New York, NY 10010
212-696-5233
www.newyorkcomedyclub.com

Broadway Comedy Club
318 W. 53rd St.
New York, NY 10019
212-757-2323
www.broadwaycomedyclub.com

Comedy Cellar
117 Macdougal St.
New York, NY 10012
212-254-3480
www.comedycellar.com

National Comedy Theatre
347 W. 36th St.
New York, NY 10018
212-629-5202
www.manhattancomedy.com

Comix
353 West 14th St.
New York, NY 10014
212-524-2500
www.comixny.com

Comic Strip Inc
1568 2nd Ave. # 1
New York, NY 10028

212-861-9386
www.comicstriplive.com

Stand-Up New York
236 W. 78th St.
New York, NY 10024
212-595-0850
www.standupny.com

Laugh Lounge NYC
151 Essex St.
New York, NY 10002
212-614-2500
www.laughloungenyc.com

Upright Citizen's Brigade Theatre
307 W. 26th St.
New York, NY 10011
212-366-9176
www.ucbtheatre.com

Dangerfield's
1118 First Ave.
New York, NY 10021
212-593-1650
www.dangerfields.com

People's Improv Theater
154 W. 29th St.
New York, NY 10001
212-563-7488
www.thepit-nyc.com

Uptown Comedy Club
2290 12th Ave.
New York, NY 10027
212-981-1200

Governor's Comedy Cabaret
90 Division Ave. # A

Levittown, NY 11756
516-731-3358
www.govs.com

Pip's Comedy Club
2005 Emmons Ave.
Brooklyn, NY 11235
718-646-9433

North Carolina

Goodnight's Comedy Club
861 W. Morgan St.
Raleigh, NC 27603
919-828-5233
www.charliegoodnights.com

The Idiot Box Improv Comedy Club
348 S. Elm St.
Greensboro, NC 27401
336-274-2699
www.idiotboxers.com

Comedy Worx
431 Peace St.
Raleigh, NC 27603
919-829-0822
www.comedyworx.com

DSI Comedy Theater
200 North Greensboro St.
Carrboro, NC 27510
919-338-8150
www.dsicomedytheater.com

Laugh Out Loud Comedy Club
8928 US 70 Bus Hwy. W.
Clayton, NC 27520

919-359-8565
www.lolcomedyclubclayton.com

Charlotte Comedy Theatre
1308 The Plaza
Charlotte, NC 28205
866-467-7681
www.charlottecomedy.com

Ohio

Funny Bone Comedy Club
145 Easton Town Ctr.
Columbus, OH 43219
614-471-5653
www.columbusfunnybone.com

Dayton Funny Bone
88 Plum St. Suite 200
Dayton, OH 45440
937-429-5233
www.daytonfunnybone.com

Wiley's Comedy Club
101 Pine St.
Dayton, OH 45402
937-224-5653
www.wileyscomedyclub.com

Funny Stop Comedy Club
1767 State Rd.
Cuyahoga Falls, OH 44223
330-923-4700
www.funnystop.com

Go Bananas Comedy Club
8410 Market Place Ln.
Montgomery, OH 45242

513-984-9288
www.gobananascomedy.com

Connxtions Comedy Club
5319 Heatherdowns Blvd.
Toledo, OH 43614
419-867-9041
www.connxtionscomedyclub.com

Bogey's Comedy Club
28060 Chardon Rd.
Willoughby Hills, OH 44092
440-944-9000
www.bogeyscomedyclub.com

Hilarities 4th St. Theatre
2035 E. 4th St.
Cleveland, OH 44115
216-736-4242
www.pickwickandfrolic.com

The Cleveland Improv Comedy Club
2000 Sycamore St.
Cleveland, OH 44113
216-696-4677
www.improvupcoming.com

Funny Farm Comedy Club
5580 Youngstown Warren Rd.
Niles, OH 44446
330-652-4242
www.funnyfarmcomedyclub.com

Mad Hatter's Comedy Theatre
1697 Mentor Ave.
Painesville, OH 44077
440-354-1428

Laff House Comedy Club
24900 Euclid Ave.

Euclid, OH 44117
216-797-4900

Oklahoma

Loony Bin Comedy Club
8503 N. Rockwell Ave.
Oklahoma City, OK 73132
405-239-4242
www.loonybincomedy.com

Bricktown Joker's Comedy Club
229 E Sheridan Ave.
Oklahoma City, OK 73104
405-236-5653

Oregon

**Harvey's Comedy Club
& Restaurant**
436 NW 6th Ave.
Portland, OR 97209
503-241-0338
www.harveyscomedyclub.com

Jester Comedy Club
15450 SW Millikan Way
Beaverton, OR 97006
503-626-6338
www.jestercomedyclub.com

ComedySportz Portland
1963 NW Kearney St.
Portland, OR 97209
503-236-8888
www.portlandcomedy.com

Pennsylvania

Helium Comedy Club
2031 Sansom St.
Philadelphia, PA 19103
215-496-9001
www.heliumcomedy.com

Wise Crackers Comedy Club
15 S. Pennsylvania Ave.
Wilkes Barre, PA 18701
570-788-8451
www.wisecrackers.biz

Improv Comedy Club
166 E. Bridge St.
Homestead, PA 15120
412-462-5233
www.improv.com

JR's Last Laugh Comedy Club
1402 State St.
Erie, PA 16501
814-461-0911
www.jrslastlaugh.com

Improv Comedy: The N Crowd
The Actors Center
257 N. 3rd St.
Philadelphia, PA 19106
610-505-4019
www.phillyncrowd.com

Philly Improv Theater (PHIT)
407 Bainbridge St.
Philadelphia, PA 19147
267-233-1556
www.phillyimprovtheater.com

**Comic Energy Sketch
Comedy Troupe**
216 S. 11th St.
Philadelphia, PA 19107
215-397-3040
www.comicenergy.com

Comedy Works
1320 Newport Rd.
Bristol, PA 19007
215-741-1661
www.thecomedyworks.net

Comedy Cabaret
625 N Main St.
Doylestown, PA 18901
215-345-5653
www.comedycabaret.com

Laff House
221 South St.
Philadelphia, PA 19147
215-440-4242
www.laffhouse.com

Rhode Island

Shorebreak
3 Beach St.
Narragansett, RI 02882
401-783-1022
www.theshorebreak.com

Comedy Connection
39 Warren Ave.
East Providence, RI 02914
401-438-8383
www.ricomedyconnection.com

Catch a Rising Star
Twin River
100 Twin River Rd.
Lincoln, RI 02865
401-723-3200
www.twinriver.com

South Carolina

The Comedy House
2768 Decker Blvd.
Columbia, SC 29206
803-798-9898
www.comedyhouse.com

Hilton Head Comedy Club
430 William Hilton Pkwy.
Hilton Head Island, SC 29928
843-681-7757
www.hiltonheadcomedyclub.com

Comedy Cabana
9588 N. Kings Hwy.
Myrtle Beach, SC 29572
843-449-4242
www.comedycabana.com

Comedy Zone
Broadway At the Beach
Myrtle Beach, SC 29577
843-222-5653

Mac's Comedy Club
507 West Georgia Rd.
Simpsonville, SC 29680
864-967-8384

Tennessee

South Street Comedy Club & Lounge
559 Wiley Parker Rd.
Jackson, TN 38305
731-668-1447
www.baudos.com

The Comedy Barn Theater
2775 Parkway
Pigeon Forge, TN 37863
865-428-5222
www.comedybarn.com

Zanies Comedy Night Club
2025 8th Ave. S.
Nashville, TN 37204
615-269-0221
www.zanies.com

Comedy Catch & Giggles Grill
3224 Brainerd Rd.
Chattanooga, TN 37411
423-629-2233
www.thecomedycatch.com

Texas

Capitol City Comedy Club
8120 Research Blvd., # 100
Austin, TX 78758
512-467-2333
www.capcitycomedy.com

Rivercenter Comedy Club
849 E. Commerce St., # 893
San Antonio, TX 78205
210-229-1420
www.rivercentercomedyclub.com

Improv Comedy Club
4980 Belt Line Rd. # 250
Dallas, TX 75254
972-404-8501
www.improv2.com

Improv Comedy Club
7620 Katy Fwy., # 431
Houston, TX 77024
713-333-8800
www.improv2.com

Hideout Theatre and Coffeehouse
617 Congress Ave.
Austin, TX 78701
512-443-3688
www.hideouttheatre.com

Hyena's Comedy Club
2525 E. Arkansas Ln., # 253
Arlington, TX 76010
817-226-5233
www.hyenascomedynightclub.com

Backdoor Comedy
8250 N. Central Expy.
Dallas, TX 75206
214-328-4444
www.backdoorcomedy.com

Ad-Libs
2613 Ross Ave.
Dallas, TX 75201
214-754-7050
www.ad-libs.com

Coldtowne Theater
4803-B Airport Blvd.
Austin, TX 78751

512-524-2807
www.coldtownetheater.com

ComedySportz Houston
901 Town and Country Blvd.
Houston, TX 77024
713-868-1444
www.comedysportzhouston.com

Comedy Showcase
11460 Fuqua St., # 300
Houston, TX 77089
281-481-1188
www.thecomedyshowcase.com

Laff Stop
526 Waugh Dr.
Houston, TX 77019
713-524-2333
www.laffstop.com

Third Coast Comedy
2317 W. 34th St.
Houston, TX 77018
713-263-9899
www.thirdcoastcomedy.com

Utah

ComedySportz
36 W. Center St.
Provo, UT 84601
801-377-9700
www.comedysportzutah.com

Wise Guys Comedy
2194 W. 3500 S.
West Valley, UT 84119

801-463-2909
www.wiseguyscomedy.com

Wiseguys Comedy Cafe
269 25th St.
Ogden, UT 84401
801-622-5588
www.wiseguyscomedy.com

The Comedy Circuit
7711 Main St.
Midvale, UT 84047
801-566-0596

Johnny B's Comedy Club
177 W. 300 S.
Provo, UT 84601
801-377-6910

The Comedy Scene
389 S. State St.
Clearfield, UT 84015
801-825-3866

Vermont

Higher Ground
1214 Williston Rd.
S. Burlington, VT 05403
802-652-0777
www.highergroundmusic.com

Virginia

Funny Bone Comedy Club
11800 W. Broad St., # 1090
Richmond, VA 23233
804-521-8900
www.richmondfunnybone.com

**Cozzy's Comedy Club
& Tavern**
9700 Warwick Blvd.
Newport News, VA 23601
757-595-2800
www.cozzys.com

ComedySportz Improv Theatre
7115A Staples Mill Rd.
Richmond, VA 23236
804-266-9377
www.comedysportzrichmond.com

The Comedy Spot
4238 Wilson Blvd.
Arlington, VA 22203
703-294-5233
www.comedyindc.com

Funny Bone Comedy Club
217 Central Park Ave.
Virginia Beach, VA 23462
757-213-5555
www.vabeachfunnybone.com

All Stars Comedy Club
2317 Wilson Blvd.
Arlington, VA 22201
703-739-7377
www.allstarscomedy.com

HA! Comedy Club
1910 Atlantic Ave.
Virginia Beach, VA 23451
757-333-6175

Washington

Giggles Comedy Club
5220 Roosevelt Way NE
Seattle, WA 98105
206-526-5653
www.gigglescomedyclub.com

Comedy Underground
109 S. Washington St.
Seattle, WA 98104
206-628-0303
www.comedyunderground.com

Comedy Underground
100 S. 9th St.
Tacoma, WA 98402
253-272-2489
www.comedyunderground.com

Laughs
12099 124th Ave. NE
Kirkland, WA 98034
425-823-6306
www.laughscomedy.com

Unexpected Productions Improv
1428 Post Alley
Seattle, WA 98101-2034
206-587-2414
www.unexpectedproductions.org

Jet City Improv
5510 University Way NE
Seattle, WA 98105
206-781-3879
www.jetcityimprov.com

The Upfront Theatre
1208 Bay St.
Bellingham, WA 98225
360-733-8855
www.theupfront.com

West Virginia

Comedy Zone Charleston
400 2nd Ave.
Charleston, WV 25303
303-414-2386
www.comedyzonecharleston.com

Funny Bone Comedy Club
26 Pullman Square Dr.
Huntington, WV 25701
304-781-1000
www.wvfunnybone.com

Wisconsin

Dells Comedy Club
591 Wisconsin Dells Pkwy.
Wisconsin Dells, WI 53965
608-253-9453
www.dellscomedyclub.com

Jokerz Comedy Club
11400 W. Silver Spring Rd.
Milwaukee, WI 53225
414-463-5653
www.jokerzcomedyclub.com

Comedy Club On State
202 State St.
Madison, WI 53703

608-256-0099
www.madisoncomedy.com

Skyline Comedy Cafe
1004 S. Olde Oneida St.
Appleton, WI 54915
920-734-5653
www.skylinecomedy.com

Comedy Cafe
615 E. Brady St.
Milwaukee, WI 53202
414-271-5653
www.jdscomedycafe.com

Comedy Sportz
420 South First Street
Milwaukee, WI 53204
414-272-8888
www.comedysportzmilwaukee.com

Giggles Comedy Pub
19115 W. Capitol Dr.
Brookfield, WI 53045
262-437-5653
www.gigglescomedypub.com

ComedyCity
380 Main Ave.
De Pere, WI 54115
920-983-0966
www.comedycityonline.com

Index

THE EVERYTHING SERIES!

BUSINESS & PERSONAL FINANCE

Everything® Accounting Book
Everything® Budgeting Book, 2nd Ed.
Everything® Business Planning Book
Everything® Coaching and Mentoring Book, 2nd Ed.
Everything® Fundraising Book
Everything® Get Out of Debt Book
Everything® Grant Writing Book, 2nd Ed.
Everything® Guide to Buying Foreclosures
Everything® Guide to Fundraising, $15.95
Everything® Guide to Mortgages
Everything® Guide to Personal Finance for Single Mothers
Everything® Home-Based Business Book, 2nd Ed.
Everything® Homebuying Book, 3rd Ed., $15.95
Everything® Homeselling Book, 2nd Ed.
Everything® Human Resource Management Book
Everything® Improve Your Credit Book
Everything® Investing Book, 2nd Ed.
Everything® Landlording Book
Everything® Leadership Book, 2nd Ed.
Everything® Managing People Book, 2nd Ed.
Everything® Negotiating Book
Everything® Online Auctions Book
Everything® Online Business Book
Everything® Personal Finance Book
Everything® Personal Finance in Your 20s & 30s Book, 2nd Ed.
Everything® Personal Finance in Your 40s & 50s Book, $15.95
Everything® Project Management Book, 2nd Ed.
Everything® Real Estate Investing Book
Everything® Retirement Planning Book
Everything® Robert's Rules Book, $7.95
Everything® Selling Book
Everything® Start Your Own Business Book, 2nd Ed.
Everything® Wills & Estate Planning Book

COOKING

Everything® Barbecue Cookbook
Everything® Bartender's Book, 2nd Ed., $9.95
Everything® Calorie Counting Cookbook
Everything® Cheese Book
Everything® Chinese Cookbook
Everything® Classic Recipes Book
Everything® Cocktail Parties & Drinks Book
Everything® College Cookbook
Everything® Cooking for Baby and Toddler Book
Everything® Diabetes Cookbook
Everything® Easy Gourmet Cookbook
Everything® Fondue Cookbook
Everything® Food Allergy Cookbook, $15.95
Everything® Fondue Party Book
Everything® Gluten-Free Cookbook
Everything® Glycemic Index Cookbook
Everything® Grilling Cookbook
Everything® Healthy Cooking for Parties Book, $15.95
Everything® Holiday Cookbook
Everything® Indian Cookbook
Everything® Lactose-Free Cookbook
Everything® Low-Cholesterol Cookbook

Everything® Low-Fat High-Flavor Cookbook, 2nd Ed., $15.95
Everything® Low-Salt Cookbook
Everything® Meals for a Month Cookbook
Everything® Meals on a Budget Cookbook
Everything® Mediterranean Cookbook
Everything® Mexican Cookbook
Everything® No Trans Fat Cookbook
Everything® One-Pot Cookbook, 2nd Ed., $15.95
Everything® Organic Cooking for Baby & Toddler Book, $15.95
Everything® Pizza Cookbook
Everything® Quick Meals Cookbook, 2nd Ed., $15.95
Everything® Slow Cooker Cookbook
Everything® Slow Cooking for a Crowd Cookbook
Everything® Soup Cookbook
Everything® Stir-Fry Cookbook
Everything® Sugar-Free Cookbook
Everything® Tapas and Small Plates Cookbook
Everything® Tex-Mex Cookbook
Everything® Thai Cookbook
Everything® Vegetarian Cookbook
Everything® Whole-Grain, High-Fiber Cookbook
Everything® Wild Game Cookbook
Everything® Wine Book, 2nd Ed.

GAMES

Everything® 15-Minute Sudoku Book, $9.95
Everything® 30-Minute Sudoku Book, $9.95
Everything® Bible Crosswords Book, $9.95
Everything® Blackjack Strategy Book
Everything® Brain Strain Book, $9.95
Everything® Bridge Book
Everything® Card Games Book
Everything® Card Tricks Book, $9.95
Everything® Casino Gambling Book, 2nd Ed.
Everything® Chess Basics Book
Everything® Christmas Crosswords Book, $9.95
Everything® Craps Strategy Book
Everything® Crossword and Puzzle Book
Everything® Crosswords and Puzzles for Quote Lovers Book, $9.95
Everything® Crossword Challenge Book
Everything® Crosswords for the Beach Book, $9.95
Everything® Cryptic Crosswords Book, $9.95
Everything® Cryptograms Book, $9.95
Everything® Easy Crosswords Book
Everything® Easy Kakuro Book, $9.95
Everything® Easy Large-Print Crosswords Book
Everything® Games Book, 2nd Ed.
Everything® Giant Book of Crosswords
Everything® Giant Sudoku Book, $9.95
Everything® Giant Word Search Book
Everything® Kakuro Challenge Book, $9.95
Everything® Large-Print Crossword Challenge Book
Everything® Large-Print Crosswords Book
Everything® Large-Print Travel Crosswords Book
Everything® Lateral Thinking Puzzles Book, $9.95
Everything® Literary Crosswords Book, $9.95
Everything® Mazes Book
Everything® Memory Booster Puzzles Book, $9.95

Everything® Movie Crosswords Book, $9.95
Everything® Music Crosswords Book, $9.95
Everything® Online Poker Book
Everything® Pencil Puzzles Book, $9.95
Everything® Poker Strategy Book
Everything® Pool & Billiards Book
Everything® Puzzles for Commuters Book, $9.95
Everything® Puzzles for Dog Lovers Book, $9.95
Everything® Sports Crosswords Book, $9.95
Everything® Test Your IQ Book, $9.95
Everything® Texas Hold 'Em Book, $9.95
Everything® Travel Crosswords Book, $9.95
Everything® Travel Mazes Book, $9.95
Everything® Travel Word Search Book, $9.95
Everything® TV Crosswords Book, $9.95
Everything® Word Games Challenge Book
Everything® Word Scramble Book
Everything® Word Search Book

HEALTH

Everything® Alzheimer's Book
Everything® Diabetes Book
Everything® First Aid Book, $9.95
Everything® Green Living Book
Everything® Health Guide to Addiction and Recovery
Everything® Health Guide to Adult Bipolar Disorder
Everything® Health Guide to Arthritis
Everything® Health Guide to Controlling Anxiety
Everything® Health Guide to Depression
Everything® Health Guide to Diabetes, 2nd Ed.
Everything® Health Guide to Fibromyalgia
Everything® Health Guide to Menopause, 2nd Ed.
Everything® Health Guide to Migraines
Everything® Health Guide to Multiple Sclerosis
Everything® Health Guide to OCD
Everything® Health Guide to PMS
Everything® Health Guide to Postpartum Care
Everything® Health Guide to Thyroid Disease
Everything® Hypnosis Book
Everything® Low Cholesterol Book
Everything® Menopause Book
Everything® Nutrition Book
Everything® Reflexology Book
Everything® Stress Management Book
Everything® Superfoods Book, $15.95

HISTORY

Everything® American Government Book
Everything® American History Book, 2nd Ed.
Everything® American Revolution Book, $15.95
Everything® Civil War Book
Everything® Freemasons Book
Everything® Irish History & Heritage Book
Everything® World War II Book, 2nd Ed.

HOBBIES

Everything® Candlemaking Book
Everything® Cartooning Book
Everything® Coin Collecting Book
Everything® Digital Photography Book, 2nd Ed.

Everything® Drawing Book
Everything® Family Tree Book, 2nd Ed.
Everything® Guide to Online Genealogy, $15.95
Everything® Knitting Book
Everything® Knots Book
Everything® Photography Book
Everything® Quilting Book
Everything® Sewing Book
Everything® Soapmaking Book, 2nd Ed.
Everything® Woodworking Book

HOME IMPROVEMENT

Everything® Feng Shui Book
Everything® Feng Shui Decluttering Book, $9.95
Everything® Fix-It Book
Everything® Green Living Book
Everything® Home Decorating Book
Everything® Home Storage Solutions Book
Everything® Homebuilding Book
Everything® Organize Your Home Book, 2nd Ed.

KIDS' BOOKS

All titles are $7.95
Everything® Fairy Tales Book, $14.95
Everything® Kids' Animal Puzzle & Activity Book
Everything® Kids' Astronomy Book
Everything® Kids' Baseball Book, 5th Ed.
Everything® Kids' Bible Trivia Book
Everything® Kids' Bugs Book
Everything® Kids' Cars and Trucks Puzzle and Activity Book
Everything® Kids' Christmas Puzzle & Activity Book
Everything® Kids' Connect the Dots
        Puzzle and Activity Book
Everything® Kids' Cookbook, 2nd Ed.
Everything® Kids' Crazy Puzzles Book
Everything® Kids' Dinosaurs Book
Everything® Kids' Dragons Puzzle and Activity Book
Everything® Kids' Environment Book $7.95
Everything® Kids' Fairies Puzzle and Activity Book
Everything® Kids' First Spanish Puzzle and Activity Book
Everything® Kids' Football Book
Everything® Kids' Geography Book
Everything® Kids' Gross Cookbook
Everything® Kids' Gross Hidden Pictures Book
Everything® Kids' Gross Jokes Book
Everything® Kids' Gross Mazes Book
Everything® Kids' Gross Puzzle & Activity Book
Everything® Kids' Halloween Puzzle & Activity Book
Everything® Kids' Hanukkah Puzzle and Activity Book
Everything® Kids' Hidden Pictures Book
Everything® Kids' Horses Book
Everything® Kids' Joke Book
Everything® Kids' Knock Knock Book
Everything® Kids' Learning French Book
Everything® Kids' Learning Spanish Book
Everything® Kids' Magical Science Experiments Book
Everything® Kids' Math Puzzles Book
Everything® Kids' Mazes Book
Everything® Kids' Money Book, 2nd Ed.
**Everything® Kids' Mummies, Pharaoh's, and Pyramids
        Puzzle and Activity Book**
Everything® Kids' Nature Book
Everything® Kids' Pirates Puzzle and Activity Book
Everything® Kids' Presidents Book
Everything® Kids' Princess Puzzle and Activity Book
Everything® Kids' Puzzle Book

Everything® Kids' Racecars Puzzle and Activity Book
Everything® Kids' Riddles & Brain Teasers Book
Everything® Kids' Science Experiments Book
Everything® Kids' Sharks Book
Everything® Kids' Soccer Book
Everything® Kids' Spelling Book
Everything® Kids' Spies Puzzle and Activity Book
Everything® Kids' States Book
Everything® Kids' Travel Activity Book
Everything® Kids' Word Search Puzzle and Activity Book

LANGUAGE

Everything® Conversational Japanese Book with CD, $19.95
Everything® French Grammar Book
Everything® French Phrase Book, $9.95
Everything® French Verb Book, $9.95
Everything® German Phrase Book, $9.95
Everything® German Practice Book with CD, $19.95
Everything® Inglés Book
Everything® Intermediate Spanish Book with CD, $19.95
Everything® Italian Phrase Book, $9.95
Everything® Italian Practice Book with CD, $19.95
Everything® Learning Brazilian Portuguese Book with CD, $19.95
Everything® Learning French Book with CD, 2nd Ed., $19.95
Everything® Learning German Book
Everything® Learning Italian Book
Everything® Learning Latin Book
Everything® Learning Russian Book with CD, $19.95
Everything® Learning Spanish Book
Everything® Learning Spanish Book with CD, 2nd Ed., $19.95
Everything® Russian Practice Book with CD, $19.95
Everything® Sign Language Book, $15.95
Everything® Spanish Grammar Book
Everything® Spanish Phrase Book, $9.95
Everything® Spanish Practice Book with CD, $19.95
Everything® Spanish Verb Book, $9.95
Everything® Speaking Mandarin Chinese Book with CD, $19.95

MUSIC

Everything® Bass Guitar Book with CD, $19.95
Everything® Drums Book with CD, $19.95
Everything® Guitar Book with CD, 2nd Ed., $19.95
Everything® Guitar Chords Book with CD, $19.95
Everything® Guitar Scales Book with CD, $19.95
Everything® Harmonica Book with CD, $15.95
Everything® Home Recording Book
Everything® Music Theory Book with CD, $19.95
Everything® Reading Music Book with CD, $19.95
Everything® Rock & Blues Guitar Book with CD, $19.95
Everything® Rock & Blues Piano Book with CD, $19.95
Everything® Rock Drums Book with CD, $19.95
Everything® Singing Book with CD, $19.95
Everything® Songwriting Book

NEW AGE

Everything® Astrology Book, 2nd Ed.
Everything® Birthday Personology Book
Everything® Celtic Wisdom Book, $15.95
Everything® Dreams Book, 2nd Ed.
Everything® Law of Attraction Book, $15.95
Everything® Love Signs Book, $9.95
Everything® Love Spells Book, $9.95
Everything® Palmistry Book
Everything® Psychic Book
Everything® Reiki Book

Everything® Sex Signs Book, $9.95
Everything® Spells & Charms Book, 2nd Ed.
Everything® Tarot Book, 2nd Ed.
Everything® Toltec Wisdom Book
Everything® Wicca & Witchcraft Book, 2nd Ed.

PARENTING

Everything® Baby Names Book, 2nd Ed.
Everything® Baby Shower Book, 2nd Ed.
Everything® Baby Sign Language Book with DVD
Everything® Baby's First Year Book
Everything® Birthing Book
Everything® Breastfeeding Book
Everything® Father-to-Be Book
Everything® Father's First Year Book
Everything® Get Ready for Baby Book, 2nd Ed.
Everything® Get Your Baby to Sleep Book, $9.95
Everything® Getting Pregnant Book
Everything® Guide to Pregnancy Over 35
Everything® Guide to Raising a One-Year-Old
Everything® Guide to Raising a Two-Year-Old
Everything® Guide to Raising Adolescent Boys
Everything® Guide to Raising Adolescent Girls
Everything® Mother's First Year Book
Everything® Parent's Guide to Childhood Illnesses
Everything® Parent's Guide to Children and Divorce
Everything® Parent's Guide to Children with ADD/ADHD
Everything® Parent's Guide to Children with Asperger's
        Syndrome
Everything® Parent's Guide to Children with Anxiety
Everything® Parent's Guide to Children with Asthma
Everything® Parent's Guide to Children with Autism
Everything® Parent's Guide to Children with Bipolar Disorder
Everything® Parent's Guide to Children with Depression
Everything® Parent's Guide to Children with Dyslexia
Everything® Parent's Guide to Children with Juvenile Diabetes
Everything® Parent's Guide to Children with OCD
Everything® Parent's Guide to Positive Discipline
Everything® Parent's Guide to Raising Boys
Everything® Parent's Guide to Raising Girls
Everything® Parent's Guide to Raising Siblings
**Everything® Parent's Guide to Raising Your
        Adopted Child**
Everything® Parent's Guide to Sensory Integration Disorder
Everything® Parent's Guide to Tantrums
Everything® Parent's Guide to the Strong-Willed Child
Everything® Parenting a Teenager Book
Everything® Potty Training Book, $9.95
Everything® Pregnancy Book, 3rd Ed.
Everything® Pregnancy Fitness Book
Everything® Pregnancy Nutrition Book
Everything® Pregnancy Organizer, 2nd Ed., $16.95
Everything® Toddler Activities Book
Everything® Toddler Book
Everything® Tween Book
Everything® Twins, Triplets, and More Book

PETS

Everything® Aquarium Book
Everything® Boxer Book
Everything® Cat Book, 2nd Ed.
Everything® Chihuahua Book
Everything® Cooking for Dogs Book
Everything® Dachshund Book
Everything® Dog Book, 2nd Ed.
Everything® Dog Grooming Book

Everything® Dog Obedience Book
Everything® Dog Owner's Organizer, $16.95
Everything® Dog Training and Tricks Book
Everything® German Shepherd Book
Everything® Golden Retriever Book
Everything® Horse Book, 2nd Ed., $15.95
Everything® Horse Care Book
Everything® Horseback Riding Book
Everything® Labrador Retriever Book
Everything® Poodle Book
Everything® Pug Book
Everything® Puppy Book
Everything® Small Dogs Book
Everything® Tropical Fish Book
Everything® Yorkshire Terrier Book

REFERENCE

Everything® American Presidents Book
Everything® Blogging Book
Everything® Build Your Vocabulary Book, $9.95
Everything® Car Care Book
Everything® Classical Mythology Book
Everything® Da Vinci Book
Everything® Einstein Book
Everything® Enneagram Book
Everything® Etiquette Book, 2nd Ed.
Everything® Family Christmas Book, $15.95
Everything® Guide to C. S. Lewis & Narnia
Everything® Guide to Divorce, 2nd Ed., $15.95
Everything® Guide to Edgar Allan Poe
Everything® Guide to Understanding Philosophy
Everything® Inventions and Patents Book
Everything® Jacqueline Kennedy Onassis Book
Everything® John F. Kennedy Book
Everything® Mafia Book
Everything® Martin Luther King Jr. Book
Everything® Pirates Book
Everything® Private Investigation Book
Everything® Psychology Book
Everything® Public Speaking Book, $9.95
Everything® Shakespeare Book, 2nd Ed.

RELIGION

Everything® Angels Book
Everything® Bible Book
Everything® Bible Study Book with CD, $19.95
Everything® Buddhism Book
Everything® Catholicism Book
Everything® Christianity Book
Everything® Gnostic Gospels Book
Everything® Hinduism Book, $15.95
Everything® History of the Bible Book
Everything® Jesus Book
Everything® Jewish History & Heritage Book
Everything® Judaism Book
Everything® Kabbalah Book
Everything® Koran Book
Everything® Mary Book
Everything® Mary Magdalene Book
Everything® Prayer Book

Everything® Saints Book, 2nd Ed.
Everything® Torah Book
Everything® Understanding Islam Book
Everything® Women of the Bible Book
Everything® World's Religions Book

SCHOOL & CAREERS

Everything® Career Tests Book
Everything® College Major Test Book
Everything® College Survival Book, 2nd Ed.
Everything® Cover Letter Book, 2nd Ed.
Everything® Filmmaking Book
Everything® Get-a-Job Book, 2nd Ed.
Everything® Guide to Being a Paralegal
Everything® Guide to Being a Personal Trainer
Everything® Guide to Being a Real Estate Agent
Everything® Guide to Being a Sales Rep
Everything® Guide to Being an Event Planner
Everything® Guide to Careers in Health Care
Everything® Guide to Careers in Law Enforcement
Everything® Guide to Government Jobs
Everything® Guide to Starting and Running a Catering Business
Everything® Guide to Starting and Running a Restaurant
Everything® Guide to Starting and Running a Retail Store
Everything® Job Interview Book, 2nd Ed.
Everything® New Nurse Book
Everything® New Teacher Book
Everything® Paying for College Book
Everything® Practice Interview Book
Everything® Resume Book, 3rd Ed.
Everything® Study Book

SELF-HELP

Everything® Body Language Book
Everything® Dating Book, 2nd Ed.
Everything® Great Sex Book
Everything® Guide to Caring for Aging Parents, $15.95
Everything® Self-Esteem Book
Everything® Self-Hypnosis Book, $9.95
Everything® Tantric Sex Book

SPORTS & FITNESS

Everything® Easy Fitness Book
Everything® Fishing Book
Everything® Guide to Weight Training, $15.95
Everything® Krav Maga for Fitness Book
Everything® Running Book, 2nd Ed.
Everything® Triathlon Training Book, $15.95

TRAVEL

Everything® Family Guide to Coastal Florida
Everything® Family Guide to Cruise Vacations
Everything® Family Guide to Hawaii
Everything® Family Guide to Las Vegas, 2nd Ed.
Everything® Family Guide to Mexico
Everything® Family Guide to New England, 2nd Ed.

Everything® Family Guide to New York City, 3rd Ed.
Everything® Family Guide to Northern California and Lake Tahoe
Everything® Family Guide to RV Travel & Campgrounds
Everything® Family Guide to the Caribbean
Everything® Family Guide to the Disneyland® Resort, California Adventure®, Universal Studios®, and the Anaheim Area, 2nd Ed.
Everything® Family Guide to the Walt Disney World Resort®, Universal Studios®, and Greater Orlando, 5th Ed.
Everything® Family Guide to Timeshares
Everything® Family Guide to Washington D.C., 2nd Ed.

WEDDINGS

Everything® Bachelorette Party Book, $9.95
Everything® Bridesmaid Book, $9.95
Everything® Destination Wedding Book
Everything® Father of the Bride Book, $9.95
Everything® Green Wedding Book, $15.95
Everything® Groom Book, $9.95
Everything® Jewish Wedding Book, 2nd Ed., $15.95
Everything® Mother of the Bride Book, $9.95
Everything® Outdoor Wedding Book
Everything® Wedding Book, 3rd Ed.
Everything® Wedding Checklist, $9.95
Everything® Wedding Etiquette Book, $9.95
Everything® Wedding Organizer, 2nd Ed., $16.95
Everything® Wedding Shower Book, $9.95
Everything® Wedding Vows Book, 3rd Ed., $9.95
Everything® Wedding Workout Book
Everything® Weddings on a Budget Book, 2nd Ed., $9.95

WRITING

Everything® Creative Writing Book
Everything® Get Published Book, 2nd Ed.
Everything® Grammar and Style Book, 2nd Ed.
Everything® Guide to Magazine Writing
Everything® Guide to Writing a Book Proposal
Everything® Guide to Writing a Novel
Everything® Guide to Writing Children's Books
Everything® Guide to Writing Copy
Everything® Guide to Writing Graphic Novels
Everything® Guide to Writing Research Papers
Everything® Guide to Writing a Romance Novel, $15.95
Everything® Improve Your Writing Book, 2nd Ed.
Everything® Writing Poetry Book